THE BEST OF ALL SEASONS

The Best of All Seasons
Fifty Years as a Montana Hunter

DAN AADLAND

University of Nebraska Press ¦ Lincoln and London

Publication of this volume was assisted by The
Virginia Faulkner Fund, established in memory
of Virginia Faulkner, editor in chief of the
University of Nebraska Press.

Chapter 9 adapted from *Sketches from the Ranch:
A Montana Memoir* by Dan Aadland. Copyright
© 1998 by Dan Aadland. Used by permission of
The Lyons Press, 246 Goose Lane, Guilford CT
06437. All illustrations courtesy of the author.

Library of Congress Cataloging-in-Publication Data
Aadland, Dan.
The best of all seasons: fifty years as a Montana
hunter / Dan Aadland.
　　p.　cm.
ISBN-13: 978-0-8032-1069-1 (cloth: alk. paper)
ISBN-13: 978-0-8032-4347-7 (paper: alk. paper)
ISBN-10: 0-8032-1069-8 (cloth: alk. paper)
1. Hunting—Montana—Anecdotes. 2. Aadland,
　Dan. I. Title.
SK99.A13 2007
799.29786–dc22　　　　　2006026327

Set in ITC New Baskerville.
Designed by A. Shahan.

CONTENTS

ILLUSTRATIONS

A Note to the Reader

This is not a book about hunting record book trophies or about stopping charging Cape buffalo in Africa. Nor does it attempt to settle the persistent questions about the nature of hunting, its ethics, its morality, or its place in the twenty-first century. This is a book about an ordinary hunter whose life has been enriched for more than half a century by pursuing, with family and close friends, wild game under Montana's big sky. For us hunting has been an essential part of the good life, a natural role in our cherished outdoors. Its absence would be unthinkable.

In writing this story I've again relied on Emily, my wife of forty-two years, as number 1 editor and, increasingly, photographer and manipulator of digital files. I dedicate this work to her, to my sons, and to my brothers and friends who have shared time in the saddle, campfires under the Milky Way, and tales on the hunting trail.

THE BEST OF ALL SEASONS

1

And the Clock Stopped

Mrs. Gaustad was the fastest walker in town. Actually, she didn't walk—she charged. Whether through the classroom door in the little sandstone elementary school, where she was my teacher for both fourth and fifth grades; whether toward my desk when I stared dreamily out the window toward the dryland hills east of town, thinking about my dog; whether west across town to the little farm her family operated on the edge of the woods near the river, to milk the cow, Mrs. Gaustad moved with a mission. But today, she told us later, she stopped in midstride.

It was not that she was unaccustomed to hearing shots. During fall's deer season the sound of big game rifles directed at mule deer near town rolled and echoed across the valley like distant thunder. Her children, like all the town kids, had .22 rifles and practiced with them frequently. She herself thought nothing of grabbing the single barrel shotgun standing in the porch corner and launching a frontal assault on the occasional skunk that had the temerity (and bad judgment) to invade her chicken house. But these shots were different. She couldn't place them.

She was walking from her school classroom toward the church to prepare her Sunday School lesson (yes, she taught us there as well), and the shots stopped her near the parsonage. Were they from far away, originating in the coulee above the dairy farm east of the church, floating over the pasture toward her? Or were they closer? She couldn't tell. There was something muffled about them.

On the front porch of the parsonage, from his rug in the shade, the black and white dog named Boots rose stiffly, tantalized by the prospect of a stationary Mrs. Gaustad. Perhaps a pat from her wasn't out of the question. He stretched and then trotted her way. But now she was moving again, this time directly toward the back door, and she gave him no mind whatsoever. Boots dropped his tail and walked back to the front porch.

Mrs. Gaustad stood a moment, cocking her head this way and that until her sonar fixed upon the parsonage. The muffled shots seemed to originate from there, perhaps in the basement. Perhaps, too, she was misinterpreting (she hoped so), and the sounds actually had something to do with the pastor's many power tools. Maybe he was working in his basement shop on something that periodically banged.

In any case, Mrs. Gaustad wasn't the type who would seize this opportunity to speculate or gossip, to form a juicy mystery about the pastor that she could bounce off customers over the counter at her husband's hardware store. That sort of thing was for women who had the time to wile away summer afternoons watching soap operas on the one television station that squeezed its signal into our valley in the foothills. She had cows to milk and kids to raise. So she did what came naturally to her. She marched to the back door, disappointing Boots, opened the screen door, and gave several sharp raps.

My mother greeted Mrs. Gaustad at the door. I wasn't there to hear the conversation between them, but I'm sure my mother offered coffee with a smile and reported the source of the shots, a mini–firing range in the basement. Mom probably shrugged and made it clear she didn't quite approve. I doubt whether Mrs. Gaustad lectured her in any way. She probably limited herself to a question. "Are you sure it's safe?"

That was enough for Mom. We were shooting only .22

shorts, we protested, after Dad called a good friend who knew more about guns than he did. Chuck Kem, like Mrs. Gaustad, was gentle but decisive. Yes, the backstop, a cement wall, was solid enough, and the plywood in front of it should prevent ricochets. But even the little lead bullet from a .22 short, should it go awry, might penetrate the floor.

And so Dad called a halt to our basement shooting range. He had instigated it in the first place, this Lutheran minister with no real shooting background of his own, had led us to the joys of splintering at fifty feet Mom's emptied sewing spools lined up on a plank in front of the backstop. He had bought us the .22 a few months earlier, a single-shot, long-barreled Winchester model 67A. Chuck had guided him toward that particular rifle, pointing out its lack of a magazine, its long barrel, and its inability to fire until you cocked the knurled knob on the back of the bolt.

Strict lessons for all of us had followed. Never pick up the rifle without opening the bolt to make sure the rifle was clear. Always point it in a safe direction. Never aim it at anything you don't wish to destroy. Watch for ricochets off stone, metal, or water. Don't shoot at anything on skyline. When walking in a group, the one with the rifle leads, and no one passes him, ever. We lapped up the lessons greedily, took them seriously, sobered by news that the son of one of Dad's minister colleagues in another Montana town had died in a shooting accident.

I don't recall any major sorrow over the loss of our indoor range. There were no houses in the field behind the parsonage, and the unincorporated town had no restrictive laws. As long as Mr. Maxwell's Holstein cows were in the pasture to the south we could safely shoot east at tin cans lined up along the back fence behind our garden. The backstop then was the valley wall, bald foothills studded with sage, juniper, and yucca, hills that had beckoned to us the very first day we arrived in our Montana town, when we called them mountains and were quickly corrected by Mrs. Gaustad's daughter Mary. "They're just hills." She pointed south to the blue, snow-covered Beartooth range of the Absaroka Mountains. "*Those* are the mountains!"

It's not as if we had come from the city. We had moved out from eastern South Dakota, country nearly as rural, but flat and seeming to us to have been quite domestic compared to south-central Montana in the early 1950s. We had relished the move. I remember guilt at the contrast between the tears of a family of friends who were seeing us off and my own enthusiasm. We were going to Montana! There would be cowboys.

And in Baker, Montana, while pausing at a dusty restaurant, all of us stared at one of them, a cowboy in a booth nervously fingering a drink from the adjacent bar while being scrutinized by a big tribe of wide-eyed children. I remember that he pointed to his glass on the table and said to the man across from him, "They don't like my habit."

My mother, overhearing, said to him, "Oh, no, they're just staring because you're a cowboy." What he was drinking was last thing we'd noticed. But we had seen the boots on feet thrust carelessly into the aisle, the Stetson hanging on the hat rack supplied in those days by all indoor establishments, the western shirt over his broad chest, and the silver buckle on his belt. He had everything but a gun.

Eastern South Dakota had already sown seeds. Pheasant hunting was popular, and although I never got close to it as a small child, the sound of distant autumn shotguns was a familiar one. Once on a hike down a county road we discovered under a bridge the rather gruesome remains of a dozen pheasants, heads and entrails, and thought it the result of a poacher.

We learned later that it was common practice for a group of pheasant hunters to stop in one location and field dress their day's kill.

Occasionally we children stayed in homes of my father's parishioners while he and Mom attended the church convention in Minneapolis. One year I found myself "farmed out" alone, not with the friendly, chattering family I knew well but with an austere old couple and their equally quiet grandson. It was one of those good old Midwestern farms in a day when farmers raised most of their own food. (Today many of those who remain on the consolidated farms have converted barnyards once teaming with chickens and pigs into golf-course sized lawns and have torn down the fences that once held cows. The deck is thus cleared for raising a single crop of corn or soybeans which the more affluent farmers harvest before heading to their winter homes in Arizona.)

Besides being lonely during the week on that farm, I remember just one other thing, the first time I saw a rifle fired. A crow landed on a fencepost at what seemed to me a long distance from the barnyard. The farm boy emerged from the house with the only grin I saw all week. He was carrying a rifle. I watched him kneel down and take aim. The rifle cracked, and the crow ducked to one side, then flew. The boy was disappointed. I, in turn, was impressed that at such long range the bullet came close enough for the crow to take notice.

I saw, during my time in De Smet, South Dakota, just one deer. This was, of course, years before the whitetail population explosion. We were walking somewhere north of the town on the same county road by which we saw the pheasant remains, a gang of us ducking into the barrow pit each time a vehicle came by so as to evade its plume of dust. The rest of the time we walked down the center of the road. One of the boys pointed toward a tiny object far in the distance moving very rapidly across our front toward the road. We all stared. It was too big for a dog and too small for a cow, and of course, a cow couldn't move nearly so fast.

Suddenly someone shouted, "It's a deer!" The animal bulleted from left to right, jumping the fences on each side of the county road, sprinted across the next farmed field toward a tree line, and then was gone. We were as incredulous as we'd have been if we had all just witnessed a flying saucer.

We arrived in south-central Montana during a December chinook. Long before I learned that *chinook* meant "snow-eater" in an Indian language, I thought it a beautiful word for a beautiful thing, the warm wind sent down by the mountains to melt the snow and give you a few days of short-sleeve weather. The chinook is Montana's compensation for snowstorms and frosts that fall earlier and later than those in the northern Midwest.

The Gaustad kids were playing on swings in the schoolyard. We went over and joined them. I remember feeling totally at home. Yes, we were told, we could walk to the top of the hills—not mountains—behind our house in an hour or so, but we'd have to be driven to the real mountains, the snow-covered ones ringing our view to the south. Even though they looked close enough to touch, they were twenty miles away.

We were soon allowed to go to those hills that beckoned, those grassy dryland foothills that rose from the pasture a hundred yards behind our house. We climbed three hundred feet or so to the top where the valley wall leveled off into a plateau. The mountains from there looked crisp and cold, half encircling us to the south. Prickly pear cactus hid in the grass, so we quickly learned to watch our step and scrutinize the ground before sitting down to rest. The yucca plant, too, could poke through your jeans if you walked too close.

My memories of these early forays are spiced with the scent of sage. We were I suppose, my brothers and I, about as free as boys can be. The local landowners were tolerant of our trespassing. Even town kids normally had enough sense to keep gates closed so that cattle would not escape. Hiking the hills became our primary entertainment, and we were soon joined by the stray dog Boots, who had been fed by my father and had made the parsonage porch his home. During nice spring days at school we longed to go, and Saturdays were rarely consumed by anything else. Sometimes we walked many miles. And always, long before the arrival of the .22 or even the bows and arrows we built ourselves, we were hunting. Whether for cottontails that ducked under spreading junipers, rock chucks that scurried back toward their holes at the sight of Boots, or mule deer bounding from the coulees on pogo-stick legs, we were always looking for game, and always smug about finding it.

It's too deep in human beings to be called habit, custom, or even tradition, this compulsion to find, shoot, and retrieve edible prey. It's truly an instinct, a drive, and if denied, I believe, finds its way into some other activity, good or bad. Golfers are passionate about targeting a distant hole. But many children today, instead of wandering the hills, pursue their "game," too often of the human sort, on video screens.

Before the arrival of the .22 rifle we worked our way through the earlier hunting stages of Man. We made spears from straight willow staves, fire-hardening their points, and slingshots from branches that naturally forked to make a handle topped by a nice symmetrical V. Such a branch was a find, a treasure. Here we were much helped by our father, who had been something of a slingshot guru during his boyhood in Minneapolis. We begged the service stations for fresh but exploded inner tubes, told by Dad that the red ones, of natural rubber, already getting rare in the 1950s, were superior. Leather tongues carved from old shoes made the best pouches to attach to the rubber strips we cut from the inner tubes. These held the carefully chosen and matched pebbles we used as projectiles.

Again inspired by our dad, who simply built things he couldn't afford, we made and discarded many bows and arrows, each a little more serviceable than the last, green willow our favorite material. Pigeon feathers for arrow fletching were easy to find under highway bridges where the birds nested, and chicken feathers from the Gaustad place, split with our pocketknives, worked just as well.

At just what era during my elementary school I first met in the library a big, tattered book named *Two Little Savages* by Ernest Thompson Seton I'm not sure, but I know it became my Bible until eventually replaced in that role by *The Adventures of Huckleberry Finn*. The Seton book, rarely idle on the library shelves, ping-ponged between Larry Pederson and me. Each of us would wait for the other to work through it, eyeballing his progress during reading time in our fifth grade class, the process then reversing.

Larry came closer than I to living the life Seton described, and only partly by choice. Tall, slim, and dark, Larry lived with his grandmother on the fringes of town, the cottonwood bottom his back yard, ran a trap line, cleverly constructing whatever he needed—snares, arrows, quivers—for hunting, fishing, and trapping. For Larry the Seton book was probably more of an instruction manual than a good story or a poetic treatise. I did not think of him and his grandmother as poor at the time (there was little extra money in my own family), but I know now that they were, that the pelts Larry caught and the small game he found were staples to them. What I was doing as a hobby, he was doing for a living. But he loved it as much as I did.

The Winchester .22 was a whole new world. It was designed for safety, a single-shot with a twenty-seven-inch barrel, long enough that pointing it at yourself was virtually impossible. A bolt action, the rifle required deliberate, manual loading of a single cartridge into its chamber. That accomplished, you still had to cock the knob on the back of the action before the rifle could fire. Should you choose not to fire, you could either twist a safety piece into place or de-cock the action by grasping the knob and lowering it gently while depressing the trigger. That was the trickier of the two operations, but probably the safer in the long run. We were taught to disarm the rifle with that method while pointing it at a soft piece of ground.

Early firing sessions were under strict supervision, but we were eventually allowed to take the rifle on our hillside jaunts. A typical Saturday involved a midmorning march down the main street of our town, the child with the rifle in front followed by the other kids and the dogs. There was nothing remarkable about this. Kids with rifles or small-bore shotguns drew not a second glance from the town residents. I've heard it claimed that modern violence is attributable to the "ever increasing availability of guns." But at least in rural America (and far more of the country was rural in the fifties than it is today) I believe the opposite was true—access to firearms was universal. The farmer's shotgun stood in the corner, ready for whatever attacked the chicken house, and most children knew how to load and fire it. But they did not do so unless allowed, and they did not take their guns to school.

We left after the requisite safety lecture, which we took quite seriously. We had seen how deeply the .22 could punch its tiny holes through boards we stacked for just such experiments. We read on the cardboard flap every time we opened a box of cartridges, "Range one mile—be careful." We imagined maudlin scenarios of tragic accidents for which we were responsible, for which we faced our father, our tearful mother, my dad's congregation. Fear may not be a perfect motivator, but in certain circumstances it works very well. But we were kids and we were human, so we were not infallible.

Before I tell how it happened, I must tell you about my father's clock. He had ordered it from one of the electronic supply houses from which he collected catalogs to furnish another of his hobbies, that of building short wave radios and phonograph amplifiers. He was quite proud of the clock. When he first mounted it on the wall he pointed it out to guests who did not notice, and he never complained of its loud ticking, even when listening to his favorite violin concertos on Sunday afternoons. Gold trimmed with a white face, the clock resembled a giant pocket watch, its face about one foot across, its gold chain hanging artfully from a peg beside it. I didn't think of this at the time, but maybe the clock recaptured for Dad something he had once lost, for I can recall a time of family financial crisis years earlier in South Dakota, when Dad had to sell some family treasures including his father's pocket watch.

I could blame it all on Bruce Reiner, but that would not be fair. Although what Bruce did was careless to a degree nearly criminal, I should have caught it. Besides, even if Bruce occasionally irritated the hell out of me, I liked him. Like Larry, Bruce lived in circumstances that made even children of a small-town minister feel rich and privileged, and he worked very hard. Raised by elderly grandparents, Bruce helped feed the three of them with a small menagerie in their backyard. There were bum lambs that he bottle fed and domestic rabbits for meat. For hay Bruce would harness his old, gentle dog to a radio flier wagon with raised sides he'd built of lathe. The pair would then meander down roadways, Bruce cutting alfalfa and clover plants in the barrow pit with a small scythe and forking them into the wagon until he'd loaded all the hay the old dog could pull.

We became good friends, the friendship having the flow and ebb common during growing up. There were many adventures hunting rock chucks and trying to start old abandoned automobiles left on the hilltops of dryland farms. We progressed through adolescence, hunted with the Amos boys, and helped Bruce's old cowboy friend Si get loads of baled hay to haul to his horses in an ancient pickup. It was Bruce who first pointed out to me that my tomboy friend Mary was, in fact, becoming a girl.

It was for a jackrabbit hunt with the Amoses that Bruce borrowed my .22. The critters were at the high end of their population cycle, and the market for them was good because mink farmers would buy the carcasses as feed for their fur-bearers. Robert Amos was the entrepreneur, driving his Studebaker, chained up when necessary, over wind-blown, snow-encrusted flats. No processing of the jackrabbits was needed to please the mink farmers. Their carcasses froze hard during the night in the trunk of the Studebaker, and Robert sold them when he accumulated enough to make the trip to Billings pay for his gasoline and a little more.

Bruce returned my rifle around suppertime. I'd been upstairs reading and did not hear him stop. I remember feeling relieved when told he had come by, the rifle being a prized possession about which I had worried. I hadn't been particularly happy about letting it out of my sight.

The Lutheran parsonage was laid out in a linear, rather unimaginative fashion. Its south side had in succession four rooms, a back porch, kitchen, dining room, and, separated by half-room dividers, a living room. There was line of sight through the doorways for the entire length of the house, from back porch to the west wall on which, incidentally, hung my father's clock.

There is, in all humans, a sort of blind spot, a potential for unexplainable error, for doing that which is completely contrary to all they have learned. It is this fallibility that makes guns, airplanes, and automobiles potentially dangerous. After someone hollered up the stairs to me where I lay reading—my "room" was a sort of cubbyhole at the top of the stairs—that Bruce had returned my rifle, I strode rapidly down, marched to the back porch, and picked up the rifle to visually inspect its stock for new scratches or dents. Seeing none, I threw the gun to my shoulder, aimed quickly at the center of Dad's clock ticking at the other end of the house, settling the sights on the round brass disk out of which extended the hands of the clock, and squeezed the trigger.

There was, as the firing pin struck, instead of the expected dry-fire click, the loud report that even a small caliber rifle makes when confined within four walls. The bang was punctuated simultaneously by the exploding screams of mother and sisters, the yowl of our cat, the howling of Boots on the front porch, a loud, "Hey, you boys!" from Dad downstairs in his workshop, and then his thunderous footfalls on the basement stairs, which he was clearing three at a stride. And, of course, the clock stopped.

My brothers have told me that my face was white, that I stood frozen looking down at the rifle as if it where some strange implement I had never seen before that moment. I don't recall what I said. I probably stumbled out something lame about not knowing that the gun was loaded, embarrassment compounded by recollection of the song lyrics: "I didn't know the gun was loaded, and I'm so sorry my friend." I must have either pointed toward the clock or muttered something about aiming at it, because I remember Dad and the older brothers flying to that end of the house and gathering around it. Perhaps it was Andy who said without derision, as merely reporting to an audience, "Missed!" By that he meant that the small .22 caliber hole was about one inch left of center on the clock, thus missing the root of the hands.

There was from Dad the expected anger about the demise of his clock, but I don't recall corporal punishment, something from which we weren't immune even in our teens. I suspect he saw "punished" written all over my pale face. Inspection by Dad and brothers quickly revealed that the lead bullet had lodged somewhere in the wall, slowed enough by the mechanism of the clock that it didn't emerge outside. "Well-built clock," Dad said, "to slow the bullet down so much."

"Good thing," said a brother. "Otherwise it might have beaned someone who was walking down the sidewalk."

A few years after the clock stopped, Peter, Paul, and Mary sang the refrain, "There but for fortune go you and I." Most of us can recall defining moments when the slightest difference in timing or circumstances might have caused drastic changes in the events of our lives. Had my millisecond's lapse in judgment resulted in an accident that killed or injured someone, perhaps today I would instead be writing about gardening, or perhaps not writing at all. Who knows?

As it stands, however, the accident was a stumble, not a fall, in this "portrait of the hunter as a young man." True, its effects, some good, were lasting. I've never had another accident with a firearm, cannot force myself to pick one up without opening the action while it's pointed in a safe direction.

Dad's anger over the clock dissolved into eventual amusement. He wrote a letter to the manufacturer detailing the chronology of the accident, and they sent him a brand-new movement for the clock—for one dollar! This triumph of

1. The beat goes on a generation later. Steven Aadland practices with his dad's carbine.

Dad's extended my embarrassment in perpetuity, because the story had to be told to everyone who visited the parsonage. It is still told.

And yet, the incident isn't the central one in my memories of dogs and brothers and .22 rifles. Dominant is a medley: It consists of sage and juniper, of crocuses peeping from spring snow, of sharptail grouse startling us as they thundered into the air, and of endless summer nights when we stayed out in the hills long after the chilled Montana air stung our arms. It's a memory touched by longing, as all the best ones are, in this case for a simpler time when a .22 rifle in the hand of a boy or girl climbing the foothills on the side of a valley seemed to everyone as wholesome and healthy as only a few of us today know it to be.

2

Robert and the Basin Buck

He was waiting for me after school, leaning in his characteristic slouch against the Studebaker's front fender, one hand in an affectionate caress over the hood, the other cupping a cigarette. Though eighteen and several years out of school (none of the Amos boys graduated), he did not flaunt the cigarette. Neither the presence of the students threading past him nor that of the supervising teachers on the playground had deterred him from lighting up, but there would have been no comfort for him in making a show of it.

The kids in small, chattering knots mostly ignored him, an occasional older child saying, "Hi, Robert," but looking more at the car than at this slim, smallish, muscular boy with the sloping shoulders of a lightweight prize fighter. Most did not know him. Few if any (my friend Bruce being an exception) knew him as I did. Robert was a breadwinner, regularly topping off a big chest freezer (one of the few modern appliances in his family's ruined rented ranch house) that never emptied so long as he could scrape together the money for .303 Savage shells, or when that failed, a box of .22 long-rifle ammunition.

There were in an annual succession behind Robert twelve younger Amoses. There was a black-eyed, strikingly good-looking father who earned decent money at the mine but drank up most of his paycheck each night at the Y-Bar on the way home. I rarely saw him. There was a good-humored mother with forearms like a man's, a woman who challenged us boys in our game to see who could hit the other harder in the shoulder. (The rule was that you stood with your side to the opponent, feet planted no more than a foot apart. The hitter's goal was to land a blow on the shoulder powerful enough to make the victim shift his feet. When the woman hit us we more than shifted. We went down, laughing and hurting at the same time.)

In this squalid mess of a house, on a floor long given up to the mud, there were children everywhere. The wood-burning kitchen range was the central magnet, and on it always, it seemed to me, sat a big cast-iron pan with venison frying. Spiced with sage, the aroma wiped out nearly everything else, masking and mellowing conditions that would have shocked even a slum-patrolling social worker. There was, you see, no hunger here. And that was because of Robert.

The time of year did not matter. Robert was stealthy, not only with the deer but with the ranchers and mine workers whose houses dotted the feet of the mountains. If the warden knew, he also knew why, and he did not try very hard. Just how many whitetail and mule deer Robert shot, then retrieved at night, processing them with his mother in a boarded up garage before cycling them through this chattering hoard of brothers and sisters, none of us knew. Twenty per year perhaps, maybe thirty, maybe more.

So you'd have thought there would be in Robert little zest for the beginning of actual hunting season, that hunting deer would be so mundane to him that he might instead wish for a vacation from it. But it was quite the opposite. When the buckbrush on the foothills tinged red and the quaking aspen turned yellow, when the wind from Granite Peak in the morning smelled moist and blew with it a few scattered snowflakes, Robert was as anxious as I was.

And that's why he showed up on this blustery day and why I knew he would be there. I had agonized through algebra, my last class of the day, tried to keep my eyes off the plate glass windows and the slate-colored sky, tried to ignore those sparse, dancing snowflakes that blew toward the glass and then careened off with the wind. So I was not surprised to see him leaning against his beloved car, the Studebaker the same grey as the sky this day, a kid from another world, and to see him wave me over.

"Hi, Dan. Camel?" I glanced over my shoulder to see if anyone was close.

"No." If I took the cigarette it would be later, in the car. I slid into the passenger side and checked the interior for recent developments. I'd seen earlier the pair of dice hanging from the mirror, but the gearshift knob, a naked woman under transparent plastic, was new. The car smelled dusty.

He slid in behind the steering wheel. "Football done for the year?" I nodded. He started the car, then twisted the knobs on the radio, which soon crackled on. "I pulled the radio out of the wrecked one. Works better." He had at home, propped up on blocks, a nearly identical Studebaker which he periodically cannibalized for parts.

Robert was not the sort to rev the engine near the school, to "rap his pipes" as we called it. Instead he worked his way through the gears, each with a precise "snick" as he shifted, then lining out in high, drew deeply on his cigarette and said, "So I guess you'll be wanting to do some hunting."

"Can't go Sunday, opening day. I was thinking about next Saturday."

"Good. It wouldn't work as soon as Sunday anyway. The folks have been awful hostile." I did not know what Robert meant by saying his parents were hostile. I did not want to know.

"I'll have to find me some .303 Savage shells. They don't have them at the Y anymore, and when they do they want so damn much." He was referring to the Y-Bar. Inside the log building, behind the bar to the left of the liquor on display there were always a few boxes of ammunition for sale to hunters, but only the more common calibers. The .303 Savage was no longer common.

"You could use my 30-30. I'm going to take the new one, the .303 British." Robert smiled, thinking, I knew, that my offer would get him out of scrounging a couple more bucks. There was nothing new (except to me) about the British gun, a .303 that took a considerably different cartridge than his Savage. This was a bolt gun, the famous SMLE (Short Magazine Lee-Enfield) that had accompanied soldiers of the British Empire to two world wars and several smaller ones. So cheaply were these now being sold mail order to the American public—$14.95 if I recall correctly—that at least three sons of my minister father had come up with the money to buy one.

My particular rifle had a very short buttstock that intensified its recoil. The first sighting-in session had beaten my left cheek black and blue, and Dad, noticing, had said, "I'll fix that for you." He disappeared with the rifle into his basement woodshop, and by the time he emerged the butt of the stock had been lengthened with a piece of walnut beautifully cut to a scroll design and inlaid into the old blond birch stock, which I had already refinished in the process of "sporterizing" the rifle. "Neat, Dad. It will need a buttplate of some kind. Since the butt is bigger now, the old one won't fit." Dad sat back at the supper table thinking of this next phase, which had not yet occurred to him. He was not a hunter or a rifleman.

"I've got some black plastic in the basement. We'll make a buttplate after supper." And so we did. We appropriated the thick plastic from an old jukebox Dad was salvaging for the amplifier and speakers. He cut it to shape, and I heated a soldering iron and pressed lines into the plastic in a checker-

2. The author's .303 British, with his father's handiwork.

board fashion to keep it from being slippery. I still have the rifle.

I was in my first stage of ballistics study, reading voraciously the writings of firearms scribes in the big three, *Outdoor Life, Field and Stream,* and *Sports Afield,* subscriptions to all of which Mom, a magazine nut herself, had sent in for me. I had learned to look upon my faithful first deer rifle, the Sears/Marlin 30-30, as something rather lowly, with rainbow trajectory and limited effectiveness. I was wrong to do so. I was also wrong to become fixated on the drop of the 30-30's blunt bullets, a fixation that caused a spate of terrible missing because of unnecessary holdover. During this particular hunting season I was convinced that the bigger British cartridge, though no flatter shooting with the loads I was using, was a significant improvement, and so I would use it instead.

The Studebaker cruised south out of town, up the valley

a mile or so, furnishing time to plan. "Can we get into the basin?"

"Right now," he said, flicking the ashes of his cigarette out the window, "you could get the Ford up the logging road, but we'd probably just as well walk. I've run into good bucks on the way."

"Yeah, it takes quite a bit of snow to stop the Ford," I bragged. "Remember the time we put Billy and Bruce on the back bumper for traction and went like hell. Got up there and those Billings hunters with a new Jeep and chains on all fours looked at us like we were scum." We took time for a laugh over that. Today I still remember the red faces sticking out from blaze orange, the hunters, well-heeled urbanites by our standards, proud of their new outfit and its backcountry capabilities, shocked to see this crowd of unruly boys show up at "their" hunting spot propelled by a hoodless, madly driven 1947 Ford with bald sawdust traction tires and two boys on the back bumper leaning forward across the top cheering on the driver, the whole crew having altogether too much fun.

"Better get back to town," Robert said, pointing to the gas gauge. We turned around at the south entrance to Lover's Lane and cruised gently back. The dryland hills on either side of the valley were brown, cattle browsing the remains of the summer's grass. At the gas station I kicked in six quarters—paper delivery money—which, when combined with Robert's dollar, bought seven gallons of gas.

Through the whole of that next week I ached to go. To a young hunter, "nice" weather is not the sunny sort. "Nice" weather promises snow in the high country. "Nice" weather makes you stand for a moment on the walk home from school facing the wind that blows down from the mountains, taking deep gulps of it. And it was that sort of week. The anticipation was made worse by early reports of success from other young hunters. Larry Pederson came to school and pointed down to the bloodstains on his tennis shoes. "Four-point buck," he said. "Uncle Slim helped me dress him out."

But the seemingly endless week finally passed. Thursday night I cleaned the two rifles, assembled hunting license, knife, ammunition of both types, and some new but cheap mail order snow packs I'd sent for. It had snowed heavily in the mountains. The white toward the tops of the peaks had that deep, velvety look, even from twenty miles away. Friday after school Mom helped me make some sandwiches. Then, after checking the oil and the gas gauge level of the old Ford I cranked its flathead six into life and headed up the valley.

What a victory; what a release! To be sixteen years old (Montana kids could legally drive at fifteen, and still can), with an aged car to call one's own, a rifle with which to hunt, and freedom, finally, from four schoolroom walls; to be driving toward snowy mountains inhabited by deer, moose, and elk, pulled toward adventure by the throaty roar of an engine whose oil you changed yourself. I was Odysseus headed out, Huck Finn casting off, Daniel Boone aiming for the Gap.

My memory, through the selective sift of time, retains little from the twelve hours that followed my parking the Ford by the decrepit Amos cabin. There was, no doubt, Mrs. Amos's venison, the dull roar of many children confined to the house by snow outside, the boys' sleeping area, a built-on lean-to with potbelly stove kept red hot by Robert's periodic attention (he jammed it full of wood every couple of hours on through the night). I do remember the heat it threw toward one side of me being barely adequate to balance the chill of my other side, the one toward the drafty wall by which I'd found a stretch of floor on which to unroll my sleeping bag. But none of this matters.

What is there for me, as sharp as if it were yesterday, is

standing outside long before dawn, shivering, going over in my mind whether I'd retrieved everything important from the Ford, smelling the first puff of Robert's cigarette mingled with morning smells of snow and pines and wood smoke from the chimney. Even now we were hunting, so we talked in whispers. "Let's wait a few more minutes," he said. "No sense spooking a big buck when it's still too dark. Then we'll walk up the logging road through the ranch and toward the basin." I nodded. No plan hatched by Robert would have drawn a protest from me.

"The ranch," as Robert called it, a big, well-heeled outfit that took dudes in the summer, was posted. We did not particularly worry about this because its owners had shown tolerance for hunters who merely crossed the property on their way to the forest service land above. Would we, in that day and age, have taken a buck on our way through that private land if temptation had presented itself? Probably. But it was a different age. On the one hand landowners had not then commercialized hunting to the degree it is today; they seemed to feel hunters had some inherent right to the game. Further, they didn't have to worry as much about destruction and theft, about someone setting up a meth lab in any old shack or house in a back pasture, about someone being injured on their property and suing even though they lacked permission to be there.

The logging road, illuminated by moonlight on the snow, threaded through cottonwoods on the creek bottom, the occasional aspen grove (we always called them "quakers," never "quakies" as in Colorado), and finally into second-growth lodgepole pine. There were manmade clearings ahead, the now-brushy sites of abortive attempts to find oil. Near the basin it was not uncommon to stumble into the capped casing of a well that did not produce. These clearings were prime places to catch a buck in the open, so we walked very slowly, straining for light, not wanting to get to the best places too quickly.

Holding our rifles over the crooks of our arms while walking side by side, muzzles pointed outboard, we communicated by reaching out and touching the other. No two hunters stalking water buffalo in the African bush could have been more intense, with senses more alive. The slight breeze in our faces was perfect. But morning light soon came, turning the snow bluish, our eyes now watering from the chill and from straining to see between the trees, and there were no deer.

By the time we reached the edge of the huge basin we had checked several of the logged clearings to no avail. There were many fresh tracks. But when Robert stopped under a spreading Ponderosa pine, took a deep audible breath, and reached for a cigarette, I knew that phase one was over. We had not surprised a buck at dawn. The cold morning sun now stabbed over the mountaintop, though most of the basin was still in shade. "We'd just as well take a rest," he said.

"Lots of tracks."

"Can't eat tracks." I could have predicted that. We waited until the morning frost had just begun to find my toes. Robert snuffed the cigarette. "Let's head up this trail," he said, indicating right, a trail I knew well that angled west along a sidehill and gradually ascended a ridge. From it, looking left and south, you could see down into a promising coulee at the edge of the basin, a coulee bottomed with beaver ponds and quaker groves. "Go ahead first, Dan."

"That's okay. You go." He had made the offer and now did not argue, stepping out smartly up the trail, my 30-30 in the crook of his left arm, its muzzle facing the direction of likely action, his dark eyes in their usual squint. I am not sure why I let him go first.

It happened very quickly. The pull of the climb had removed all chill from my toes, and my hands, too, had warmed, gloves now in my coat pockets. My eyes watering from the wind, I saw no more than a flash of tail, the glinting horns that said buck and a good one, and Robert's fluid drop to a knee. The 30-30 tracked for an instant, then bellowed. There was a crash of something heavy falling into dry, crackly brush, and then silence. Until I could hear again the wind rustling the lodgepole pines above me, Robert did not move, the 30-30 still at his shoulder as he squinted down the sights toward the bottom of the coulee. Only then did he say softly, "Got him."

It took both of us to pull the whitetail buck from the patch of brush at the edge of the beaver pond, to get him onto a nearly flat spot of snow where we could dress him out and really look at him. He was magnificent. With thick antlers two feet wide, four points on each side plus the brow tines, a four-point to us, a ten-point to Easterners (and now, in our age of superlatives, a five-point to many Westerners who have forgotten the rules), the buck looked like those of dreams. "Pretty as anything I've ever seen in *Outdoor Life*," Robert said, echoing my thoughts. And then, "But he's your buck. You were supposed to be ahead of me, and it was even your rifle. We'll just say you shot him."

I said nothing. We field dressed the buck, marveling at the fat everywhere under his hide, the fat that left our hands sticky with tallow wherever his blood touched us. "He'll be some fine eating, Dan." He was even more than that, and respect for the buck quieted the two of us. It was as if a king had come down to our level, leant himself to us. Dragging him up the steep slope to the trail, I would wince when we had to jerk his body to get it unstuck from buck brush. We were as gentle as we could be.

But once on the trail, for two successful hunters, boys in shape, with the lubrication of snow on the trail and then on the logging road, and with the assistance of gravity, the going was easy. Each of us took a side of his beautiful horns, wrists in a fork of the tines, and walked at nearly unburdened speed. Periodically we'd switch sides to ease the ache of the arm we had been using. In little more than an hour we scented the pine smoke from the Amos chimney, and Robert said, "Hell, there'll still be time for more hunting. We can put your tag on this one, then go look for another one for me."

I had been thinking of this buck hanging from the rafters of the old doorless garage by the church. Everyone would admire him. Larry Pederson would come to look. Bruce would be full of envy and grudging admiration. Dad, never shy about superlatives, would tell everyone about the massive buck his son got and dragged down from MacDonald Basin.

When we were in sight of the Amos house a dog barked, and then the parade began, led by Billy, the quiet one, also a hunter, a train of younger brothers and sisters behind him. And just as Robert opened his mouth to speak to Billy, I said, "Your brother's a helluva shot. Got this one on the run, right behind the shoulder. Give us a hand, Billy, and we'll get him hung up."

Billy looked his brother in the eye and said under his breath, "It's daylight. Better tag him." Robert pulled out his wallet, fished for the tag, retrieved it and started to attach it. "Better punch it," Billy insisted. We snaked the buck out into the cabin clearing, Billy relieving me, found a single-tree in the junk pile, and hung him up.

"There's time to go up again, Dan."

"That's okay, Robert. I think I'll head home." Mrs. Amos had come to the front door. I thanked her for the food and for letting me stay and then got into the Ford. I wanted to feel noble, but I couldn't. I knew that feeding that hungry mob of kids some of the most select venison they would have all year had nothing whatsoever to do with my blurting out quickly that Robert had shot the buck. I was a young hunter, but I already knew that the best of it has nothing to do with competition, with showing off, and that those who hunt for those reasons are just shooters of game, not hunters. Robert was a hunter. It was his deer. I could have taken no pride in it, perhaps could not have even been able to hide the truth when the people at home were patting me on the back.

It was only noon. As I drove the Ford I reached into the sack on the seat behind me and pulled out one of Mom's turkey sandwiches. There would be time for a short hunt with brother Steve that afternoon, maybe out beyond the dump. If we went, I would take the 30-30.

3

Little Brothers and the Rifles of the Empire

I looked him in the eye. Now, at the threshold of his teens, Steve was already afflicted with the nearsightedness that would catch up with all of us brothers, so he wore glasses that to me seemed thick, and his look through them conveyed indignation at my doubt. He held the old military rifle at what I'd learn later in the Marines was "port arms," shook it once, then braced the butt against his knee to free one hand, pointed at the tall, fold-down peep sight, and said, "Why in the world wouldn't it work? Why would the English government put a sight on this thing that wasn't akret?" (We never pronounced all the syllables in "accurate.")

"That's not what I meant. You said you'd just click it up to three hundred or five hundred yards if that's how far away the deer was, and it would be no sweat hitting him. What I mean is that the sight was probably regulated for military ammo, which might not be the same bullet weight or velocity as the soft point bullets you're using. The trajectory wouldn't be the same. Besides, you'd have to estimate the range almost perfectly, otherwise you'd shoot either below or above him. Even if everything else was perfect, your rest would have to be steady as a rock."

He looked at me blankly. He had not pored over every treatise of Jack O'Connor, Clyde Ormand, Elmer Keith, and Warren Page that he could lay his hands on, as I had. He did not nightly revisit a stack of dog-eared *Outdoor Life* and *Field and Stream* magazines as I did. He knew nothing but unreasoning faith in one of the world's large governments. If they installed a sight on the rifle that helped win two world wars, a sight with a dial on top and graduated increments marked in yards all the way up to one thousand, then, by golly, it ought to be "akret." "Well," he said, "I still think it'll work."

Andy, the brother between Steve and me in age, less passionate about hunting than we were, looked on with mild interest. He, too, had sent for one of the $14.95 surplus rifles along with a couple of boxes of discolored ammunition advertised to be "non-corrosive," probably military rounds with bullets pulled and replaced by soft-nosed spitzers. Andy wasn't worried, and we did not worry about him. He had, after all, the "luck of the Andy." A better athlete than either of us, for all we knew he would beat us to the top of the mountain, pull down on a Boone and Crockett buck, shoot it through the heart from the hip, then drag it down in time for basketball practice and a little girl-chasing afterwards. And he would think there was nothing remarkable about any of it.

But Steve and I were more influenced by the tough but pessimistic Norwegian tradition that expected no favors from wind or weather, no luck beyond the mathematical odds. Mule deer hunting to us meant cold, wind-blown hillsides, the range grass having lost the dazzling ornamentation of fall's scarlet buck brush as November shut things down. But for Steve there was this silver bullet: a rifle all his own, ammunition in its ten-round clip, and an "advanced" peep sight on the receiver with clicks all the way to a thousand yards.

We would get as far into big-buck country as the old Ford would take us, then walk the big coulees with in-line deer drives that placed one hunter on the ridge, another halfway down, and a third in the bottom. For all the wind and cold, it would be exciting, the country open and wild, sagebrush flats bordered by patches of dark timber that dropped steeply into the coulees.

3. The author's brothers circa 1962: Andy Aadland (left) holds Dan's .30-30 carbine while he flanks a nice mule deer buck with brother Steve, who holds his .303 British. Because of a testicular abnormality, the buck was still in velvet in October.

Enough years have passed to make many mule deer hunts with brothers and friends melt together in memory. Usually it was mule deer, because although whitetails existed in the river bottoms, their population explosion had not yet occurred, and they were less accessible. Almost always it involved the 1947 Ford or one of the Amos brothers' Studebakers. Only once did it involve a more suitable vehicle, a Jeep, but that was unpleasant, with brother Andy and me stuffed into the rear jump seats, cold feet, moving on two big bucks too early, the friend's father angry with us for blowing the chance.

More than the vehicles, there was the walking, miles and miles of it, because to boys whose greatest Saturday joy was hiking the foothills with dogs and .22 rifles, walking was not a chore. There was a profound lack of money. Rounds of big game ammunition were counted individually, treasured and hoarded. Food came from Mom: huge slices of her home-made bread sandwiching last night's main dish, whatever that had been.

None of us ever shot a trophy buck or even a very good buck. During my spate of missing with the 30-30, my ballistic studies having skewed any faith in the gun so that I tended to overestimate range and shoot too high on first impulse, I did have several chances at true trophies. Once, Robert Amos and I were ascending a ridge in deep snow, and suddenly, there was the buck. I did not take time to sit down. The shot whistled harmlessly over his back, and he was gone. Robert issued the only reprimand I ever remember from him: "Dan, *never* do that."

Another time, with another friend, I labored through knee-deep snow on a frigid morning all the way to the top of a mountain ridge several thousand feet above the valley floor. This onset of winter had been early, at the beginning of hunting season, so we did not believe we'd hiked so high we were above the deer. But I wondered. Through deep timber, aspen groves, and open clearings we struggled along, wishing for snowshoes, seeing only trackless snow, an endless expanse of whipped cream. And then, in a patch of scrub fir, there was a deer partially obscured by brush. It was no more than fifty yards away, frozen, its nose and eye and rump visible. I was certain I had seen horns but now could make out nothing with unaided eye, the iron-sighted 30-30 in ready position. Melvin had the only binoculars. He studied and studied, then proclaimed decisively, "Doe!" Does were legal, but we weren't about to drag one down through deep snow from a mountaintop. We both lowered our rifles and let out deep breaths. And, from the brush, the "doe," tree-branch antlers on "her" head, launched. In three giant jumps he/she was over a little ridge, out of sight.

We stood for a moment with our mouths open. I needled, but just a little. "Pretty big horns on that doe."

"Yeah," he said, as dejected as I was. Then we both laughed. We'd been beaten fairly. The big buck had given us a thrilling jolt, had reminded us that as hunters we were really still boys, had left us only a series of pyramid patterns of tracks in the snow where all four feet landed before each of his giant mule deer jumps, to proclaim that he had not been a phantom after all. It was worth the hike.

But today was another hunt. As Steve, Robert, his phlegmatic brother Billy, and I slammed the doors of the old Ford in front of the Amoses' ramshackle house, we were hopeful but not confident. We knew the realities. A chinook wind was blowing so hard we could hardly stand on the glazed ice of the gravel driveway. Warm winds from the southwest that sweep over the tops of the mountains, blowing snow thousands of feet into the air so that the mountaintops are shrouded in artificial clouds, the chinook winds are nearly always welcome. But the country around Nye, Montana, is already known for its winds. Add a chinook and, yes, the snow will melt all right. But the deer, too smart to stand in the wind, will bed down in the junipers, their grey coats melting into the sagebrush. And they will stay there unless you stumble upon them.

The muffler on the Ford was long gone, but I liked the resulting rumble of the flathead six. Backing onto the county road, I gave the accelerator an unnecessary goose. "Where we goin', Robert?"

"Midnight Canyon. It's deep enough to get us out of this damn wind."

"The rancher will let us across the private land?"

"Yeah. I helped him brand last spring, and he said it was okay."

That was a little tenuous, and more so when he flipped his cigarette out the window, its spark arcing toward the snow in the barrow pit and said, "Just don't stop." Oh, well. I was sixteen. Robert was nearly twenty. He would take the heat if we got into trouble traversing the half-mile of private road that fronted the BLM and forest service land to the north. He was well known, admired for what stability he gave a family that would have had none without him, so if he interpreted our privileges a little too broadly, the consequences would not be severe. We would probably just be made to understand that we were not to cross the tract again.

After a couple of miles we left the county road, passed through a wire cattle gate, which Robert opened, then held as we passed through. He was already hunting, I noticed, his dark eyes scanning the low ridge we would cross on the two-track ranch road. Given the chinook winds, I'd been concerned about mud, but the ranch tracks ascended the ridge on the side of a shallow coulee, mostly shaded from the sun, the surface still solidly frozen. The earlier wind, the cold one before the chinook, had bared the road of snow, so the occasional drift was shallow, the Ford able to punch through with a quick downshift and thump on the accelerator. If the road thawed while we were hunting we'd make it back out okay, because gravity would be on our side.

There were two more gates, the second the one putting us safely onto public land. I suspect Robert took the normal ribbing from the back seat about opening gates, for the most comfortable passenger seat, in front on the right by the door, carries that duty with it. The "real cowboy," the western saying goes, is smart enough to get out of opening gates by sitting in the middle of the front seat.

Once through that last gate, we abandoned the car. We knew better than to continue on the Jeep road that descended into Midnight Canyon, knew that climbing back out, especially as it thawed, would be beyond the Ford's capabilities. Besides, hunting to us was walking, and this was a landscape that beckoned, a mosaic of brown range grasses bared off by the wind, small white drifts of snow, patches of pines nearly black in the stingy light from a slate sky. To our left was the big canyon, mostly timbered. We would avoid hunting too deeply into it because of the tough uphill drag we would face if we were successful. One of us said, I'm sure, the old, "Shoot one down in there, and you'd better have a frying pan with you and just eat till it's gone."

So we would skirt the top of the canyon and the little timbered pockets to the east, looking for deer bedded out of the wind in the small coulees feeding the canyon. But before we hatched any plan involving the four of us, we were suddenly three, because Billy was simply gone, faded into the timber. He was that way. He had a plan, we knew, and he would be back when the time came for him to be back, and we would not worry about him.

After so many years I cannot claim to remember clearly the details of the day. I remember seeing deer, but at a distance, small groups betrayed by the contrast of their rump patches, otherwise blending perfectly with sage and juniper as I tried to discern them through eyes watered by wind. The deer were quicker to leave their beds than we had expected them to be, spooky just as horses are when the wind blows hard, and too often up and bouncing away long before we were close enough for a shot. There seemed to be no bucks, or if there were any, all must have been spindly horned forkhorns or spikes with antlers scarcely visible at a distance. Nothing in the several groups that cleared the ridge to our front and briefly paused on skyline bore the heavy horns of my dreams.

Robert acted as guide for Steve, who at the beginning of his hunting years was ready to be much satisfied by any deer. (Our tags were for either sex.) I paralleled the two of them at a distance. There was, I'm sure, a small fire at midday, kindled by Robert, while we ate Mom's sandwiches. And there is this picture, sharply imbedded: eager little brother Steve, hair blond, nearly white, next to dark, long-haired, wiry Robert, the younger boy peering toward his guide, matching his movements, looking where he looked. Steve's unmodified military rifle was heavy in his hands, and he frequently switched it from right to left.

Steve was with me when I shot my first deer. Too young for a hunting license, he was still as eager as I was. At fourteen, like most of the town kids, I was allowed by my parents to drive without a driver's license, and although the grey Studebaker of our town deputy Fearless Fred slowed menacingly a couple of times, the lined, stoical face of the old cop staring with penetrating eyes, its flashing lights never came on.

We drove after school on the winding dirt road north of

town, past the town dump, and hiked across a plowed field toward some mini-buttes around which we had hunted rabbits the previous year. Once across the plowing, on the late-season brown range grass mottled by yucca, prickly pear, and juniper, walking was much easier. The scent of sage at that time of year tickles your nose. I remember the day as warm, the scene wrapped by the view to the south from this high ground with the great wall of the Beartooth Mountains, purple, new snow on the peaks.

My first success on deer was not of the storybook sort I had seen on the pages of *Outdoor Life*. There were no big antlers, no photo opportunity of boy hunter and father flanking a giant deer head, the father wringing his son's hand with pride (although when we finally got our meat back to town Dad was celebratory enough). With two either-sex deer tags in my pocket I wanted success and meat. I could use the second tag for the dream buck. It did not take long to fill the first one.

In a little pocket between the small buttes we jumped a band of mule deer at close range. There were no bucks. I did have the presence of mind to sit down (narrowly avoiding a prickly pear) as I levered a cartridge into the chamber of the new 30-30, then swung on one of the does in the line that loped casually across our front at seventy-five yards. I waited a trifle too long. By the time the rifle fired, the doe I had chosen was approaching alignment with the setting sun, though not yet on skyline, and I was a little surprised to see her pace slacken. Then she fell. Steve and I rushed to the scene. She was still moving slightly, so in haste I fired a finisher, a head shot, learning first hand something about the destructiveness of even a modest big game caliber up close.

I was shaking. I wished the doe no suffering. Steve and I conferred, agreed quickly that she had suffered little if at all, the kill of the sort you call "clean." But now the things I had studied only in books were stark reality. Lacking a hunting mentor, even the opportunity to go along with anyone, I had never seen on the ground a dead, bloody deer, killed by a hunting rifle. I had studied what came next, had read and memorized how-to photo sequences on field dressing game animals, but I had never seen it done. I had a huge impulse to forget the whole thing and walk toward the car, but Steve's wide-eyed jubilation at my first deer was contagious, and, of course, stigmas against waste and breaking the law made impossible any alternatives to carrying the task through.

So, in time, the shiny hunting knife, a birthday gift from Dad, came out of its leather sheath (on which I had wood-burned my name), and little brother was assigned the task of holding out the doe's hind leg while I made the first cuts. It actually went quite well. Everything was exactly as the photos had shown. My one mishap after removing the entrails was a step backward, landing one foot squarely on the stomach of the deer, which now lay on the grass near the carcass. That was a lesson in the digestive process of mammals I did not particularly need at the moment.

But with the field dressing of the deer came the transformation known to all hunters and meat eaters, the deer now not a dead creature that was alive only a half hour earlier, nor an animal in any way to be pitied. The deer was now meat. The meat was clean (if only we could keep it that way), red, little ruined by either bullet (my first had gone high through the rib cage). We had eaten enough good venison donated by Dad's parishioners to relish it. But with the killing of my own deer the blanks were filled in, the equation balanced, and I knew I'd savor its meat. I had bought a rifle, sighted it in, driven my own car to the right place, found a deer, killed it, and dressed it out. Shock was now being replaced by pride.

One major lesson remained. Steve and I quickly discov-

4. A mule deer doe.

ered the meaning of dead weight, even that of a smallish yearling doe. Worse, we discovered the agony of dragging such a
weight over soft, plowed ground.

Late in the day of Steve's first deer there was a rendezvous of
Robert, Steve, and me on a ridge overlooking the big canyon.
We spotted Billy a half mile away walking toward us. As strong
as he was quiet, Billy would reach the car not long after we
would, though he had much farther to travel. We had come to
that point you discover on many hunts when the excitement is
worn down by the walking, and the car heater becomes a pleasant thought. There would be other days in Montana's long
hunting season, days when the wind blew less strongly and the
deer were less spooky. The rut was beginning. Maybe my imagined buck would show up as they eventually do, lured beyond
his powers of common sense. I was ready to call it a day.

So was little brother. Talking loudly now, we dropped out of hunting mode, laughed and ribbed, walking a beeline to the car. And, of course, as so often happens while hunting, our lapse in concentration corresponded with the sudden appearance of game. There was a shallow coulee to the northeast near the parked car, and crossing the bottom of it was a small bunch of mule deer, six or eight of them, their gaits alternating among walk, trot, and lope, not really hurrying, but moving out just the same. They were already out of practical range for our rifles. I trotted to where Steve and Robert conferred. Robert was saying, "Well, if you're going to shoot you'd better, 'cause they ain't getting any closer."

Steve flopped onto his belly in prone position. "How far?"

"Too far," I said, but I knew he was going to do it anyway. The deer had moved up the far side of the coulee. "It's got to be four hundred yards." Steve pushed the long range sight up from its folded position, squinted at the numbers on it, and cranked the dial. The deer were piling up against a barbed wire fence, jumping it one at a time. As Steve aimed I watched the muzzle of the rifle do an unsteady little dance, then stop just an instant before the rifle bellowed and recoiled.

At first I saw nothing. The deer, in late afternoon, their grey so perfectly blended with the grass and sage, were hard to see at all at such long range, and from what I could tell all were moving normally. The last of the bunch jumped the fence, then slowed, and then Robert yelled, "Hey, it's down!" Billy had appeared. Both of the Amos boys had eyes like hawks, and one of them said, "Sure as hell. It ain't goin' nowhere."

It was then that Steve answered me, asserted his claim to be right about something, little brother status or no. It came with one word, before he even got up from the ground. He craned around to look at me, pointed at the peep sight on his rifle, and said, "See?"

Yes, I saw. I saw that compared with the stark evidence of a deer dead on the ground after one shot, a deer lying nearly a quarter of a mile away, that all the ballistics knowledge, all the Jack O'Connor evidence, all talk of bullet weights, trajectory, and the effects of wind on flying projectiles, was now as effective as a handful of rocks. I felt like Huck Finn trying to argue with Jim.

The other three hurried toward the fence, where the deer, it turned out, was a little button buck, shot squarely through the lungs. I took my time. I wanted to pace the distance to check my estimate. Besides, Steve's field dressing job was in good hands with the help of Robert and Billy. After four hundred and ten long, deliberate paces, as close to a yard apiece as I could estimate them, I arrived at the deer and announced the distance. That kicked off a renewed chorus of exclamations, congratulations, slaps on the back, and protestations from Steve that it was mainly luck. Assuming that the trajectory of the bullet matched the graduations on the sight relatively well (and this seemed evidence that it did) I could have claimed some credit for the accuracy of my estimate. Fifty yards wrong in either direction would have meant a miss. But I kept what little satisfaction that gave me to myself. Any way you stacked it, it was a hell of a shot. I found myself proud of the brother.

I hurried back to the car, planning to juggle it down the hillside toward the coulee bottom to shorten the dragging distance, but it was little use. I'd no sooner arrived, cranked the six into life, and started down, than I saw the hard-muscled Amoses dragging the deer at a near trot, Steve walking to the side carrying his rifle. They were halfway to me before I got the car moving.

There is in Montana during the foreshortened days of fall, when light changes very quickly, a magical moment between sunset and darkness, especially when you look east.

The grasses change from brown to reddish brown, and then to red. For just a moment the scene seems very bright, the colors saturated, then subtle, then gone. I watched this progression through the windshield of the old Ford as the three figures neared. Quick as they were, it was gone by the time they arrived. We loaded the buck into the Ford's generous trunk. On the way down to the county road we needed the headlights.

4

A Christmas Buck

As the years pile up I find myself thinking of past experiences less in the first person and more in the third. I'm afraid that as you age a certain toughness is lost, and I look back on my actions and those of people closest to me with wonder. Not that the "characters" were truly heroic, but they certainly seem braver and in many ways more capable than I could be today.

So this is the story of a Marine lieutenant on leave and his little blond wife named Emily, and I see them now in a certain way that doesn't correspond to "she and I." I see them as if from a low-flying helicopter hovering over a piece of terrain with which I am intimate. They are walking away from a tiny blue Toyota car parked at a ranger station. He has a rifle slung on his shoulder. Against the snow on the ground, the blue car and their orange vests contrast sharply. Over the steep timbered ridge toward which they walk briskly the sky is very blue and very bright with white clouds that reflect the low winter sun.

This is a return home for both of them, to the ranch on which she grew up and on which he worked, and for him, to a hunting ground he knew with friends and brothers. Behind the ridge toward which the couple walk lies a place called Bad Canyon, a name well earned. In front of the ridge is a thin strip of private land, irrigated hayfields, then owned by a tolerant landowner who, although he did not allow you to hunt there, didn't mind if you walked through it the quarter mile east to reach the steep timbered ridge, which is on forest service land.

Driving to Bad Canyon was always impossible after the first snow, and in any case couldn't be attempted with the little Toyota. Walking toward the ridge that fronts it, the lieutenant has much to recall. There were insane drives up a treacherous road cut into the side of a canyon, the old Ford goosed, two boys standing on the back bumper for traction, their bellies flat along the rounded contour of the car body, in the posture (if you could remove the car) of Olympic ski jumpers. In darkness and deep snow, he and a friend hiked off the ridge, trying several routes that dead-ended at cliffs, working their way around each of them, cold and wet but more worried about being late for the school carnival, at which they were scheduled to work, than about returning with their limbs intact.

It was off one of those cliffs on another trip that his brother Andy dropped the Sears/Marlin 30-30, breaking its buttplate. Andy returned it to his older brother with that sheepish grin that allowed him to slide out of so many touchy situations with his father, and it worked here, too. It was hard to be mad at Andy.

It was on this ridge, too, that he missed a huge mule deer buck and received the only words of reprimand he remembered from Robert Amos. Today, he and Emily will not look for a giant buck. Any deer will do, really, though a buck will be better. Whatever comes along they will take, because they have just one day for this late season "damage" hunt, scheduled fortuitously by the Fish and Game department. The purpose is to have a hunt together and if possible take home some venison for Emily and her parents.

The road that took them from Montana and then returned them here, he for a brief season before Christmas, she to an aunt's cottage near her parents' house on the ranch where she will stay while he is gone, has been both beautiful and bumpy. They go back a long way. She was with him in the third grade class in the school where he played on the swings with the Gaustad kids during the December chinook that welcomed his family to Montana.

But the more immediate past, since their early marriage, has been dominated by the rest of college, then collisions of forty pairs of combat boots on the squad bay floor in the barracks at Quantico, Virginia, where he went for Marine officer's training. She went, too, living nearby during the early stages of his training, then with him when allowed. The winter was cloudy and wet with a cold wind off Chesapeake Bay that felt like nothing in Montana.

There was a war, and most of them would be going to it. There were, however, during the most dismal days of winter, some bright spots for both Emily and him. The Quantico backcountry, when he could tune out the barks of the drill instructors, was rugged and pretty, rolling hardwood hills watered by many small creeks and springs, with deer trails everywhere. Hunting was allowed, but there was no time for it.

During training that required locking step with many others, he longed often for solitude, and he got it on one fine day during a map-and-compass examination, an individualized hike that tested land navigation, one of the few areas of military academics in which he felt supremely confident. He hiked all day through the snowy woods, finding with little difficulty the numbered boxes that would prove his course. It was the closest thing to hunting he had that year, and it was very good. He stopped once on a logging road to watch a string of whitetail does cross. Three does in a row, then a pause. He froze. Then he came, a magnificent buck, crossing the road after the does had done so unmolested.

Marine life in southern California was better, the uniforms more casual, the sprawling breadth of Camp Pendleton retaining, because development was denied, a touch of the West.

There was much open country there. Housing developments had not yet enveloped all the land surrounding the base, so there was room for the two of them to roam with their dog and a neat little rifle he'd purchased, a Marlin lever-action rimfire in .22 magnum.

But, of course, this duty station soon would end with written orders, as they all do, and in this era most orders were to go "across the pond." His orders were to Okinawa, at least initially. Both knew where he would likely go from there, but they spoke of it little. The war to them was not a matter of good or bad, but simply reality, and he would likely have his part in it and she, hers.

So they have come home, she for a year or more, he for a few weeks. And during the bustle of preparation, of unloading household goods during the year's first snow, finding a Christmas tree, seeing his family (who have moved to Minnesota), of doing anything they can to make the ranch cottage more tenable for her during his thirteen-months absence, they have gained this opportunity to hunt. Mule deer are at the high end of a population cycle, and the Fish and Game has decided to reduce their numbers before winter snows set in and accomplish the reduction through starvation instead.

And so, the two of them begin to climb the ridge. They will not go all the way to Bad Canyon. They are not prepared for that. They should find mule deer in the many rough breaks and timber patches that contrast darkly with the snow. He has always found them there.

For the first time in his hunting life, he has just the right rifle. In the last days the U.S. government trusted its citizens to buy hunting rifles through the mail, he has ordered from (of all places) the Spiegel catalog a Savage model 110 left-handed bolt action .270 and mounted on it an inexpensive 4X scope. He has, now, what Jack O'Connor's writings extolled, the classic American caliber, a flat-shooting but light-recoiling western rifle. He will reload cartridges for it when there is time, but for now, while still in California, he has sighted it in with factory Silvertips to impact three inches high at one hundred yards, O'Connor's standard open-country trajectory.

Where the snow is light, blown off the stony knolls, they walk side by side. On game trails and where the snow is deeper, he walks in front with the rifle. They ascend, dots against the snow, checking patches of timber, the vapor of their breaths rising in clouds. It is hard work, but they are young.

They have climbed perhaps five hundred feet in elevation when they spot them, a line of mule deer nearly three hundred yards above, working their way to the right on a ledge trail. There is a buck with the group. They confer excitedly. From long training he is thinking in 30-30 terms, of slow blunt bullets, of a need to get closer, and then he remembers what he holds in his hands. He sits down in the snow and wraps his arm in the military "hasty sling." The mule deer are progressing at a trot toward a patch of brush that will hide them. He swings the rifle gently with the buck, the crosshairs just in front of him, and squeezes the trigger. She is sure she sees the buck flinch. The group enters the patch of brush and in a few seconds emerges on the other side. The buck is not with them.

There is not much more to tell. They ascend again, the slope so steep that it takes half an hour to reach the deer trail. The buck is there. He has died nearly instantly, as quickly as anything can die. In twenty minutes he is no longer a deer, but field-dressed winter venison, and the snow coupled with the steep descent makes the buck drag as easily as a child's sled most of the way. On tougher places she helps him drag, the two of them linked by the buck's horns, her right hand on one, his left on the other. When they must walk single file, she walks ahead carrying the rifle, leaving both his hands free for the dragging.

Soon they are back at the ranger station, smiling. They strap the deer across the rear deck of the Toyota. Elmer, Emily's father, loves venison and will be glad to see it. Along with Emily and her mother, Nora, Elmer will relieve the lieutenant of butchering duties, for there is little time left before he leaves and much to do. The car sputters to life, its exhaust flume rising, and aided by the added traction of the weight of the deer over its drive wheels, plows through the snow on the road from the ranger station, heading down the valley toward home and destiny.

Fast-forward five years. I am a graduate student in the English department at the University of Utah. Friends are over for dinner, and Sam, a fellow student from New Jersey, is idly leafing through one of our photo albums on the coffee table. He stops at a particular page and says sharply, "Dan, I'm ashamed of you."

At first I think he's kidding. Then I look at his eyes, and there is no humor there. He points down toward a photo, and I lean over, curious, and see that the photo is of me, holding the .270, orange vest in place, next to a mule deer buck tied across the trunk of a little blue Toyota. Sam is close to tears. "I can't image you killing an animal."

I say nothing. There is a great gulf between us, and I'm speechless, unable to cross it. Since the two of us are in a class on Shakespeare's tragedies together, I'm tempted to quote, "There are more things in heaven and earth than are dreamt of in your philosophy, Horatio." But I hold my tongue. Emily's and my winter meat, taken together at a time of terrible beauty, is murder to Sam. And I'm powerless to change that.

5. Author with winter meat for Emily, Elmer, and Nora (but murder to Sam) taken on the hunt with Emily just before author left for Southeast Asia.

5

Antelope

She thought we were driving straight toward the far end of the earth, and she wasn't bashful about saying so, this Montana ranch girl who craved elbow room but who was now seeing thousands of acres more of it than she'd bargained for. My feelings were close behind hers, though I was reluctant to admit it. Our home environment, the foothills of south-central Montana, ringed by the blue Beartooth Mountains, is one thing. The vastness of eastern Montana is another. Driving toward Jordan, we had turned at a wide spot in the road named Winnet, driven another hour or so in eager anticipation of a town named Mosby, passed it without being aware of it, and now were cruising down a totally unpopulated stretch.

Except where the highway passed through an occasional coulee wet enough to sustain a lonely cottonwood or two, there were no trees. The country wasn't flat, exactly. It was broken frequently by small buttes and rimrocks, and sometimes in the distance were blue hills covered with scrub pine. But the overall impression was that of being perched in our car on a vast bare globe, the sky so big it nearly encircled us. There were occasional cattle, and now and then a bunch of mule deer bedded in the shade of junipers. But there were always pronghorn antelope. There were so many that a herd was nearly always in sight, though sometimes so far away that you could only discern the distant white flecks of their rump patches.

I had finished graduate degrees at the University of Utah

and was set to be a college English professor. There was, how-ever, a dearth of jobs. Campuses that had been swollen by the ranks of those who found study more attractive than Viet Nam were now downsizing, and when my job search came up empty we decided to do what for us came naturally: head back to Montana. The cottage on the ranch was available to us as temporary quarters. We'd camp there while I stacked hay for ranchers and looked for something to sustain us.

It came with the interview opportunity toward which we now drove. We fancied ourselves true Montanans, impervi-ous to agoraphobia, renewing now our craving for the big open. That craving had been too long on hold. We had lived near Washington DC, in North Carolina, near San Diego, and in Salt Lake City. Perhaps, though we'd never admit it, the urban life had rubbed off on us just a little. Driving across a county half as large as Massachusetts but containing only 1,700 people was a jolt in the opposite direction, like jump-ing from a sauna into a snowbank.

Emily was very pregnant. The baby would arrive before our move from the ranch, but this trip to the interview proba-bly did little for her confidence that she could expand the secure nest that already contained David, our four-year-old. I'd assured her that Jordan, the only town in this county, had a hospital, and that in any case Miles City was only eighty-four miles away, Circle, in the other direction, only sixty.

After I accepted the job of teaching high school English in Jordan, Montana, there were many adjustments to be made, but they came quickly. The endless space around us, around the mobile home we bought and perched on high ground on the north side of town, eventually became such an addiction that whenever we returned to more domestic surroundings we felt claustrophobic. In addition to adjusting to the space, we adjusted to the people. They were archetypical Westerners, self-sufficient and tough. Ranch women thought nothing of hooking big gooseneck trailers to their pickups, loading up a dozen cows for market, filling the cab with kids, and heading for Billings 175 miles away. There they would unload the cows at the stockyards, drop the trailer, head for the shopping mall, stock up at K-mart, pick up the trailer, and then drive home. Such things were no big deal.

Jordan, Garfield County's county seat and only town, was so isolated that the high school where I taught had a dormitory to accommodate students whose ranch homes were eighty miles away. In spite of its low population, the county contained more one-room elementary schools than any other in Montana. Some of these schools were tended by dedicated, steady teachers, and others by people to whom such a teaching job had sounded quaint and interesting. One idealistic teaching couple from the East liked the idea of isolation, but not the reality. They fled in the night, two weeks into the fall term, and the kids arrived the next morning to a cold, empty, and silent classroom.

There were hardships, particularly the first winter, which was so cold that our propane bill each month nearly disintegrated my meager monthly teacher's salary. One morning, after getting my old pickup to cough into life, I eased out the clutch, hit a small bump, and heard a "ping," the snapping of a rear spring at forty below. That same old pickup jump-started the vehicles of many students, both after school and during the middle of icy nights when we returned from speech and drama meets at schools a hundred miles away. My teaching load was crushing. We never adjusted to the water. But there were always antelope.

Along with growing friendships, delightful little boys (Jonathan had joined David), and a good boss, we were sustained through our years in Jordan by the antelope. The bag limit was two. Add a mule deer, and the freezer began to contain serious heft. One antelope was always reserved for transformation by Mr. Ryan, the town grocer, who performed magic with spices and smokehouse, converting the animal into a summer sausage equally delicious whether on a sandwich, fried with eggs, or substituted for hamburger in the little one-burger electric grills that were popular at the time.

But it was more than their meat that sustained us. The antelope were wild and free, with room to run their fifty-mile-per hour sprints on ranches hundreds of square miles in size. Rarely could we drive any direction from town for more than five minutes without seeing them. As a hunter, they challenged me. As a father with a family to feed, they satisfied me.

There had been some hunting for me in Utah. Even then hunting was of marginal political correctness in the environment of an English graduate student. However, one colleague lived for both trapshooting and upland game hunting, while another was passionate about chasing waterfowl with his Labs. Better yet, my graduate committee chairman, Don D. Walker, an American scholar of renown, had, along with several of his cohorts, just enough residual western redneck to make him interesting. Literature of the American West was this group's side area of scholarship, and they didn't only study it—they lived it. They owned rifles, horses, and small ranches to which they would escape as soon as their quarter's grades were posted.

The group contained, too, the Chaucer specialist, who looked and acted like *Canterbury*'s monk. He would drive across state lines to buy just the right sort of ale, and like all in the group honored the monk's interpretation of scripture: They "gave not a plucked hen for any text which said hunters be not holy men."

Once a year Dr. Walker would host certain colleagues and former students, now professors, who had in common a bent for things Western, to a "rendezvous" at his ranch. An invitation during one's second year of graduate school to this well-known party was an honor, and attending it renewed Emily's and my touch with the West. There was a little ranch house nestled in oak brush and a pole corral with horses, along with campfire, barbecued turkeys, jackrabbit hunting, and loud academics in brief exile. We drank, told stories, and generally reveled in surroundings confined only by distant horizons and the stars above.

Later, Walker invited the hunters among us to his ranch to look for mule deer. It was a meat hunt, all of us with doe tags, the group progressing on a broad line through the oak brush with several hundred yards between us. I got the only shot. The doe ran through the brush and across a gap. I shot badly, too far back, but put her down. I split the deer with Dr. Walker, he insisting on taking the more damaged half. So I found myself under a lantern in a shed standing elbow to elbow with the same somewhat austere academic I'd known in graduate classes, his questions to students involved and terrifying, but now wielding a knife as I did while we jointly pulled the hide off a mule deer doe. Hunting can be a great equalizer. But I never could bring myself to call him Don.

To me, though, hunting was Montana and Montana was hunting. I'd enjoyed it briefly in other places, including in the middle of Iowa where Alan, a college roommate, took me back to his father's farm. We walked the corn rows with his older brothers as pheasants ran out of range in front of us, then cackled into the air at the border of the field. Alan's sisters-in-law cooked the pheasants that night along with dumplings and the rest of the bounty to be expected on old-fashioned Iowa farms. It was fine. But there was no blue line of mountains on the horizon and no country so wild that you could hope to encounter a bear or an elk.

I did renew my acquaintance with horses, though, in that Iowa country, enough to awaken dreams of hunting the mountains some day with horses of my own. The only Montanan on that particular campus, I'd been nicknamed accordingly: "Montana." Many knew me by no other name. Because I was from Montana, everyone assumed I was a cowboy, even though I never dressed like one or claimed talents in that direction. I did consider myself a horseman, however, perhaps somewhat prematurely, because the nature of horsemanship is such that later in life no real horseman looks back on his nineteenth year as one in which he deserved such a title.

Alan had a striking gelding, not large but beautiful, so red that "sorrel" doesn't capture it—the horse was nearly scarlet. I'd seen this arch-necked gelding once where it wintered on an uncle's farm five miles from Alan's parents' place. One March day Alan was puzzling how to get the horse over to the home place, since he had no horse trailer and didn't want to bother his busy father and brothers. Could I, perhaps, ride the horse over?

"Is he broke?" I asked.

"Well, I've been on him."

"Okay," I said, and therein bit off a bigger hunk than I knew. There was no rodeo, just a long, cold meander up a country road bareback on a horse that knew nothing. He was not mean. He did not try to buck or run away. It's just that he had absolutely no rudder, no rein, so that I'd haul him left and he'd go too far, all the way to the left shoulder of the road, then zigzag back when I tried to correct. Luckily there was little traffic. But I do remember this, as a college freshman with a future that I knew would take me even farther from

Montana, probably for many years: I would, someday, be hunting there again. I sat on this sweaty pony facing a humid Iowa wind on a gravel road where patches of wet March snow still clung to the shoulders, looking for mountains that weren't there, but still happy to have elbow room around me. I could wait. There would be smaller pleasures along the way.

Jordan, Montana, did not have mountains, but there was much rugged country, particularly in the Missouri River breaks to the north. I did not have horses, except for Sugar and Rosie, Emily's and my retirees back on the ranch, but good hunting horses weren't far in our future. My supervisor at school showed us a spirited gaited mare that, unknown to us at the time, would become a relative of our own stock, the first colt I'd raise and train from scratch.

So just as it occurred to me while sitting on Alan's colt, that the worst day outside straddling a horse beat hell out of most of the other days I'd recently experienced, it soon seemed to me that the toughest environment in Montana suited me far better than many alternatives. It took a while. I missed academia, my position as argumentative challenger among teaching fellows at the university, the bantering of ideas with peers. I was taken aback by the workload of a small-town high school English teacher, who teaches six classes every day, each with a different preparation, then is expected to handle extracurricular duties while finding work on the side to supplement his meager salary. But I was back in Montana, and I was hunting.

And soon, frequently emerging from his Ford Bronco in the parking lot of our trailer court, often near mealtime, came Hopkins. I remember him in those years as a plumpish young man in a leisure suit. (Ye gods, I wore them too!) He was quick-witted, his nimble hands darting precisely as he talked, and his talk was nearly always about guns and hunting.

His first name was Steve, but in a family replete with Steves he was more often, simply, Hopkins. He taught in the junior high school, then came across the parking lot to the high school to handle ninth-grade English, two large, badly behaved classes that gave him fits the first year. Later, he would develop mastery over this difficult age group, a teasing, humorous, quick-moving style that made the most recalcitrant junior high kids putty in his hands. But his first year of teaching, as it was for many of us, was rocky. Our warm trailer, Emily's supper cooking, little boys playing on the floor, seemed to furnish him welcome relief.

So did talk of guns and hunting. After years in academia I had nearly forgotten there were others as fascinated with ballistics, handloading, and accurate hunting rifles as I was. Steve was a wealth of knowledge and a constant source of humor, some of it in a language we called Hopkinsese: "Have a hunch, bet a bunch;" and regarding students, "Infamy, infamy, they all have it infamy." The gun language, however, Emily simply referred to as "code," and she was as adept at tuning it out, with an upward roll of the eyes, thirty years ago as she is now.

The people of eastern Montana are hospitable and helpful. Break your vehicle down on a county road, and the very first "outfit" to come along will stop to help. You can count on it, the only possible exception being the occasional vehicle bearing an out-of-area license plate. The hospitality carried over to hunting. A boy could give you fits all week during your class, and then invite you to hunt on his parents' ranch. We'd verify with the parents, arrive before dawn, and find that a sumptuous breakfast had been prepared for us. To the students it was an honor to have their teachers come and hunt, and students would compete for us. But, come Monday morning, the kid would resume giving you fits. He was a different personality in class than he was while driving his father's pickup and acting as guide, a light-years maturity gap between the two, but he saw no inconsistency whatsoever.

There was also near Jordan a massive prairie dog town, some two full sections (square miles) of mounds, the little misnamed rodents scurrying everywhere. There was little grass, the voracious critters having mowed every blade down to the dirt as is their habit. These champions of overgrazing have today become darlings of some environmental groups that hope, I suspect, that protected status for the critters would result in federal control of the vast lands they inhabit.

In the 1970s no one was talking about that. The rancher involved, however, tired of seeing two full sections of his rangeland devoted to rodent feed and the resultant holes that threatened the leg bones of his horses and cattle, was considering plowing the area. With the marginal reasoning of enthusiastic boys, Hopkins and I could justify "thinning" the creatures, thus keeping the town from spreading and perhaps saving the balance of it. This we did frequently, keeping our barrels hot and our marksmanship sharp.

To those who don't look closely, this vast eastern half of the country's fourth-largest state, this mix of grain fields, open prairie, piney buttes, and steep coulees may look barren indeed. To such, the blue mountains in the distance seem fertile gardens, the preferred environment for many types of wildlife. But Lewis and Clark ate well on the prairies and nearly starved in the mountains.

Truth is, what looks barren to the urbanite is a smorgasbord for a tremendous array of wildlife, something I quickly learned at Jordan. Many species have the best of both worlds: the natural protection and food sources of places such as the Missouri Breaks, supplemented by the husbandry of farmers, who grow nutrition-rich grain and alfalfa crops. Thus turkeys

6. Hopkins in the prairie dog town in the mid-1970s.

and deer (and today, elk) can live during the daytime in country so rough you nearly break a leg just looking at it, then emerge at night onto the fattening fields. I shot my first turkey in such country, with Hopkins and Gallahan, the basketball coach, as the birds began to retreat to the sheltering pines of the breaks. The turkey was delicious.

I can't say the same for the sage hens. Yes, I too admire this largest of the grouse family. On a field trip with students we stopped the bus for a fascinating distant view of their strutting, circular breeding dance, the males puffed up in the center of the circle of admiring birds of lesser stature. But all admiration stopped at the dinner table. We barbecued, fried, baked, soaked, marinated, and to us they still tasted like muddy sagebrush.

Hitting them was easy, even for me, a mediocre hand with my Savage side-by-side double. They looked like loaded B-52s as they nudged into the air. Hopkins and I told our students that we'd discovered the proper way to shoot them. On first flush you hollered "hoverrrr . . .," holding onto the "r" and the birds would beat their wings in place like a helicopter, making the shot an easy one.

The Missouri Breaks can be hunted on foot (and in some areas on horseback) but care is required. The country is incredibly rugged. I've watched hunters pass up standing shots at mule deer bucks of trophy quality at only two hundred yards, because between them and the deer were coulees with nearly vertical sides, hundreds of feet deep. Lacking a helicopter, retrieval would be almost impossible.

This is territory that laughs at four-wheel-drive if even so much as a quarter inch of rain has fallen. The gumbo soil simply rolls up on the tires. Jordan natives never tired of watching out-of-area rigs roll in sporting the biggest and widest tires, those labeled nearly unstoppable by their four-wheeler magazines, then head for the breaks while soils were wet. Invariably a beleaguered hunter would end up walking out to a county road to hitch a ride and seek help.

During warm weather you soon learn to either avoid the breaks entirely or to be prepared, should it rain, to wait it out. In that climate, rain is infrequent, and things dry fast. During hunting season we did our driving early in the morning when frost had stiffened the mud. In the evening we sometimes built a campfire and waited for temperatures to drop below freezing before storming out, keeping up momentum over the soft spots.

I never shot a really good mule deer buck in the breaks, but they exist there, and today, trophy elk as well. A small bunch had been planted north of Fork Peck Reservoir before our years in the area. An elk would occasionally cross the ice during winter and stir the desires of locals who had to travel to western mountains for their elk hunting. Those elk have since thrived, and the area has become a bonanza for bowhunters, many of whom base their hunts from boats on the reservoir.

Hopkins and I did share in a dandy buck. Improbable as it sounds, we shot simultaneously. Neither of us was aware that the other had fired. The buck dropped in his tracks. We each waited to be congratulated by the other until, as we both ejected our spent shell casings, it dawned on us that a .270 and a .264 had combined in the effort.

But memories of Jordan keep coming back to pronghorns. They were "antelope" to us, and sometimes "goats" to the locals, although biologists tell us they're really neither. What they are is a creature so magnificently adapted to its environment that you must look upon them with wonder. They may well be the world's fastest land mammal if distance is factored in at all. They seem to loaf as they run, their backs traveling as smoothly as that of a gaited horse, with none of the pogo-stick bounce of the mule deer or side-to-side dodging of the white-tail. Should you shoot at one on the run without leading it considerably, your shot falls behind. Meanwhile, the critter kicks up into the next gear, doing so deceptively. You increase your lead, but the accelerated pronghorn still outruns your shot.

Antelope seem to be far-sighted, some people claiming their distance resolution equals that of a human's supplemented by 8x binoculars. I believe it. Look at a spooky herd through your binoculars when they're so far away you've picked up only on the faint white sprinkling of their rump spots, and they're usually already looking at you. I've stalked them with belly crawls up ridges, careful to peek over with just the top of my head, just far enough that I can see, and found that they've been spooked even by that, at many hundreds of yards.

Conversely, they seem confused by objects near them. I've driven a pickup truck over a rise and dropped suddenly among a herd straddling a two-track ranch road, and had them mill around long enough to allow me to get out and take a shot, this while a herd a mile away has spotted the same truck and has lit out in high gear. Bowhunters readily fool antelope with decoys, behind which they hide. Often the curious creatures can't resist coming over to check things out. Indeed, when the first settlers came and the antelope were more innocent, they were lured within shooting range by a rag held aloft with a stick. Curiosity was often their downfall.

There is much bad hunting of antelope. Too often they're chased by vehicles, the "hunters" piling out and blazing away. Perhaps the modern idea that antelope are inferior eating has stemmed from too many being shot while adrenalin-charged during this sort of chase. In contrast, the mountain men considered antelope among the tastiest creatures, as did Teddy Roosevelt. Antelope were the primary staples for Roosevelt and his ranch hands during North Dakota winters, preferred to the beef they raised. A veteran guide and outfitter friend of mine considers antelope better eating than even elk and moose, but he's extremely particular. His routine: the antelope must be shot at dusk, skinned, hung just overnight, then cut up the next morning. He will not hunt antelope unless his schedule, and that of his wife, allows following this scenario.

I've always had good luck walking for antelope. Country that appears billiard table flat usually contains little dips and coulees that provide cover. The vehicle-bound hunter thinks he's seeing the whole picture and that the herd of antelope in the distance is unapproachable. Or else he sees none, and assumes there are none. But antelope country is nearly always more broken than it appears. Rarely have I launched out on foot in good antelope territory without finding them.

The challenge, of course, is to get within range. The animals key much less on scent or sound than deer or elk do. They rely almost exclusively on their vision. There's nearly

7. The next generation: Jon and David watching antelope.

always a vigorous wind in antelope country, so perhaps scent, tending to be blown toward the next state, has never been a reliable tool for their protection, and their sense of smell has thus not developed to be as acute as that of a deer or elk, creatures that spend some of their time in heavy cover. When you spot antelope at long distance, you must get out of sight as rapidly as possible, because they've already seen you. If they haven't bolted, they're watching to see what direction you go. If cover is impossible, walk away from them. Then, when a depression becomes available, drop into it. Usually a stalk is possible using the terrain, taking your time, staying low.

Antelope are not nocturnal as deer are. This is the reason relatively few are hit on highways, even in country loaded with them. Yes, it occasionally happens, normally in broad daylight. But at night, while deer are being frozen in head-lights, then smacked by vehicles, antelope are bedded down, often just over a ridge where they'll be protected from the wind. Sometimes early-morning hunting works, when you can approach their bedding area protected from sight. I've seen them bedded down in tight formation like sheep, fifty or so in an area no larger than a city lot.

I took one of the most memorable of the Jordan bucks by going up, rather than down. A small herd of antelope was grazing gradually to my left, nervous and watchful, but not quite ready to run. Between them and me was a pretty butte, flat-topped, a couple of hundred feet tall, rimmed with sandstone. I ducked down and crawled through the sagebrush until the butte blocked the herd's vision of me, then trotted to its base and started to climb. A few feet from the top I took a long time-out to allow my heart to slow and my lungs to quit heaving.

Then I eased over the top. At first I saw nothing, so I darted across the top of the butte, bent at the waist, and flopped down behind a patch of buckbrush. Again, I saw nothing for a moment, until I realized that, like the antelope, I was looking too far off into the distance. The herd was below me a mere seventy-five yards away, and the big buck fell to an easy but satisfying shot from my .270. While it's true that many antelope are taken at long range, a good number are also shot in just this way, relatively close at the end of a good stalk.

There is another hunt that stands out indelibly in my mind, as do many of the best hunting experiences, and not so because of the size of the animal taken. The big pronghorn buck I'd shot earlier was being processed in Mr. Ryan's smokehouse. The second either-sex tag would allow us fresh antelope steaks. We went after school, Emily and I, the little boys between us on the seat of the old GMC pickup.

Mr. Harbaugh, our school board chairman, was generous in allowing teachers to hunt on his ranch, considered modest in size by Jordan standards, where it takes many acres to graze a single cow. I believe the ranch was some one hundred sections (square miles) in size, and Mr. Harbaugh often used his small

airplane to check cattle. This particular day we did not have
to drive far into the ranch interior to find antelope. We spotted a small herd within a half mile of the dirt road and parked
out of sight. After a short stalk I shot a fat doe. Before I field
dressed the animal I was able to signal Emily to negotiate the
pickup my way—the terrain was gentle enough to allow driving to the downed antelope.

She arrived as I finished the dressing chore and let the boys
out of the pickup to play. David, six years old, checked out
the antelope, seemed impressed, and then found a small hill
to climb. Jonathan, at two, we'd keep closer. We had always
spoken freely around the boys about food, where it came
from, how the animals Dad hunted became good meat to
eat. Jon was probably too young to assimilate much of that.
He showed interest in the antelope, but no upset.

He was playing near the animal, occasionally looking its
way, and then, quite suddenly, toddled over to it. He squat-
ted down, his white-blond hair reflecting the setting sun, and
reached out and gave the animal one long pet down the hair
of its neck. Then, all smiles, he turned and resumed playing.
His face revealed no shock. What he understood about death
at this young age we could not tell, but this was not a pet of
pity or of sympathy. The act exuded respect, perhaps even awe
at the beauty of the creature. But more than that, it was simply
connection. He connected with the antelope during that
touch, and I think, at that moment, he became a hunter.

It's a difficult principle for nonhunters to understand, this
connection, this affinity, this near oneness with the animal
a hunter pursues and eventually eats. But it's there. It is
revealed in the cave paintings of early humans, in the utter-
ances of hunters from Chaucer's monk to Aldo Leopold to
Teddy Roosevelt. It is there, mysterious and powerful, in the
Massaum Dance of the Cheyenne. It was there that day in the
touch of a two-year-old boy.

8. Jon, who first touched an antelope at age two, with a nice antelope buck.

6

Rosie and Rockytop, Major and Mack

There are left in life on planet Earth few sensations like planting your left foot in a saddle stirrup, grabbing a handful of mane, and swinging onto a good horse that carries your rifle in a scabbard and your "possibles" in saddlebags. You instantly feel an affinity with the great hunters of the past—Boone, Crockett, and Roosevelt—and with fictional ones as well, Cooper's Leatherstocking and A. B. Guthrie's Dick Summers. More, you're sharing in the superior speed and power of the original all-terrain-vehicle, not as fast as its exhaust-spouting, elk-frightening mechanical counterparts, but able to take you places those machines cannot go. A horse can pack your camp in and your elk out. With his superior senses he can negotiate a trail in the dead of night and sniff out game ahead of you on the trail.

From boyhood, I needed no convincing. Hunting with horses would be the real deal, and I would do it someday. I would ride to the high country like Jack O'Connor and hunt out of a real camp, searching the rimrocks for heavy-antlered mule deer bucks and the dark timber for bull elk.

Since from the beginning my innate attraction to horses seemed as strong as my drive to hunt, I found ways to get close to the critters even though I was a town kid. Ranchers who invited the preacher's family to Sunday dinner sometimes let us ride their old reliables, savvy ranch horses that were gentle enough but talented at seeking out the slightest weakness or inability in the rider. We were easy pickings. My sister once mounted a palomino that headed for the barn at a dead run the instant she settled into the saddle. I remember her body swaying first forward until she nearly lay on the saddle horn, then backward until she nearly touched the horse's rump. Luckily, it was on one of those backward dips that the palomino stormed through the barn door, Carolyn barely clearing. She was unhurt.

Tomboy friend Mary Gaustad and I, in our country wanderings, were attracted to every horse we saw as if by magnetic force field. We would catch horses loose in the pasture when we could and ride them if we could get away with it. Sometimes this was not good. In a meadow fringed by woods with no houses in sight we once saw two friendly looking horses, grazing contentedly with halters on. We caught them easily enough and vaulted onto their backs. Mine did nothing. Mary's gave a tremendous buck and launched her into the unyielding, rocky ground.

I thought she'd been killed. Her face was deathly pale, and only very slowly did she rise to a sitting position and then shakily to her feet. She kept muttering that she was okay, but nothing about her—her color, her tentative steps, her weak tone—suggested that was true. This was the toughest kid on the block, packaged, it happened, in female form, a girl I'd never seen cry. I had a hitherto unknown impulse to put my arm around her as we walked slowly back to town—but I resisted it.

Along with teen years came the need to make a little money beyond weekly delivery of *Grit Magazine*, and the only attractive option to me was summer ranch work. That was where my equine education truly began. There was little stereotypical "cowboy" work, but there was an occasional need to move cattle or to check fences where vehicles could not go. The junior kid on the ranch does not get the best horse. I learned much about spoiled, recalcitrant animals that resisted work, and if made to work, tried bucking first. I learned too that most such creatures were bluffers, that if you could get past their initial resistance and convince them that you were more stubborn than they were, you'd have an easy day.

Although hunting with my own horse was many years away, I did start forming opinions about what sort of animal seemed most suited to the task. Brother Andy and I once walked up a long finger ridge perpendicular to a larger ridge behind which we intended to hunt. Parallel to us, on a similar finger ridge, a steep coulee between them and us, two horseback hunters progressed toward the same objective. The distance and terrain they needed to cover to reach the good hunting on the other side of the big ridge was similar to ours, but to our surprise, we outdistanced them, our "shank's mare" moving along more rapidly than their actual equines. When we met them on top I saw that their horses, short-legged, wide-bodied, over-muscled animals of the type now stereotyped as "western," were well lathered. My brother and I were not even sweating.

I would, I decided, have horses some day that could *walk*, because if a hunting horse could cover ground no more rapidly than I could, what was the point? Even in those days I knew that over mountain terrain the faster gaits, the trot or lope, were rarely practical or safe. That leaves the walk. What I didn't realize at that time was that arena horses had taken over the West, that horses were being bred to do everything *except* walk. They were being bred to accelerate, to be effective at in-close speed events, but not to cover ground rapidly all day long. Since they arrived at those arenas in horse trailers pulled on paved highways, not under saddle, smoothness of gait and endurance over distance were unimportant.

Enter Elmer, my future father-in-law. Emily, the little blond I'd known since the third grade (but who seemed to take no interest in me whatsoever until we were juniors in high school), was now my best friend and soon to be more. She was a ranch girl, a rider who sat a horse as well as her father, erect, with pride, the horse moving freely beneath her. Our favorite date was a ride to the dryland hills with promise of a homemade pizza when we returned to the house.

Elmer, born in 1903, was not a fan of the horse flesh he was seeing around him in the early 1960s. He once pointed at an extremely muscular Quarter Horse stallion of the "bulldog" type, favored in those days, the ad in *Western Horseman* picturing the horse from the rear to emphasize its massive gaskin muscles, and said, "When I was a kid we might have hooked that to the plow, but we wouldn't have ridden it to town on a Saturday night. That's not a *saddle* horse."

I needed a few years of exposure to Elmer before a picture emerged of just what he meant by a *saddle* horse. First, in his mind a horse had to be able to cover ground in a fast walk, or better yet, in a single-foot, a term he used for any of the smooth four-beat gaits that replace the trot in gaited animals. From reading I was aware of such gaits—the running walk, the rack, the amble—but I'd never experienced one of them under saddle. All of these gaits are four-beat, each foot of the animal hitting the ground separately, and are thus far smoother than the trot, a two-beat gait in which the left front and right rear foot hit simultaneously, followed by the right front and left rear.

Secondly, the animal had to have endurance. Elmer still thought of a saddle horse primarily as transportation. What good was a horse with speed in the short run if he couldn't take you fifty miles in a day when necessary? Lastly, Elmer's idea of proper appearance was not suited by the low head carriage coming into fashion, made uglier, in his opinion, by the "downhill" build of these modern horses, butt high, withers low, head lower yet. To him a horse should be "looking for the next town." He should walk as if he owned the place, his neck arched, his body exuding willingness to go forward, to cover some miles.

I listened, but I wasn't wholly convinced. The oldest ranchers in the valley recalled horses like those Elmer described and lit up with recognition when you mentioned a single-foot or a running walk, but anyone younger gave you a blank stare. It took a few years. I eventually learned that the Government-line Morgan stallions kept by the Army Remount Service not far to the east of us, to which many old-time ranchers bred their mares, were indeed single-footers. I learned that fore-runners of the American Saddlebred were favorites out west. I studied photos of early Montana cowboys and saw horses similar to the ones in Elmer's early photo albums, narrower in build, shorter in back, higher-withered than most of the horses now prevalent in our valley. And I learned that many of these early cow ponies were gaited, for tough as their riders must have been in those days before horse trailers and high-ways, there was nothing attractive even to them about being beaten to death by a rough-gaited horse when they had miles to go before they slept.

Teddy Roosevelt, a contemporary of Emily's grandfather Magnus, passed down in writing what Magnus gave us in oral tradition. Magnus cowboyed in central Montana, bought horses from the Crow Indians to break over winter and sell to neighbors, and was always able to find something for himself with a single-foot gait. Roosevelt, devastated by the loss of his first wife, came west to rebuild himself physically and mentally. His ranches on the western border of the Dakotas were home base for hunting sojourns into Wyoming, all of Montana, Idaho, and southern Canada. Always he was horseback.

Accustomed to the groomed Thoroughbreds of the East,

Roosevelt considered the western cow ponies to be small, but he reports in *The Wilderness Hunter* how he soon grew to admire their toughness and to appreciate their smooth gaits: "My foreman and I rode beside the wagon on our wiry, unkempt, unshod cattle ponies. They carried us all day at a rack, pace, single-foot, or slow lope, varied by rapid galloping when we made long circles after game; the trot, the favorite gait with eastern park riders, is disliked by all peoples who have to do much of their life-work in the saddle."

Elmer never read the above. Had he, he would have been justified in a smiling "told you so."

Rosie, my first horse, was not a paragon of the virtues I'd choose today for the ideal hunting horse, but she had her strong points. She was a Quarter Horse–Thoroughbred mix, athletic, fast on cows, and fairly amenable to new learning, although more given to unreasoning panics than the average horse. Elmer gave her to me. He had sat all day at a horse sale in Billings, decrying the fact that nothing came through the ring with anything like a single-foot, but then, impressed by Rosie's owners, bought her. We needed another horse on the ranch. Brownie and Tommy, though still capable, were getting old. Both harkened back to that earlier sort of horse Elmer loved, Brownie moving fluidly with the pride of a horse carrying a Confederate general. Both retained enough gaited genes to rein back into a swift rack if you simultaneously spurred and collected them, but the genes were of distant origin and not strong.

Along with Rosie's good points she had one really bad one: she pulled back. Horses, if tied sloppily or by thin leather reins, can condition themselves to be impossible to tie. Tied poorly, they spook, break the reins, and teach themselves that freedom is just one sharp pull away. This is the reason that smart hunters always tie a horse with a stout lead rope attached to a halter rather than with the reins.

Rosie had learned she could break any rope in the tack shed. Elmer, intent on curing her, went to town and bought a length of three-quarter-inch nylon rope. No horse in the world can break three-quarter-inch nylon. You can pull trucks out of ditches with that sort of rope. Elmer tied one end around Rosie's neck with a bowline, the only knot I know that can take a tremendous pull without tightening up and choking, yet still be easy to untie when the tension is released. He then tied the rope to a snubbing post consisting of a railroad tie set four feet into the ground.

Rosie felt the tension, hesitated a moment, and then flung herself back. There was an explosion of frantic horse flesh. Dust flew, and we scrambled to stay out of her way. She squealed and struggled. After about twenty seconds of this, with no sign of abatement, soft-hearted Elmer pulled out his pocket knife. Timing his move to protect himself, he slipped in and cut the rope. "She wasn't going to stop, Dan. All she'd do was mess up every muscle in her body. It's not worth it. You'll just have to carry hobbles."

Luckily, hobbles worked relatively well with Rosie. She had a big appetite, and she never learned to travel while hobbled as well as some horses I've had since, several of which could actually run with their front feet fettered. If there was good grass to eat, Rosie normally stayed put. I'd hobble her, then fix fence, watching her out of the corner of my eye, not letting her stray too far.

In spite of her quirks, Rosie really became *my* horse. We gained that rapport that only comes with much daily use of a horse. The mare became tuned to my slightest touch, turning on a dime when asked to head a cow, taking me in a smooth, rocking lope across the east range through the sagebrush when I needed to get somewhere quickly or maybe just wanted to feel the wind dry the sweat on my face. I taught her to pull from the saddle horn, impressing Elmer once by removing a large tree that had fallen across an irrigation ditch. He had noticed it the day before, and now asked, "What happened to the tree?"

"I pulled it off the ditch with Rosie." He acted surprised, but then smiled. He'd expressed doubts as to whether the mare's disposition would allow that sort of work.

And Rosie took me hunting. We had no horse trailer, so my first horseback hunting was confined to the ranch, but I have fine memories of mule deer in the pungent sage of October. Emily was always with me in those early, pre-child days of our marriage, piling off to hold the horses when I got a shot. I had no saddle scabbard and could not dream of affording one. Instead I slung the 30-30 across my back with the web sling Emily had sewn me. I'd scraped enough money together for an inexpensive 2½ power scope and found it liberating, even with the range restrictions of the caliber.

Elmer was not a hunter, but he loved venison and helped in the effort to get it whenever he could. The great resurgence of the whitetail deer was just beginning. We had a few on the ranch, but I'd never shot a whitetail buck. Once, the three of us rode single file through the thick cottonwoods on the river bottom. Elmer stopped. "Dan, why don't you get off and check that clearing just through the brush there? It's a pretty good place."

Elmer held Rosie while I sneaked to the downwind side of the clearing, then eased toward it. Elmer could not have been more correct. A big buck stood across the little park, facing me but totally unaware of me. Intent on being as silent as possible, I worked the lever of the Marlin slowly, too slowly, apparently holding the rifle out of vertical, and the result was the first jam I'd ever experienced. Frantically I plucked at the action, cleared it, closed the lever, aimed at the buck's chest and pulled the trigger. He went down.

Jubilant, I dashed back to Emily and Elmer and announced that I'd just shot a big whitetail buck. We tied the horses, went to where the buck lay, and discovered that in the heat of the moment I'd noticed the size of the antlers rather than their shape. The buck was a mule deer that had uncharacteristically holed up in the brushy river bottom where a whitetail ought to have been. My disappointment was very slight, however. This was the largest buck I'd shot to date, hog fat, with a coat that shone in the morning sun. While Emily and I were dressing it, Elmer disappeared. By the time we were done with the chore, we heard the put-put of the Jeep, which Elmer had managed to jockey across the river to retrieve the buck.

During a decade of college, the Marine Corps, and graduate school, hunting with horses had to be a dream deferred. There were these things to be done in life, and certain other things had to wait. It was during our early years of ranching, when teaching paid the bills—barely—and we worked to buy the home place and stock it with cattle and equipment, that a good horse became a necessity. Ironically, it was then, some years after Elmer's death, that we began breeding horses of the sort he had described to us and had longed for in his later years.

I needed a ranch horse and at first made a bad purchase, a Rosie-like mare that was still green in training. Rosie's quirks had been annoying; those of this mare, nicknamed W. B., were dangerous. She would proceed along normally enough, but sensitive to that exact second when I relaxed. Then she'd explode from a dead quiet walk to a full bucking run. Three times she did this, and three times I managed the "one-rein stop," the horseman's survival valve, that of pulling the animal around into a tight circle from which it has less ability to either buck or run. The fourth time she got me. I hit the ground head first, rolled, and came up not seriously hurt but sore through every fiber of my body. I walked very tenderly for a week.

The folks who had sold me W. B. were good people. They had entrusted an old horseman to ride the mare hard for a month to ready her for sale and now were convinced the work had not been done. They refunded my money, but they also let drop later on that the mare had always been a difficult one, that the initials stood for "Witch Bitch." I felt a little like Mark Twain when he learned that the title given to that bucking bronco in Nevada—"Genuine Mexican Plug"—was not a compliment, except to dudes and innocent buyers.

Still sore from my encounter with W. B., I went to a dispersion sale at the Flying Mule Ranch held by an outfitter who was going out of business. In a corral full of mules, lighting the place up, was a big sorrel mare with socks and blaze, a registered Tennessee Walking Horse of the good old-fashioned type, rugged but still beautiful, heavy in foal to a gaited stallion owned by the man who had been my principal while I taught at the high school at Jordan. We knew the stallion, a horse called Montana Traveler, three-quarters Tennessee Walking Horse and one-quarter Morgan. Emily and I looked at each other, looked at the price for Mona on the private treaty sales list, shook our heads and walked away.

But nothing that day sold. The poor man hosting the sale had bought kegs of beer and plates of barbecue, and people enjoyed the outing as much as any county fair. But they did not buy. We took the sales list home, and the next morning, with pangs of conscience for taking advantage of the situation, called the hungover host. I offered him 20 percent less than the asking price. There was a long pause. Then, "Yeah, that would be okay."

If I'd had pangs of conscience thus far, they grew so strong when we drove up to get the mare that I almost backed out. We still owned no horse trailer, but I did have a stock rack on my old GMC pickup, which had been initiated by hauling the Holstein calves we raised. I looked around the outfitter's corrals, expecting to see the sort of loading ramp common to such places, built to load a stock truck with cattle or horses. I saw nothing of that sort.

The outfitter emerged, leading Mona, and behind him a crying little girl. "You're selling Mona?" she asked her dad, and then, receiving his answer, retreated to the house. The outfitter looked me over, read my eyes, repeated the price I'd offered on the phone, and making retreat impossible said, "A deal's a deal."

"I don't see a loading chute," I said.

He almost scoffed. "You don't need one. Open 'er up." I dropped the tailgate of the pickup and pulled the rope that raised the back gate of the stock rack. "Get in, Mona," he growled. The huge mare, so wide with the foal inside her that I worried she wouldn't fit through the opening, studied the stock rack, then half-reared to the point that her front feet rose over the tailgate. She gave a deft, controlled leap, and was suddenly in, the pickup swaying on its springs. Her value, in my eyes, had just doubled.

Mona started it all. With her began our quest for the gaited "using" horses that fulfilled Elmer's requirements, proud, smooth to ride, capable of nearly any task including, of course, hunting in the mountains. Over subsequent years we would collect mares, reject some, breed for a short back, easygoing disposition, eagerness to cover ground, big bone, good feet, and pretty heads. Not everything in the Tennessee

Walking Horse breed would do. Some show stock was too fine in bone and too hyper in disposition. Some animals would prove too pacey, preferring that rough, two-beat gait (both feet on one side hitting the ground simultaneously), another showring anomaly fostered by trainers who can hang weights and chains on a pacey horse's front feet and more easily satisfy show judges who reward artificiality. We were breeding for horses that would have made Elmer (and his father, Magnus, and Teddy Roosevelt) happy.

But first there was Rockytop Tennessee. On a May morning we looked out our north window toward the corral, and where Mona alone should have been there were two horses, not one. The colt was sorrel like his mother, a beautiful leggy creature lit up with a blaze and socks and a look that said, "I'm here, world."

He grew like a weed. At two, sixteen hands tall and still a stallion, he became nearly unmanageable. Reluctantly, since the owner of the colt's sire considered Rockytop to be stud material, I called our veterinarian. I've come to believe strongly that with horses of the male persuasion, castrate first and ask questions later. The best gelding is that horse you thought might have made a fine stallion. Stallions are reproductive machines, and no matter how well trained, remain stallions and can revert when circumstances dictate. They are not horses with which to lead pack strings or stand picketed on a highline in mixed company. There are a very few exceptions, but this big, proud, high-strung colt would not have been one of them if left intact. I needed an all-purpose horse, and to qualify, Rockytop had to be gelded.

Our vet at the time was a big, no-nonsense woman named Diana. We drugged the colt and laid him down. Diana did the surgery while I touched to his left shoulder Elmer's brand, which Emily and I had inherited, a reverse E, lazy J in brand language. The second phase of his life had begun. Diana read my mind. "You were saying you'd done some ground work. If you haven't been on him yet, this week, while he's a little sore, might be a good time."

Rockytop Tennessee was the first colt I raised and trained from scratch. He's still alive today as I write this, though time is running out for him. I trained him and he trained me. I've heard it said that the best vessel with which to learn to sail is not a beamy tub, overly safe in design, but instead a boat that's responsive and subtle. Much the same can be said for horses and horsemen. It was spirited old Brownie that made Emily into the rider she became, and it was Rockytop that made me a trainer and a rider. Yes, I'd ridden most of my life, but this colt was a whole new world. We got through it without getting hurt.

I had hunted elk with an old Marine friend a couple of times using Mona while Rockytop was growing up, but I think of Rockytop as my first hunting horse. He was not perfect in that regard. By my standards today he was unnecessarily tall and too long in the back. He was snorty about silly things, some to which he never adjusted. Tearing open the Velcro on your jacket made for a spook, always, every time, no matter how much you did it. The horse just didn't like Velcro.

But the two of us covered some miles and saw some territory. As age and experience settled him down, Rockytop carried my sons in turn. Concerning him there are many pictures in my mind, many memories, but one is particularly vivid. During a weekend-long, special season elk hunt near Gardiner, Montana, the Eagle Creek parking lot was jammed with vehicles. Much snow had fallen earlier, and the surface of the big parking area was packed to glare ice. Outfitters with horse trailers were nursing their clients onto unfamiliar horses, and the harvested elk of successful hunters were being loaded into vehicles. It was cold.

I had shot a cow elk about a mile out from the trailhead. Many elk had been taken in the area since the snow had fallen, so dragging trails had formed, these icing over during the night and converging toward the parking area. The trails were like bobsled runs. The horse labored a little while dragging the cow through deep snow, but when we reached the dragging trail and the cow slipped down into the icy groove, Rockytop's ears went forward, he smelled home, and he picked up his pace to a running walk. This would be a rapid retrieval.

We hit the parking lot at a running walk dragging an elk, Rockytop and I, threading our way through vehicles and horse trailers, and all activity stopped. We were a one-man, one-horse parade, the heads of humans, horses, and mules swiveling to watch the spectacle of a big Tennessee Walking Horse, neck arched with pride, dragging an elk with the same attitude he'd have had in a showring, his rider with the fixed grin that the smoothness at speed of a gaited horse tends to bring on. We reached our outfit, and I dropped the dragging rope. Activity gradually resumed. But one outfitter left his clients and strolled over. "What kind of a horse is *that?*" he asked.

There is in Montana, to the north of Yellowstone Park, a fabled valley where a stream named Slough Creek flows south. Crystal clear and loaded with trout, the creek winds among the stately trees of semi-open parks, through the campsites of sourdoughs from ages past and through newer ones, too, for the area has long been Mecca to those seeking elk during the early bugling season. (The federally mandated wolves have now changed that, but that's a tale for another time.)

I had spent much of my life longing for Slough Creek. I'd

heard of it since boyhood, particularly from the rancher/out-fitter who brought hay bales to my brother and me where we labored on summer days to build solid haystacks. Now and then he felt such a compulsion to talk about hunting that he turned off the tractor, gave us a break, wiped sweat off his brow and said, "God, would I like to be up on Slough Creek right now. I'd lie in the shade half the day, and catch a few fish for supper when it cooled off." When work was less pressing he'd tell us about bull elk slain, about dudes he had guided, about pack strings and mules and camps in the aspens.

The name of the place had become magic to me, but I'd reached into middle age without seeing it. Eventually, I'd had enough. I would go by myself riding one horse and packing another. I would see this valley, and then I would cross the mountains and travel down the Stillwater River to a trailhead near home. Emily shook her head, knew it was some sort of "man-thing," and although apprehensive about my traveling through grizzly country and over mountain passes alone, took me to my selected jumping-off point. I left her and the boys in a drizzling rain, knowing it would be snowing up higher, and that in this year of much lingering snow, my trip in early July might mean I'd be the first traveler of the year over the high passes. There was no one with whom I could "inquire locally." No one would know whether the high trails were still blocked with drifts.

I had with me two companions, two horses only three years old. Sugar was carrying the packs. I rode Major. Normally I would not have selected such young horses for a challenging trip, but Sugar's packs were light, and Major had matured early. He was already burly and muscular, and he had always been gentle. There was a level of trust between us I've been unable to feel with many horses considerably older. Major would be my chosen mount for the moose hunt scheduled that fall (I'd been lucky enough to draw a tag), and he was now taking me on one big scouting trip. As if to confirm that early in the game, on the upper reaches of Slough Creek we rode into a herd of cow elk bedded with their calves under dark green spruce.

Horse breeding (like horsemanship itself) is a lifetime quest. It takes many years to clarify in your own mind just what you want and then to achieve it. Horses are long-lived as animals go, and slow to reproduce. We never breed a mare before she is three, and then it's another three years at least (one of gestation and two for the foal to grow) until you start her colt under saddle. Six years have passed before you have a true idea of what you have bred. Nudging your breeding program in the correct direction is the quest of a quarter century.

We've homed in on what we want, but it has taken nearly thirty years. We started out with Mona and Rocktyop, and they were good. Each successive generation of horses has been better. Major arrived relatively early in this process. Big and heavy-boned, he was born blessed with some of the best old-time genes, gentle genes that carried with them a running walk natural and smooth. By my standards today, Major is (he's still healthy and useful) a bit too much the Mack truck, but on the trip over the Beartooths I appreciated every bit of that.

It was not an ordeal, but the trip was plenty to fill the plate of a man nearing fifty and traveling solo. We were in true grizzly country, crossing an area where a teenage elk hunter was once slam-dunked from behind by a grizzly sow with no warning whatsoever. He was stalking an elk and was hit so hard he likened it to being smashed by a vehicle while standing on the shoulder of a highway. He survived, but only because a surgeon was camped on Slough Creek for the early elk hunt.

9. The author rests while Major looks on with apparent disapproval.

So as I crossed this territory, my Ruger Bisley .44 magnum loaded with hard-cast 300-grain bullets was never so far away that I couldn't reach out and pat it.

Twice we had to backtrack, once because a trail was closed and another time because I lost it in a maze of old mining roads that predated this area's wilderness status. We crossed a snowfield because we had no choice: the trail disappeared into it and reemerged three hundred yards away. I worried the horses would either bog down or slide down the mountain (a cliff with no bottom I could see dropped off to our left), but the old packed snow was just right: the horses' hooves sank in just six inches or so, good for traction.

The three of us were cold and wet much of the time. The second night I experienced a brief, violent illness that shook me to the core both mentally and physically. I wondered whether in the morning I'd have strength to continue, but whatever brought this strange visitation turned during the early morning hours and left: I was a little weak but mostly recovered.

And, yes, we had fun. The horses were tuned to new sights around each bend, the only one causing undue concern being a big bull moose that fed in a stream near the trail. He minded his business, but the horses eyed him carefully and snorted with suspicion. I saw the late afternoon sun hit a mountain that rose from velvet forest surrounding it and wondered whether anyone, ever, had camped at its foot. I saw lakes and streams that until now had been only names on the map: Wounded Man, Froze to Death, Horseshoe. And, cemented forever, confirming all previous experience with horses, I learned just what true trust between man and beast means and what it can accomplish. We were a team of three, each keeping up the morale of the others in turn, each capable of injecting humor into a difficult situation, each lending strength. I was never alone.

In a book called *Sketches from the Ranch: A Montana Memoir* I told of a remarkable stallion named Mack that I lost too young. He left me with two fine foals, a broodmare that proved to be one of our best, and a spunky gelding named Little Mack. Smaller than Major and much smaller than Rockytop (to whom he was related through his dam), Little Mack was kept on the ranch partially for sentimental reasons (I had treasured his sire) but also because there was something willing and just a little cocky about the guy. He, too, is sorrel, with a blaze and hind socks. I didn't start him until the Christmas before his third birthday. Even then he was like a gangly teenager, but the fact that he would never mature to the size of those earlier geldings was something he never noticed.

I rode Little Mack in the round pen on a few warm winter days, then back-burnered his training during frosty, muddy late winter. Toward spring I took him out to the hills exactly once. He was, as the Spaniards say, much horse. Today, at thirteen, he throttles down to the ability level of anyone I put on him, then reverts to his butt-kicking earlier self the instant my own toe touches the stirrup. He knows when work will be expected of him, and he relishes it, particularly chasing cows, which he does with a little too much gusto for the first half hour or so. Then he simmers down.

Shortly before Little Mack's third birthday, the colt still having had only one ride outside the round pen under his cinch, two friends and I planned a spring bear hunt. Our expectations were meager where bagging a bear was concerned, but quite high on the index of contemplated fun around the campfire while sipping Yukon Jack. I would ride Major and lead two packhorses, an experienced one and Little Mack, who needed the packhorse duty as training. My friend Cliff would ride his own horse and pony a mule, while Roger would ride a big gentle gelding of ours named Marauder. But our best laid plans were disrupted when Major started coughing and it became clear he was having a bout with the heaves that precluded any exertion.

"Okay, Kid," I said to Little Mack, "you're on. It's time to be a real horse." But another side of me was saying inwardly, "Dan, you are a fool. You're going to lead a pack string over mountain terrain with a high strung colt that's been ridden outside a round pen exactly once, that doesn't yet neck rein, that's likely to spook and bolt and dump you in a heap by the trail, then get the packhorses and Cliff's mule involved in one colossal wreck." I was younger, braver, and more foolish ten years ago.

But it went well, if a little on the white-knuckle side. It was a fast trip. Slowing the colt down while guiding him and holding onto the lead rope of the front pack horse was a challenge. Little Mack, seeing a beautiful stretch of the Rocky Mountains in front of him, could see absolutely no reason not to have a peek at the west side of the Continental Divide. Yet, by the time we got to camp, he was becoming a mountain horse, and by the time we packed out a few days later he had gained my trust. Even at that stage of training I would have gladly taken him nearly anywhere.

A week after the hunt Emily and I had occasion to take our young horses to a clinic taught by a first lieutenant of the famous trainer Pat Parelli. I rode Little Mack around the grounds the night before, noticing that the instructor was observing in clandestine fashion. The next morning we were introduced to the Parelli "games," ground exercises considered in that school of "natural" horsemanship to be essential ingredients in a horse's education. When introduced to them Little Mack was completely befuddled. He looked at me quizzically. "What's all this about?" he seemed to say. "Saddle me

10. David and Little Mack, one of the author's best hunting horses.

up, and get me out of this stupid arena. Let's head for the mountains."

Somewhere during this process the instructor looked over and said, "You know, Dan, that horse isn't ready to be ridden."

"I know," I answered, "That's probably true. But he's already led a pack string to the mountains." What I really *wanted* to say to the instructor was, "There are more things in the world of horsemanship than are dreamt of in your philosophy." But he was a nice guy, a friend, riding the crest of a trend that puts method as more important than final result. So I held my tongue.

Little Mack became, during my decade of resisted middle age (from fifty to sixty) my number one hunting horse, always game, always willing, even when loaded up with a heavy body and far too much gear. He once smelled out a herd of elk on the trail, one of which would have become winter meat for me if I'd only listened to him.

We were progressing down a forest service trail at first light. Little Mack's ears went forward. He stopped dead in his tracks, eyes and ears fixed on a spot in the murky woods ahead of us. I could see nothing. An outfitter friend was working this area with his dudes. I had passed their camp and noted that they had hit the trail ahead of us, and I wrongly assumed Mack's running walk had overtaken them, that Mack's attention to the trail ahead was to horses and mules. So I failed to do the right thing. I did not dismount, pull my rifle out of the scabbard, and walk down the trail leading the horse with rifle at the ready.

Thus, I rode right into the middle of a herd of elk bedded in the forest straddling the trail. I piled off my horse and jerked out the rifle. Elk bodies were everywhere in the trees, but I possessed a permit that allowed only taking a cow. Even shooting a spike would have the local warden reaching for his very pricey ticket book, so I had to study carefully to make sure there were no horns, this while elk were ducking in and out of the thick lodgepole pine. I never fired. In seconds they were gone. I felt very foolish, and I still do.

For more than a quarter century I have made part of my living by raising horses, training them (and having them trained), selling them primarily to backcountry riders, and writing about the process for such magazines as *Equus* and *The Trail Rider* as well as for book publishers. I'm often asked what sort of horse is "perfect" for the Rocky Mountain hunter. Of course "hunter," as a term applied to the horse rather than the rider, has a completely different connotation in the equine world. There the term means a horse intended to carry a rider and very light tack over hill and dale at a gallop, jumping fences on its way. This is hardly the emphasis pertinent to the elk hunter trudging through deep snow, his horse burdened with rifle, warm clothing, and survival gear.

The earlier portion of this chapter gives a good idea of what for me makes the ideal hunting horse, but here's a quick synopsis: I want a medium-sized horse, 15.1 to 15.3 (61–63") in height, perhaps 1,000-1,100 pounds in weight. Taller horses tend to be less athletic, while heavier ones, sturdy as they appear, are burdened by their own weight, particularly if it is muscle designed for a purpose other than carrying weight or covering ground. The chest should be moderate, not wide, and the hindquarters muscular but not massive. In human terms, we're looking for a moderate build, neither the hugely muscled one of a power weight lifter (Quarter Horse of the bulldog-type) nor the extremely slim one of the marathon runner (endurance Arab). We're looking for a Greek god, the equine equivalent of the decathlon athlete.

This ideal horse should have a short back, with withers that seem to rise out of the middle of its back. The withers should be prominent for several technical reasons and one very practical one: they hold the saddle in place. I like an uphill build (withers higher than rump or croup), because it tends to go with smooth gaits and walking ability, while the reverse, rump higher than withers, tends to go with racing ability.

The big game hunter's horse ends up with much weight on his back, often too much. Weight-carrying ability requires a short back, but is also connected with another conformational trait, that of a broad loin. Feel the space behind a horse's rib cage but ahead of its hip bones. That space should be short, front to back, but rather flat. You can trace with your fingers from backbone on down, pressing the loin muscle until it drops off on each side. That muscle should be wide, extending nine or ten inches down from the backbone each way.

Good feet, if anything a little on the large side, are essential, with good hoof wall thickness and good texture. (A farrier can tell you more about this.) Good bone is equally important. Measuring the front leg just below the swell of the knee gives a good indication of bone mass in a horse. The minimum circumference should be seven inches for each one thousand pounds of weight. Again, many horses, particularly stocky, muscular animals, fall short in the bone department.

Of course, the best-built horse in the world is still not one with which you want to trust your very life on a ledge trail if he has nothing but bone between his ears. Horses vary in intelligence and disposition (personality, in human terms) as much as people do. Spirit in a horse is great if you can handle it, but flightiness is not. Horses by nature are flight animals, programmed to jerk suddenly into action and get the hell out of the territory when something threatens them. Further, they have terrific imaginations, so a strange looking rock at the side of the trail can seem as threatening to them as a mountain lion.

Good breeding and good training overcome most of the flight instinct in most horses, but some remain forever spooky no matter what you do. These don't work well as hunting horses. Neither do excessively quarrelsome horses. Any group of horses will find its pecking order, and things then normally settle down. But certain horses are always spoiling for fights with others, and such don't make pleasant companions in the mountains.

Ever since that hike up the ridge with my brother eons ago, I've insisted on a good walk in a hunting horse. Here, many western horses are sorely deficient. It wasn't always so. Teddy Roosevelt and his ranch hands (or Emily's grandfather Magnus) would not have tolerated heavily muscled, short-gaited horses that can't stretch out and *walk*, that break into a trot at two or three miles per hour. As I've said, the absence of a good walk is the result of highways and horse trailers, the breeding of arena performers that are never required to get out and cover ground, and of arena events that reward everything *except* a good walk.

And, if a fast walk is good, a running walk (or amble or fox-trot or single-foot) is even better, though in the mountains it will normally be reserved for smooth stretches of trail on the way back to camp. From what I can observe more and more backcountry riders are rediscovering the joy of riding gaited horses such as the Tennessee Walking Horse, Missouri Foxtrotter, Peruvian Paso, or Rocky Mountain Horse. For starters, the regular walk of these horses tends to be faster than that of nongaited animals.

When you want a little more speed these animals kick into another gear, a four-beat gait that replaces the trot and brings a smile to your face. Do expect derision from some "western" types who haven't read their history, who think only one breed has claim to the title "horse of the west," who will make all sorts of fantastic claims about gaited horses. They'll tell you such horses are not sure-footed, that they'll fall right off the mountain. Virtually without exception, such folks have never used the critters, have no experience with them whatsoever. Some refuse to get on one at all, considering a horse with smooth gaits to be somehow "unmanly" (and maybe fearing they'll enjoy the experience). Perhaps to be a he-man in the eyes of such poor lost souls you'd have to knock the shock absorbers from under the axles of your Jeep or ask an airline pilot to find whatever turbulence he could to make the flight more enjoyable.

The best way to educate these naysayers is to keep your mouth shut and instead go riding with one of them. At your horse's dog walk, your friend's mount will already be lagging and perhaps breaking into a trot for short stretches. Kick up to a flat walk or slow running walk and he's now riding a fast, bone-jarring trot. Ignore this completely. After an hour or so, tell your companion he's welcome to try your horse, but only for fifteen minutes. (That's all you'll be able to stand, because your gaited horse has already thoroughly spoiled you.) Grit your teeth, kick your friend's horse into a trot, and watch your companion's face turn from anxiety (he's not used to speed with smoothness) to a slow grin. That should do it.

No, there's nothing "unmanly" about horses bred to cover ground with comfort for the rider. The Roman soldiers who crossed all of Europe to the British Isles must have been some of the toughest men on earth. But they looked at the native gaited ponies of the people they invaded, were envious, and began devising cruel-looking cross hobbles in an attempt to get their Barb horses to break their two-beat trot into the smooth amble of the British horses. Since gaitedness is genetic, the effort probably was not very successful.

Those who hunt close to home sometimes own their own hunting horses, and many I know in Montana keep horses for that purpose alone. More often, though, today's big game hunter travels far and wide for his hunting opportunities. His only experiences hunting with horses may be with those of the outfitters with whom he books hunting trips in the West or in Canada or Alaska.

Gaining a little knowledge of horses, perhaps by taking riding lessons, could ease some of the anxiety and make the anticipated trip—likely an expensive one and perhaps the opportunity of a lifetime—less painful and more fun. Hunters spend big bucks on firearms, clothing, plane tickets, and nonresident licenses. They study ballistics, sight in their rifles, and practice imitating the bugle of lovelorn wapiti. Yet some assume there will be no problem getting on a horse's back, perhaps for the first time, and riding a dozen miles on a cold and snowy day to reach a base camp, then repeating the ride each morning in the dark to reach elk meadows before shooting light. Riding takes special muscles, and it stretches those new to it. Cold temperatures make it worse.

The horses of the average outfitter are likely to be sound, capable, and sure-footed. They will not be the paragons described above, however. Why? Outfitters must maintain huge strings of riding and pack animals, herds that earn them money for only a short stretch or two during the year. The rest of the time the horses or mules must be fed, doctored, and trimmed or shod. Exorbitant as the outfitter's fees may seem to the nonresident hunter, few in the profession make much money. They must earn it all in a short time each year, and then perhaps work a second job to make ends meet.

Consequently, outfitters acquire horses that are adequate for their purposes, but they can't chase after ideals. They buy what's readily available and what they can afford. The horses, used to carrying inexperienced riders, aren't above taking advantage, perhaps by lagging behind, attempting to snatch a mouthful of grass, maybe even crow-hopping a little when first mounted on a cold morning. These things aren't serious to those with a basic knowledge of horsemanship, and such knowledge can be acquired close to home before the trip begins.

The old admonition of boxing referees, "Protect yourself at all times!" applies to interaction with horses. They are, after all, big, strong animals that are fully capable of hurting or even killing you, though rarely by design. On the ground beside a horse, the safest position is close to the animal next to his shoulder, not either in front or in back of the horse. Avoid anything that would tie you to the horse in any way.

Don't wrap a lead rope around your hand while leading the animal. When going steeply uphill lean forward, but avoid leaning back when going down. In both cases give the horse extra rein.

Hunting with horses invariably involves carrying extra gear. Hauling heavy stuff behind the saddle is taboo, because it can injure a horse's kidneys. Pommel packs or horn packs that fit in front of you on the saddle are better than conventional saddlebags for bulky stuff like water bottles, cameras and binoculars. Don't leave your essentials—knife, game saw, ammunition—in any pack on the horse, because you'll end up tying up in a hurry and clambering up a ridge after some elk without the stuff. Instead wear a fanny pack or light daypack so that when you dismount the truly necessary gear is with you.

Hunters and outfitters divide sharply on the proper placement of saddle scabbards on horses. My preference is butt forward, scope up, and bolt handle away from the horse (unless a you have a fully padded scabbard that prevents the bolt from gouging the horse). Manufacturers of saddle scabbards often picture them positioned with the scope down. True, scopes and mounting systems have improved over the years, but they are still the most vulnerable parts of the firearm. I've had several rifles move severely in point of impact after long, rigorous horseback hunts, and you don't want to add to that possibility by making the scope bear the weight of a bouncing rifle.

The so-called Southwest position, butt to the rear, works well for some. Disadvantages are that unless the rifle is strapped or buckled in you could conceivably lose it without knowing it, an extremely unhappy thought. Also, should you mount the scabbard in that position, be careful dismounting. Once in a moment of carelessness, forgetting the rifle was there, I dismounted, swinging my right leg over the horse's rump, and caught it between the scabbard and the horse, an embarrassing development.

Whichever position you choose, mount the scabbard at a steep angle. Recently I read an article in a major hunting magazine written by the managing editor. He complained profusely about the pain and discomfort to his knee while riding. No wonder. A close-up of his saddle scabbard showed the thickest part of the rifle lying squarely under the stirrup leathers right at his knee. Lowering the muzzle end of the scabbard would have eased the pain, and I have to wonder why his guide did not prescribe such a change.

Complications aside, for me hunting in the West, especially for elk, would be incomplete without horses. They get you there, get you back, carry your gear, and pack out or drag your game home when you're successful. With a good horse under you, you're never completely alone. I've known some good ones. From my office window this morning I can see another, a black colt that I'm just beginning to train. He seems promising. I suspect that together down the trail we'll be seeing the sun rise on elk meadows fringed by aspen groves. We'll smell the pines and the sharp woodsmoke from the tent stove, and, with some luck, catch up with a big bull.

7

Tools of the Trade

It was hot. I was aiming the Farmall tractor straight across the furrows, just as I had been told to do, and my stomach felt like jelly. For half a day I had been harrowing a plowed field that had never (for reasons unknown to me) been disked, the usual farming procedure that comes after plowing. I'd been ordered to go directly across the furrows, the tractor pounding like a small boat in steep chop, pulling a wired-together harrow that attempted to disintegrate every couple of passes. I'd hop off with fencing pliers and baling wire, stick the thing back together, then get back at it.

After working for these people at fourteen I would go on to many pleasant ranch jobs, to work that was tough physically but gratifying in its way, for people who fed you lavishly, respected your time off, and did what they could to help a green kid learn the ways of the ranch. This first job, however, was the exception. The people were nice enough, but they were disorganized. A strange family arrangement meant that the father, the mother, and the children each had their separate livestock and registered brands. I'd "signed on" with the father, a kind enough sort, only to find that an order he gave was often countermanded by the mother, who would roll her eyes when I mentioned the instruction already given.

Later I would realize it was characteristic of this outfit to give a helper a job that none of them would do. Because I was available at four dollars a day I could be sent to the field with a small tractor and harrow to do what should have been done with a big tractor and a disk, and any discomfort could be ignored. The harrow would not do the job in one pass, but I was available to go over the field again and again if necessary.

I'd failed to bring any water with me. I remember being hot and thirsty, but mostly sick to my stomach from the constant pounding. There was dust, of course, and hot engine exhaust that, if the breeze was just wrong, hung over the seat of the cabless tractor in a foul cloud. Flocks of gnats found me. The old tractor's speed was just right for them to hover along around my face through the whole downhill pass. Turning uphill into the breeze brought some relief.

It wasn't torture, but it wasn't pleasant. Yes, I suppose it built character. In any case the job was short-lived because the couple eventually fought over whether they could afford my wages and decided in the negative. The experience taught me that you can live through much discomfort if you have a goal. And I had one.

It was on the pages of the Sears catalog. In their hunting section, sandwiched between more expensive firearms, was a Marlin lever-action rifle, a slightly cheaper version of the famous Model 336 because it bore the Sears name rather than that of its maker. The rifle was offered in two calibers, .30-30 and .35 Remington. Even in those innocent days I knew that neither caliber was ideal for country of the sort in which I now farmed, for the open sage flats, but affording one of the sleek bolt actions on the same catalog page was inconceivable. Besides, I was left-handed, and the ambidextrous Marlin was free of prejudice in that department.

During the 1950s for every scoped bolt action you saw riding in the rifle rack of a pickup truck, even in open Montana, you still saw several iron sighted 30-30's. I was sure such a rifle would do the job. The obstacle was the $75.95 price tag. At four bucks a day it would take a while. Yet each pass down the huge farmed field made it closer, and thoughts of hunting that fall with a new rifle, a real rifle, a big game rifle, made it easier to tense up my stomach muscles and brace myself on the tractor's iron seat for the next war with the furrows.

And there were other such wars during my first experience as a ranch hand. I worked hard. I remember just one pleasant evening, a horseback ride with the rancher out to his hill pasture to check the cows. He was running a palomino stud with a bunch of mares, and when the stud came charging toward us the rancher said in his curt Norwegian accent, "Get off, trow rocks." We did so, turning the stallion away. That, he explained, is the standard solution when you're horseback and a range stud comes close. "Get off, trow rocks."

We dropped back into the valley in the dark, leading our horses down one steep place, the cool Montana night air infiltrated periodically by a warm July breeze. I was not anxious to return to my basement bunk at the ranch house.

When I was terminated (laid off, let go, fired, whatever it was) after the couple's argument I caught a ride into town and pulled my check out of my wallet. It was for sixty-five dollars, signed by the ranch woman. Sitting on the couch in the parsonage living room, I opened the catalog, looked at the rifle, and looked back at the check in despair. Apparently this caught my father's eye.

There were many children in our family, and although they were intensely devoted to them, my parents' attention was necessarily diluted. There was only so much to go around, after all. When I got my share of Dad's attention it was sometimes off base—he had trouble remembering I was left-handed when it came to such things as baseball mitts—but sometimes it was dead-on. He looked at the catalog over my shoulder. "You could shoot deer with that?" He was thinking of the family larder.

"Oh, yeah, that's just what it's for."

He thought a minute. In today's dollars the rifle would have cost nearly six hundred dollars, the shortfall of my paycheck some 10 percent of that, and on a pastor's salary there was little extra to stretch. But this was a good day for me. "You've earned most of it. We'll go ahead and order it for you." So I turned my paycheck over to Dad and he ordered the rifle. I had done a little homework weeks earlier, walking into a sporting goods store in Billings and bluntly asking the man behind the counter, "Which one's better, 30-30 or .35 Remington?"

He didn't hesitate. ".30-30," he said. I had already leaned that way. I'd read that the .35 Remington was a wonderful brush cartridge, but in open Montana the 30-30 would have a trajectory advantage. So now I spent an agonizing couple of weeks waiting for a particular box in the mail. When it came, blued steel and walnut, smelling of new gun, I cleaned off the preserving oil, grabbed a cardboard box to use as a target, and headed for the hills. I had scraped the money together for a box of shells, which I remember buying at the local Outdoor Supply store in our town. They were Remington Corelocks in green boxes, but I can't remember whether their flat pointed bullets were 150- or 170-grain.

What I do remember is that the rifle kicked. I can't recall for sure whether I'd ever shot anything larger than a .22 at this point. Larry Pederson owned a heavy-barreled .410 shotgun that I may have tried, and Bruce Reiner had a Winchester Model 92 .25-20, so well-used that most of the bluing was gone. We hunted rock chucks with the .25-20, perhaps before this summer I turned fourteen, perhaps after. No matter. I'd read frequently that the .30-30 was a mild caliber. But after a walk up the hill toting the rifle, ammo, and a big cardboard box, shooting prone because there was no bench for the purpose, I decided that if the .30-30 was considered mild I was not particularly anxious to shoot anything considered really powerful.

Most carbines are light, and their stocks tend toward a fair amount of drop at heel, a concession to the needs of iron sights. Shooting prone allows no give whatsoever. The Marlin's butt plate was hard as stone, and my bad shooting form placed it against my collar bone. Long before I could truly say whether the open sights were adjusted properly my shoulder was throbbing. I suspect I'd already developed a flinch that would plague me for some years.

Also, I'd read just enough to be dangerous, to second-guess the caliber. Magazine writers loved to refer to the .30-30's "rainbow trajectory," to its range limitations, to its general inferiority, though they tritely conceded that carbines in this caliber probably killed more deer each year than rifles in either .270 or .30-06, darlings both of the gun writer crowd. Consciously or otherwise, I tended to compensate for the caliber's alleged inferiority by holding over, or at least aiming toward the top of a deer's body, even though the targets were usually closer than a hundred yards. Many misses resulted. Many deer I managed to hit were struck just below the spine, a placement that kills, but not in spectacular fashion. The saving grace of this caliber is the large flat point, soft-nosed bullets. Should shot placement be less than ideal, deer-sized game usually succumbs because expansion is sure and the wound channel large. Even today those who actually know the old .30-30 will tell you it does pretty well at reasonable ranges.

I eventually scoped the rifle, first with a bogus three-quarters inch mail-order 4x with unreliable aluminum mounts. I walked over a ridge, missed a deer, went back to the car in disgust, removed the scope, then walked back to the ridge and shot the same buck with iron sights. Much later I installed

11. The rifle earned by the author working on a ranch at age fourteen, pictured with the buck found in the clearing Elmer suggested.

a decent 2½x, still a bargain outfit, but credible at least. It served well, though scoping such a carbine removes much of its handiness and charm. With a scope in place you can no longer wrap your hand around the flat receiver.

I still have the Sears-Marlin. No, it doesn't have any sort of first-love status as a souvenir from more innocent days. It's just that I'm far better at buying rifles than I am at selling them, and the carbine justified its existence for many years as the trainer for my sons. Two of them shot their first deer with it. My recoil lesson had been well learned, so I hand-loaded milder ammunition, 130-grain flat point Speer bul-

12. A new type of ear protection while firing a big-bore handgun: sons Jon and David help out their dad.

lets to around 2,500 feet per second. So loaded, it did well for the boys. Sometimes I toy with rebarreling the rifle to .38-55 so that I can handload big cast bullets for whitetails in the brush, but I'll probably never get it done. So many rifles, so little time.

What is it about rifles? I own shotguns, and I intend to use them more when and if a slower time in my life arrives and the Brittany pups I've bought develop as I hope. I enjoy large-bore revolvers, too, and have hunted with them. A Ruger Bisley Blackhawk in .44 magnum has downed deer and has been a comfort to me on long rides through grizzly country. A shorter barreled stainless Blackhawk in .45 Colt, loaded heavily (as this action allows) with hard cast bullets has become a horseback favorite.

But write me a fat check and say, "Here, Dan, go buy yourself another gun or two," and I'll immediately think in terms of new rifles even though I own enough of them to make me blush. I could, literally, buy a rifle a week and still find myself looking at more possibilities than I could apply in the hunting fields were I to live and hunt another century.

In my defense I plead culture as responsible, at least partially. Nothing is more American than rifles and the ability to shoot them well. We grew as a nation of hunters, the constant push into the frontier often having been a live-off-the-land proposition: you shot well if you were to eat. Further, there was often a tactical requirement for marksmanship in self-defense.

For squirrels in the trees and deer in the shadows the smoothbores of the British would no longer do. Thus came the somewhat misnamed Kentucky rifle (for it was built primarily by German gunsmiths who lived in Pennsylvania), slim, elegant, long in the barrel and therefore in sight radius. After being formed around a mandrel their barrels were rifled by hand, one groove at a time, with a tool slowly turned as it was drawn through the bore. Even by today's standards, these rifles were accurate.

Such rifles were family treasures, probably as expensive in terms of relative family wealth as a luxury SUV today or even a home. Mountain men out West sometimes took half a year off to make the journey east to visit the gunsmiths who had built their rifles. While the mountain man camped nearby, the gunsmith would rebore the worn barrel to the next larger caliber, rerifle it, make him a new bullet mold to fit the larger bore, and then send him west again. Long before being replaced by the needs of the Great Plains—bigger animals, longer ranges—the long rifle, as it was sometimes called, established the United States as a nation of riflemen, of sharpshooters.

Thus I can plead two centuries of a tradition so strong it's a compulsion. To be an American male is (or should be) to also be a rifleman. It's a tradition that includes Daniel Boone and Sergeant York and sometimes Americans on the other side of the trenches, such as the unnamed Sioux sniper who did much to hold Marcus Reno and his troops pinned down on that hilltop while Custer died a couple of miles away. It's a tradition that means you could, if the chips were down, feed your family and defend it.

This tradition may or may not survive the current assault, an assault that includes misappropriating the word "sniper" and applying it to any homicidal maniac who guns down innocents at point-blank range; that has yanked marksmanship programs out of high schools and colleges; and that rates ignorance about firearms as a sort of badge of honor. (One of the highest-paid news people on network television declaimed to her audience that the DC "sniper" had something new and insidious in his gun barrel, some recent invention that made the bullet spin and therefore enabled the criminal to place his shots accurately at twenty-five yards. Had she so completely missed any other major historical development as important as rifling in gun barrels, a development centuries old, she would have been declared a village idiot.)

And so, I have owned a fair number of rifles, though my collection is meager compared to some I know. I'm sure I have not bought my last one. There is a magic in opening that box and smelling the oiled steel, in thinking of adventures ahead, of camps in the aspens, of shots to be made, and of elk tenderloins to be roasted while the hunting tales flow.

Most hunters are fascinated with the pros and cons of various rifle calibers. There are exceptions. Yes, with the right loads you really can use a .30-06 for everything from woodchucks to brown bear, and there are hunters who do just that. For many of us, though, that would be a boring scenario, which is probably the reason I've never owned a .30-06. Here is a rundown of some of the calibers that have served our family well. We'll take them approximately in order of their arriving into our hunting world, the .30-30 having been already discussed.

The .303 British

As mentioned in earlier chapters, this rimmed warhorse came to us via the British military rifles, the famed SMLE, which were sold in the United States through the mail at prices even pastor's sons could afford. The cartridge itself is a very good one, nearly identical to our American .30-40 Krag, though its bullet diameter is .311, slightly larger than conventional thirty calibers.

Our first ammunition consisted of 174-grain soft points of unknown origin sold with the rifles. I suspect these were military hardball with the full metal jacket bullets pulled out of the cases and soft points seated in. I better remember the Remington loading, a big 215-grain round nose at 2,100 feet per second. These certainly didn't improve on the open country characteristics of my .30-30, but had we been able to track down an elk, I'm sure they'd have been capable. Later in our stint with the caliber, Winchester released a sleek 180-grain power point at better than 2,500 fps, a very good load, not far behind the .30-06.

The rifles themselves were a bit crude, even by our standards, though with military stocks cut down they made decent deer guns, plenty good for boys on their first adventures. When I finally became convinced that any ballistic superiority over the .30-30 was too slight to justify the extra weight and the awkwardness of a right-handed bolt, I retired mine. It sits in my gun safe today, its customized stock a badge of my father's attention. I may handload cast bullets for it, just for fun, if I ever get time.

The .270 Winchester

Throughout my growing up, this was *the* caliber. Yes, the famed writer Jack O'Connor, gun editor of *Outdoor Life*, had his effects in this direction. His archrival Elmer Keith held the caliber in contempt, probably mainly because O'Connor preached it so strongly, but the difference between the men was largely a literary one. O'Connor, the former journalism professor, wrote well. Keith's style was heavy and awkward. The better communicator won our hearts and minds.

During my early hunting days the .270 was out of reach to me for one primary reason: I was left-handed, and the only left-handled bolt guns available were expensive custom conversions. I suppose I was aware of pump-action rifles in this caliber, but to me a big game rifle came in only two persuasions, lever or bolt. Then one day I met a friend named Bob Cook walking down the back street of our town carrying a new rifle. He was headed up the hill to try it out, but he gave me a good look first. It was a classy outfit, a Savage 110 in .30-06, with walnut stock and nice checkering. The best news of all: the rifle was available in a left-handed version.

I'll always have a sense of gratitude toward Savage for doing what other manufacturers had refused to do until that time, for making a left-handled bolt-action rifle that was affordable for an ordinary guy. Many years passed before I bought one, and by the time mine was made the company had considerably cheapened it with impressed rather than cut checkering. No matter. The thing shot just as O'Connor claimed it would. For me it was Zeus's thunderbolt.

I shot only one box of factory rounds, knocking down a mule deer buck just before leaving for Southeast Asia. Upon my return I set up to handload O'Connor's favorite load, a 130-grain spitzer in front of 60 grains of the only powder then called 4831. (Actually, O'Connor had used 62 grains but throttled back, in print at least, as we entered the modern era of sue first, ask questions later.) The 4831 powder at the time was all of the same persuasion (there are now five different powders bearing that code number, each with further letters or digits to distinguish it from the others and, unfortunately, with subtle differences in burning rate). This was still the military surplus stuff, available at a gun shop in Salt Lake City during my graduate school days for a buck a pound.

Later in eastern Montana this was the load with which I did my best to keep Mr. Ryan's smokehouse busy. I'm not sure how many deer and antelope it took during those several years. I did learn to put the bullet as precisely as possible through the rib cage behind the shoulder. Hitting a ham or shoulder meant much meat turned to jelly.

My first elk, a huge cow, fell to the .270 as well, to a relatively new bullet weight, a 140-grain made by Hornady. The range was long but she was stationary, and I had for a rest a boulder the size of a compact car over which I leaned, Hopkins at my elbow. One bullet through the rib cage did the job cleanly. On subsequent elk with the same bullet and with the Speer 150-grain I got similar results.

That said, I've come to consider the .270 rather light for elk. The elk have not changed, and bullets have gotten better since O'Connor's time. However, hunting conditions have changed. Fewer are the chances of gaining a broadside shot at a standing elk. Little as you may like it, that bull crashing away through the timber might have to be broken down with a shot at the root of the tail, feasible enough, but only with heavy bullets that can smash their way forward. If I were to use the .270 again on elk I'd handload the bullet with which my son Steve took his first one, the 160-grain Nosler Partition in semispitzer form.

And there's the other problem, that experienced by a

friend just a week ago. He hit a big bull solidly enough, but it still managed to run over a ridge where it was put down and tagged by other hunters. Dropping an animal as decisively as possible is not only the most humane set of circumstances, it just might be required to retain your animal. O'Connor's solitude in the high country is harder to come by today. Still, the .270 is a queen among calibers, relatively light in the recoil department, available all over the world, superb on antelope and deer at long range, yet capable of bigger stuff with the correct bullets placed carefully.

The .25-06

Most of what I've said about the .270 applies to this caliber as well. Based also on the .30-06 case, the .25-06 can be thought of as a varmint to deer proposition. I would not use it on elk, though in a pinch it would do with 115-grain Nosler bullets. It truly shines on antelope.

My one rifle in this caliber is a heavy varmint version of the Ruger #1 single shot. Superbly accurate, the rifle has become a family favorite for what we call "haystack sitting," hanging out on top of an alfalfa stack as the sun goes down and the whitetails arrive to browse on the third-cutting alfalfa I've left standing, conceded to them. However, I've also used this rifle in the brush. I've found I rarely have an opportunity for a second shot at a whitetail buck in close cover anyway, so the single shot is no big disadvantage, and the short overall length of the Ruger single-shot rifles makes them handy.

The 7mm-08

This is a good one. I remember so well Jonathan's first elk, our watching a clearing at long range. We were certain we'd seen an elk enter the timber just below it, but we had seen mule deer enter it too. I spotted for Jon with my binoculars, and as an animal entered the clearing said, "Deer!" Then, in close succession: "Deer, Deer, Elk!" The third in line was indeed an antlerless elk, the animal his tag prescribed. The little Browning 7mm-08 barked once, and the critter went down, struck by a 140-grain Nosler Partition.

Just as the .30-06 case has been necked up and down and has given us the .25-06, the .270, the .280, and the .35 Whelen, the shorter .308 case, introduced by the military as the 7.62 NATO, has spawned the .243, .260, 7mm-08, and .358. All have slightly less case capacity than the 30-06-based cartridges, but they have the advantage of feeding through short actions, thus reducing slightly the overall length of the rifle.

The 7mm-08 may be the best of the lot. I do wish more 7mm-08s and fewer .243s were purchased for young and female hunters. Too often the new hunter is given a .243 because its recoil is light and it is adequate for deer at moderate ranges. Then the budding hunter moves on to elk and uses the same rifle. Yes, should its tiny 100-grain bullet slip through the rib cage and into the lungs, the .243 will kill the elk. But if something goes slightly wrong, the animal is wounded instead.

The 7mm-08 is in a whole different category. Edged only slightly by the .270 in ballistics, this caliber shines for deer, and it moves into elk category because it can be loaded with heavier bullets, all the way to 175-grain if desired. It's versatile, light in the recoil department, and chambered in many short and handy rifles. I hope the caliber stays around.

The 7mm Remington Magnum and the 7mm STW

These larger 7mm's build on the theory that if a little is good, more velocity with the same weight bullets is better. Thus the 7mm Remington magnum improves considerably upon the velocities of the old 7mm X 57 Mauser and the 7mm-08, while the 7mm STW kicks it up another notch. The Remington round has become exceedingly popular, and it is indeed a useful one, a premier cartridge for deer and antelope at long range, and proven as well on elk.

I have used both of these, ironically in the same rifle, a Ruger #1 single shot that started out as a 7mm Remington magnum and was then rechambered to the longer STW round. Truthfully, I could tell little difference in effectiveness between the two, and for that matter, with similar bullets can't really claim any great superiority over the 7mm-08. On a Friday-the-Thirteenth elk hunt in Gardiner, my son Jonathan and I hit identical cows with virtually identical hits, I with the 7mm magnum and 175-grain Sierra bullets, he with the 7mm-08 and 160-grain Speers. There was no discernable difference. Each cow took two hits in quick succession right in the ribcage, each staggered a short distance and died. Jon's bullets both exited. Just one of mine did so. I've increasingly come to believe that after a certain point, given similar bullets, greater velocity flattens trajectory but doesn't do a whole lot more. The cost is greater recoil and muzzle blast, possibly packaged in a longer and heavier rifle, perhaps worth it and perhaps not.

When the 7mm Remington magnum was first released, gun writers were lavish in their praise. For large animals, they claimed the new round would be far superior to the old .30-06 (an opinion that has changed over the years), and with its heaviest factory load, a 175-grain spitzer, it was proper medicine for anything that walked the continent. Two well-known scribes headed for Alaska to prove their new rifles on Alaskan brown bear. They very nearly got their butts kicked. Yes, they killed their bears, but the critters absorbed a lot of lead before rolling over. No matter what you do to a 7mm (and much *has* been done in the bullet department), it is still only a 7mm.

This one is a wildcat, but a rather useful one. Basically, it's a blown out .30-06 case necked to 7mm. It may be thought of as a .280 Remington on steroids. The process of "improving" a factory caliber consists of sharpening the shoulder and reducing the taper of the case for added capacity. In rounds such as the 7mmJRS the process has been carried further, because the shoulder has also been moved forward.

The downside is that creating cases involves fire-forming. For the JRS cartridge I start with .30-06 brass, necking them down to 7mm but for only a short distance down the neck, thus creating a false shoulder that allows the bolt of the rifle to close but with some resistance. The false shoulder headspaces the case, holding it firmly against the blow of the firing pin. I then load these cases to somewhat below maximum with cheap bullets and head to the range. Firing these partially formed cases blows them out to their proper dimensions.

The resulting cartridge treads closely on the heels of the 7mm Remington magnum with similar bullet weights. It retains the advantages of the .30-06 family, the slimmer cases allowing a fourth round to fit in the magazine. Recoil is relatively mild. I've shot many whitetails, mule deer, and antelope with this caliber and like it a great deal. But is it worth messing with a wildcat for which you could not buy factory ammunition in a pinch? Only if you, like me, simply enjoy the messing around.

.300 Winchester Magnum and .300 Remington Ultramag

I've never used either of these, but my son Jon the mechanical engineer is an expert on both. Realizing that his handloads were pushing the Winchester version rather hard (which may be putting it mildly) he eventually rechambered his rifle for the larger round. The big .30 caliber magnums are indisputably effective on elk and other large critters. If I have any objection to them, it's that they are Mr. In-betweens: as long-range deer and antelope rifles they tend to be a bit much in terms of recoil and muzzle blast. Conversely, if you're going to belch that much smoke, why not move up to a .338 and be all the more capable of tackling the big stuff? Jon plans to counter this argument by loading extremely heavy bullets—250-grains—for his Ultramag, thus moving it into a different category. The huge case can propel such heavy bullets fast enough through the rifling to stabilize them.

.338 Winchester and .338 RUM

These, and other versions of the same theme, are perhaps the best elk calibers going, particularly if ranges tend to be long. I've used both, going to the larger version with the same philosophy as Jon used on the .30s: velocities that would max out the Winchester round are mild with the larger case.

The combination of heavy bullets of high sectional density and relatively high velocity make the .338s impressive indeed, at any range. With the best and the heaviest bullets they are at home used on any North American game. Yes, you pay a price. I found the .338 Winchester relatively easy to shoot, but I must concentrate while shooting my Ruger #1 in the Ultramag version, even though the rifle weighs 9½ pounds. I've shot just one elk with it, a cow that had bedded strategically so she could watch a heavily timbered coulee below her. She never saw me. The shot high in the neck was no test for the caliber, because a .30-30 would have done as well.

.35 Whelen and .35 Whelen Improved

These are family favorites. I'd go so far as to say that we'd have more successful elk hunters in this country if more of them forgot about ultra-velocities and four-hundred-yard shots and

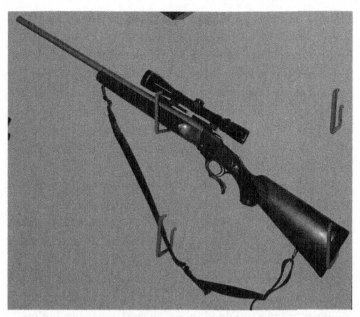

13. It's hard to beat the simplicity and aesthetic appeal of single shot rifles. This is one of the author's favorites, a Ruger #1 custom barreled to .338 RUM.

instead took to the woods with .35 Whelens. Across the world's hunting fields, one sort of ballistic combination seems to have always been effective and reliable, that of medium bore, heavy-for-weight projectiles fired at moderate velocities. These calibers include the .358 Winchester, .338-06, .35 Whelen, .350 Remington magnum, and in Europe (and increasingly here) the much-respected 9.3 X 62mm. No one who uses them speaks ill of them. With the right loads all of these can be used at ranges up to three hundred yards with only a little holdover, though some writers who apparently look too rarely at ballistic tables refer to them as "brush cartridges."

My first .35 Whelen was chambered in the Ackley improved version by ER Shaw, who installed the barrel on the same left-handed Savage 110 that started life as my first .270. This "improved" version (blown out, with sharper shoulder) did no better than the standard .35 Whelen with 250-grain bullets, 2,500 feet per second being the ceiling, but with the 225 Sierra it shaded factory loads for the .338 Winchester. My first load propelled the Sierra at well over 2,700 feet per second. With that I killed a moose. At thirty yards away in the timber the bull faced me, and the bullet entered the center of his chest. He went down decisively.

When Savage made left-handed .338s available I (somewhat too hastily) gave this rifle to my son Steve, who went on to kill a couple of big cow elk with it, one with the same Sierra load, the other with the 225-grain Nosler Partition, a bullet that hadn't been marketed in that caliber by the time of my moose hunt. The rifle performed on both as is par for the medium bores: solid hits mean that game animals go down. No muss, no fuss, no need for exotic and expensive bullets or meat-pulping velocities. The Whelen is easy on the shoulder and soft on the ears.

Recently the firm Midway began selling Adams and Bennett barrels for the Savage 110. With the right tools and a little common sense these can be installed by laymen. I made such a conversion to the standard Whelen for my son David, who promptly took a cow elk with that same 225 Sierra pushed at a bit over 2,600 feet per second. One shot, one young cow, whose tenderloin treated us under the tent canopy that evening. I'll own a .35 Whelen again someday, and I'll probably load the classic old 250-grain Speer to about 2,500 feet per second.

.375 H&H

I've had just one flirtation with the grand old girl of world class cartridges, the .375 Holland and Holland. It's really as good as everyone claims, and if one caliber is to be given the "all-around rifle" label, it should probably be the .375. You do not have to be planning a trip to Africa to covet one. All riflemen, down deep, want to try a .375. There is nothing awesome or ferocious about the .375. In a rifle weighing nine pounds or so the recoil is quite manageable. Mine weighed 9½ pounds and seemed considerably less punishing than my .338 Ultramag in a rifle of similar heft.

New bullets make the .375 an even more sensible choice as a rifle for elk and moose. Efficient projectiles in the 250- to 270-grain range can be given enough velocity to flatten trajectory adequately for any sensible rifleman. Many bullets of various configurations and weights are available to the handloader, and factory ammunition can be purchased anywhere in the world where hunting is allowed. Few North American hunters may really *need* .375s, true, but that has little relevance to those of us who enjoy hunting with them.

.325 WSM

My new left-handed Browning A-bolt in this caliber just may get nicknamed the Eliminator, but not only because it does such a good job on game. Rather, this caliber may eliminate future excuses to buy new rifles. I was initially lukewarm to the introduction of these hot Winchester Short magnum calibers in short, fat cases. As I've mentioned, boosting the velocity of .270, 7mm, and .30 calibers has become a yawner for me. It's been done in spades, after all. The WSM versions fit through short actions but at the expense of a fourth round in the magazine, perhaps a fair exchange and perhaps not.

Like many, I hoped for a .338 version on this theme, but for several reasons the engineers at Winchester had trouble making that happen. Foremost among the difficulties was the shape of longer .338 bullets. Seated deeply enough to fit through a short action, the bullets contacted the case mouth on the ogive (front, curved portion). The engineers settled on necking the WSM case to .323 caliber, also known as 8mm, but because Americans have a history of shunning 8mm calibers, their marketing folks released the caliber with a sexy new name, the .325 WSM. I think it's a winner.

My new Browning hit the ground running, the Montana general hunting season having already begun. I quickly developed handloads for two bullets, the 175 Sierra at 2,950 fps for antelope and deer and the 200-grain Nosler Partition cruising at 2,850 fps for elk. I've never developed confidence in a new rifle so rapidly. A nice antelope buck fell to the rifle's first shot on game, and it fell, literally, in its tracks at about 275 yards. A whitetail buck was dispatched with equal efficiency. And, as winter descended and my bull tag expired, the new rifle put down a cow elk at very long range with a shot that may not have anchored her with a lesser caliber. She angled steeply away, more than quartering to my right. The bullet entered her shoulder and exited between the front of the shoulder and the neck, missing the vitals. Enough damage was done, however, to keep her in one spot until I could approach for the finisher.

I've found the .325 WSM to be relatively mild in the recoil department, even in this very light rifle, except during prolonged sessions at the bench rest. But then, I've been messing with .338 Ultramags and .375s. The caliber is probably a bit much for anyone who is recoil shy. What impresses me is the versatility of the round. I can think of no other cartridge more capable for a variety of game from antelope to moose and beyond, yet packaged in light, short-action rifles. This caliber is a keeper.

Some Biases

Many things work well, and in this world our primary arbiters of preference and opinion are the experiences we've had. I've hunted enough years to have strong opinions about hunting rifles. I can't claim any unusually astute insight, but I can look back and quickly recall the experiences that have led to my biases. When it comes to big game rifles, I offer a few quick observations:

First, nothing is free. We can't evade Newton's laws, so more power means more recoil. That said, recoil is not to be feared if you simply shoot more. Professional African hunters shooting in short-sleeved shirts consider calibers such as the .375 H&H to be the light ones. Recoil can be handled well if you get off the bench rest and shoot from the normal hunting positions and protect your ears while you're doing so. Practice, unfortunately, is nearly unknown to many American hunters. They sight in their rifles from a bench rest (some don't even do that), then head for the field.

Second, if you're using one of the proven calibers such as the .30-06, the .270, or the 7mm Remington magnum, don't assume you need something bigger until you've exploited the superior modern bullets and factory ammunition now available. Once that's done, if you want more power *increase the size of the hole in the barrel* rather than buying a caliber that simply pumps the same bullets along a little faster.

Third, though I never call my hunting rifles weapons—they're tools of a very different purpose—they do have something in common with military weapons. The military considers a weapon useful only if it can be readily deployed. Custer's cavalry had Gatling guns available, but they were packed away in boxes back at the mule train and could thus not be deployed. Fancy devices are only useful if you can readily deploy them. I watched a video recently in which a hunter missed a chance at a bull moose because he was so intent on setting up his shooting sticks that the bull ducked away. The range was less than a hundred yards! With many trees to lean against, did he really need those shooting sticks on a large animal so close?

Some hunting rifles are so decked out today with huge scopes, bipods, and other paraphernalia that they won't fit in saddle scabbards. Often the attachments are vulnerable to damage. I've learned the hard way that if a rifle is to see hard use, such as riding on a horse or in a canoe all day, the scope should be short, low, and strong. Huge objective lenses also require high mounting, which not only makes them more vulnerable, but makes you more vulnerable to recoil as well. You tend to raise your cheek off the comb of the stock to see through such scopes, and that gets you smacked when the rifle rises during recoil.

Do remember that hunting videos exist primarily to sell products, not to demonstrate what's truly needed or practical in the field. The old KISS principle (Keep It Simple, Stupid) applies. The more complications involved in getting off an accurate shot when a split second of opportunity arises, the greater the chance of failure.

The "Varmint" Rounds

I'll just touch on some of the calibers we've used on smaller game ranging from prairie dogs to coyotes. Beyond the obvious .22 rimfire came the .22 rimfire magnum, chambered in a dandy little Marlin lever action. I have fond memories of the rifle and never should have sold it. During Marine years Emily and I carried the rifle for walks on two-track roads off El Camino Real in southern California, plinking at targets of opportunity while Tar, our dog, joyfully checked out every patch of oak brush. This land is, of course, long since buried by housing developments.

Later, in eastern Montana, in the two-square-mile prairie dog town, the rimfire proved its worth as long as it wasn't too windy and I stuck with shots closer than a hundred yards or so. After one spate of missing on a windy day, Hopkins commented on my fusillade while I reloaded the tubular magazine. He claims that I rejoined, "Oh, well, ammo's cheap and this is fun."

I've used just a few .22 centerfires. The .22 Hornet is particularly useful as a pest rifle on the ranch when it's necessary to eliminate a skunk or porcupine in close to the buildings without terrorizing the livestock. The .223 gets into long range territory. Chambered in several rifles and in the Remington XP 100-bolt action pistol, it has been efficient on coyotes.

I've used the .25-06 in varmint capacity as well. Loaded with 75-grain bullets it settles all arguments, but it's a bit much for prolonged shooting. My current favorite is the .22-250 that, like the .375 H&H, proved when I acquired one to be every bit as good as I'd always heard it was. Mine is a left-handed Savage 110 (what else?) in stainless steel featuring the crisp new Accu-trigger. It, like the Browning .325 WSM, is a keeper.

One can ask, of course, whether all this is necessary. The only real requirement for any hunting rifle is that it be powerful enough to kill the quarry quickly and humanely, and that it be accurate enough at the ranges at which it is used to place a bullet precisely and thus accomplish a clean kill. Much as we study subtle differences in bullet weight, velocity, and retained energy at various ranges, we rifle enthusiasts will normally admit that the old cliché is true: proper bullet placement by accurate shooting is still more important.

But most of us have crossed the line, have passed the point where we're satisfied in owning just one adequate rifle. Anticipation of the hunt is a good share of the thrill, and selecting the tool (or more likely, the tools) is central to that process. We keep wanting to open the box, to touch the walnut, and to smell the gun oil.

8

Gardiner

Those who have experienced hunting at its very best have known its poetic side. The art of hunting can seem almost transcendental, its truths going directly to the gut with startling, unsparing honesty. Anyone who has spent a day stalking—and being beaten by—a wily whitetail buck has learned worlds about both the buck and about himself.

But there is at the very base of the hunting experience, something more primitive and simple, and it is not to be despised. Hunting is, after all, the gathering of meat. It starts there, and it ends there. Hunting is locating a creature below you on the food chain, killing that creature, and converting the carcass into edible protein. This basic fact about hunting is its major strength, not a weakness. Hunting retains its honesty only when it remains rooted as a basic act of nature, and it is not made more legitimate by the gathering of trophies or by introducing the competitive elements of television sports.

A certain segment of the fly fishing world has made the grave mistake of implying moral superiority for the artful act of luring a fish to the fly, playing it on a line, taking it from the water, and then, instead of killing and eating it, returning the fish to the stream. With a fish species that is threatened or endangered or hard pressed by hordes of like-minded anglers, our fisherman may well claim ecological correctness. But he should never consider himself morally superior to the barefoot Southern child who throws worm and bobber into muddy waters and extracts a mess of sunfish for supper. Indeed, one could argue the opposite, that the child is a true participant in nature while the more sophisticated fisherman is, in fact, a spectator, one who toys with its basic laws and makes them into a game. (I say this while assuring the reader that I, too, fly fish.)

There is in Montana, due north of Yellowstone Park, late in the year, when the aspen leaves have dropped, leaving white-barked branches as frozen as Russian birches, an elk hunt that makes no pretension. It is what it is. The Yellowstone elk herd, always too big for its range (though wolves now chip away at this), migrates north out of the park to winter range around Gardiner, Montana. For many years special hunts have been held with the express purpose of reducing elk numbers to keep their appetites somewhat in proportion to the rather limited winter range.

No one would claim that these hunts represent elk hunting at its best, at its most aesthetic. The bugling season is long, long gone, and true winter in the mountains precludes pleasant camps. But these special hunts are a great improvement over the infamous "firing line" of the past, when huge numbers of Montana hunters converged on Gardiner during the last of each regular season as snow and cold brought the herd north. Tales abound of hunters shoulder to shoulder herd-shooting elk, fighting over whose bullet hit which, the whole thing a sorry spectacle of hunting gone completely amok.

Today hunters apply for special drawings and, if selected, receive a tag good for just one particular weekend sometime between the end of the regular season and the middle of February. The hunts are extremely well regulated, so much so that a few hunters grumble that there are more game wardens than hunters, that your every move is watched by a distant game warden through a 20X spotting scope perched on the hood of his pickup. But the extra scrutiny seems worth it to most for a prime opportunity to fill the larder with first-rate meat.

On their way into the Gardiner area all hunters stop at the check station and show their tags and special permits to sleep-deprived wardens, picking up maps and advice. This compulsory check-in proved a saving grace for my son Jonathan and me one year when regular elk hunting season, hard as we had tried, had proved fruitless. The cow tags we had drawn for a Gardiner hunt in February had been stashed in a hutch drawer in the dining room, insurance against an elk-less freezer during the year to come.

And so, in the darkness of a bitter February morning, we too were leaning on the counter in the converted trailer house used by the wardens as a check station. We had seen elk in the headlights on the way in, always a thrill, and the building excitement was chasing away the grogginess I had fought earlier behind the wheel. Jon, never a morning person unless hunting is involved, was wide-eyed enough, and the two horses, Rockytop and Marauder, blanketed in the stock trailer behind the pickup, stamped their impatience. Tags validated, and revved by the optimistic assessment of the wardens, we headed not to one of the fringe trailheads that they recommended, but to Eagle Creek. "They're trying to spread the hunters out, Jon, and that's okay, but cold as it is I'll bet the elk are flowing through the Eagle Creek area right now as we speak. We'll be up that draw to the south right at shooting light."

It was a good idea. Too good. The wardens' attempts to spread the hunters out had failed miserably, and the parking lot at the Eagle Creek trailhead was jammed with vehicles juggling into place, headlights and taillights in a confused jumble. "Should we go to one of the others, Phelps Creek maybe?" Jon asked.

"I hate pulling that last little hill with the horse trailer. That's the one where a game warden's pickup lost traction and slid back into George's new outfit last year. Besides, most of these hunters are on foot. We've got good, fast-walking horses. We'll just get up there ahead of everyone else." Ahead, yes, but not too far ahead, we agreed. No sense stumbling onto elk in the dark, and for sure no sense in being tempted to fire a shot even a minute before legal shooting light. "Legal Shooting Light: 6:57 a.m." had been prominently posted on a chalkboard behind the check station desk. Tales of woe abound about hunters who had jumped the gun even a minute or two before legal shooting time of one half hour before sunrise, and had paid hefty fines as a result.

Rockytop and Marauder came out of the trailer snorting, turbocharged by the cold, the vehicles, the outfitter's horseback string near us in the parking lot, and the under-breath rumblings of many low human voices they did not know. We removed the insulated blankets that had kept the horses warm in the stock trailer, curried and saddled quickly, then rattled off our mental checklists, the absolute essentials first: hunting licenses, rifles, ammunition, and hunting knives. Then, the second tier: meat saw, binoculars, dragging rope, lunch, flashlight, camera. And then we were off in a running walk, our tall, hard-charging horses weaving among the vehicles, their hooves going rat-tat-tat against the frozen parking lot.

It did not take long for us to see them, the morning light coming on just enough to let us discern the partly timbered ridge a mile to the south covered by dark dots we knew to be elk. We stopped. Only a few hundred yards out from the parking lot, Rockytop and Marauder were already breathing hard from their fast pace through deep snow, their breath vapor clouds in the icy air. Binoculars confirmed it. Elk, a huge herd, more we quickly agreed than we had ever seen. There were hundreds loosely scattered on the broken ridge over a front at least a mile wide.

Even this, however, did not mean it would be easy. The elk could drift either east or west, or even turn around and head south again, back toward Yellowstone Park. In their bionic ability to cut through the deepest snow at a ground-eating trot, they could be out of harm's way long before we could get into rifle range.

So there would be no stalk. We had to keep riding straight toward them. Yes, some would see us and move off, but the ridge was cut by many timbered pockets, and these would certainly hold elk. This was not a single herd of one mind, but a loose conglomeration of many, many animals, determined to migrate north to winter feed.

It was exciting and unsettling at the same time. In my years growing up along the Beartooth front of the Absaroka mountains there were far fewer elk, at least in that region, than there are today. I spent many days during hunting season climbing the snowy slopes through thick scrub timber, thrilled when I saw a new elk track or fresh droppings, doubly so when I heard their bodies crashing through the lodgepole pine ahead of me. To actually see one was too much to ask; to actually shoot one, would have been something of a miracle.

Indeed, we had once gone completely elkless on one of these Gardiner hunts, and on others had worked very hard for them. So it was a thrill to see spreading to our right and left for at least a mile a ridge covered with hundreds of elk, close enough now that with the added morning light their bodies showed brown, the racks of the big bulls (off limits to us) visible at a thousand yards. Jon needed no contrasting boyhood recollections for *his* thrill—he was wide-eyed as he reined Marauder close behind me in the tracks Rockytop bulldozed through the snow. I remember his face as he peered between the horse's ears, cheeks red, determination written all over it.

The unsettling part was to be *between* all these elk and all these hunters. To put it in perspective, there was plenty of room for them. This was, after all, Big Sky Country. An Ohio or Pennsylvania hunter would probably wonder what concerned us, think the terrain relatively free of humanity. But to Montanans spoiled by sojourns nearly solo, trips when few if any hunters share one's mountain, seeing today a dozen or two to our rear, scattered over half a mile made the picture seem populated indeed. My greatest fear was that just one of them, fearful that he could not buck the snow to within proper range, would forget the exact minute of legal shooting light or ignore its reputation for strict enforcement and begin shooting at long range. That, at least, was one thing that did *not* go wrong.

We stopped to let the horses blow. I was aiming us up a small finger ridge that joined the main ridge at right angles. From previous trips I remembered a large sunken pocket to the left of this smaller ridge, a mini-basin perhaps three hundred yards across and a hundred feet deep, partly open and partly covered with aspen. It could not be seen from below, so consequently elk within it would not be able to see us approaching. We were above the open, sagebrush-covered flat now, the ridge sides broken and semitimbered, and although we were catching glimpses here and there of elk out of range, it was clear the main bunch was moving off. I was willing to bet we would catch elk undisturbed in the little basin, and it would be legal shooting light by the time we got there.

It worked just that way. The terrain was exactly as I remembered, the snow deeper now, both horses laboring. But after we ducked under the snow-covered branches of a small patch of timber and emerged into the open on the other side, the little basin was there and so, too, were the elk, a dozen of them, cows and a few calves, winter meat less than two hundred yards away.

14. Jonathan and Marauder hunting elk near Gardiner.

It was then that the trolls of Friday the Thirteenth began to assert themselves one by one. I piled off my horse and yanked out my rifle. Because there was a little intervening brush between the elk and us, I intended to cover the last few yards, necessary to get into the clear, on foot. The snow was very deep. Jon, too, piled off. I raced forward, attempting to load the single-shot rifle (a new Ruger #1 in 7mm magnum) as I ran, somehow letting go of Rockytop's reins in the process. I'm an experienced horseman, and I *never* let go of my horse. But there he was, just the same, a couple yards away from me, free without knowing it yet, and since there was no place to tie him without jeopardizing the shot at an elk, I said, "Hey, Jon, Rockytop's loose. Hang onto Marauder really tight while I shoot, and then I'll grab him for you." I took a good sitting position in the snow, tried to pick out the darkest cow in the bunch (the darker coat said to be a sign of good, fat condition) and squeezed off the shot. Caught behind the shoulder the cow stumbled and hesitated while I reloaded and shot again, then walked a couple of steps and went down. It was a good clean kill.

Everything else, however, went to hell. Rockytop, taking issue with a magnum rifle being touched off so close to his nose, swapped ends and headed for Gardiner. Marauder was not about to be left behind. He weighed 1,200 pounds; Jon weighed about 130. It was not a fair contest. The boy did his best, though, holding hard to the reins as the big black horse swiveled like a discus thrower, swinging his front toward the steep downward slope of the basin and the huge drift of snow below. Jon's body went airborne, his course describing an orbit out over the edge, through the air toward splashdown head-first into the drift. When he landed he simply disappeared.

There was no time to worry about the horses. I just had to hope one of the hunters below us would grab them as they went by. Meanwhile, the snow in the drift by Jon's entrance hole began to shake, and a shape emerged, Casper the Ghost with a rifle. Standing in snow to his waist, Jon shook like a dog, then began methodically wiping off his face, then his rifle, then with a pulled-out shirttail, his scope lenses. After what seemed an eternity (but was probably no more than half a minute) Jon peered through the scope and swung on the lead cow. Though spooked, the cows had not accelerated past a trot, probably having watched this entire sorry spectacle and concluded they were safe.

"Bang!" went Jon's little 7mm-08, then "bang!" again. The cow, hit, it later turned out, twice behind the shoulder, the two shots a hand's-breadth apart, went down. Well, things were improving. We had our meat, lots of it, and Jon had survived his dunking in the snow. Then I saw that a benevolent horseman down the trail from us had snatched Rockytop and Marauder, and things were a whole lot better yet. (The horseman was very kind. Had I been in his shoes my attitude might have been far less tolerant toward hunters apparently so tyro as to let go of both their horses.) Jon headed down to inspect the elk while I retrieved the horses.

We were inclined to celebrate, but it was still Friday the Thirteenth. We stood near the cows for a moment, awed and thankful, our hearts still thumping. There was a great deal of work to do. Field dressing an elk is always a major task, and the deep snow would make it worse. But before we even got started another troll crawled from out of the snow and asserted himself this way: "Jon, we'd better get these cows tagged."

"Yeah, Dad." I took the elk tag from my wallet, punched out month and date, inserted it into a ziplock bag, and began duct-taping it to my cow's foreleg. Only then did I notice that Jon was not moving. I looked at him. His face was white, and not, this time, with snow. "Dad, my wallet's gone"

"Are you sure? Could it be in one of your vest pockets?"

"I've looked in all my pockets twice. It must have come out in the snow bank. I'll go up and look." I looked up at the snow bank, really more of a cornice formed by wind blowing snow over the ridge, and again at Jon. I was not hopeful. His face reflected my worries about where we would stand legally with two elk down and only one valid tag. "You think they'll fine us?"

I tried to be jocular. "Probably send us straight to the crowbar motel." He didn't laugh. Instead he turned back uphill toward the ridge, a good young hunter whose triumph had been compromised through no fault of his own. I, too, was worried sick, but tried to set that aside; there was much work to do. The field-dressing job was especially difficult because of the steep slope and deep snow. I gradually tramped a deep path on either side so that the elk itself remained on a sort of pedestal of snow, okay for a while until gravity took over and it slipped down into one of the deep troughs packed next to it. Nevertheless, I was nearly finished with the first elk when Jon returned dejected from his fruitless search, saying little, shaking his head as we worked.

I knew my parental leadership had been a bit deficient thus far. "We'll just have to tell the truth. Things like this must happen from time to time." Gauging by Jon's reaction, I must not have sounded very convincing. In place of a tag on Jon's elk we wrote out a note explaining what had happened, then taped it in a ziplock bag under several wraps of duct tape, just as if it were a tag, to the foreleg of Jon's elk.

Dragging out an elk dallied to the saddle horn is a formidable task, one Jon was not old enough to tackle, so we would take one elk at a time, mine first, finding a warden back at that trailhead and throwing ourselves on the mercy of the court. Rockytop seemed more tired than Marauder, so we swapped saddles. I took two dallies around the saddle horn and eased Marauder forward to take out the slack. Confused for just a moment by the resistance, the big black horse leaned into the task and the elk slid grudgingly through the deep snow. Soon, though, we dropped to what I knew to be a gravel road, closed to vehicles during winter, but easier travel for us even snowed over. And soon after that we hit a groove in the snow, iced like a bobsled run from use by several like us, a slick, elk-dragging trail that let Marauder walk along almost unfettered.

The road curved gradually toward the trailhead. We crossed a big open flat, a snowfield marked only by sagebrush tips poking through the deep snow. I was attentive to the elk I was dragging, glancing behind frequently, when Jon said, "Look, Dad, buffalo!" To our front, in a herd of thirty or so, spanning the road, were bison all right, cows, calves and bulls, pawing through the snow for the grass underneath. They saw us and stared. We stopped to study the situation, our horses now snorting at this strange breed of cattle, the bison considering whether they should move out of our way, while I pondered whether I had the guts to ride through the middle of the herd while dragging an elk.

Choices were limited. The bison were between the trailhead and us, and they straddled the easiest route. I had no desire to veer off the road, away from our elk/bobsled trail, into deep snow with tangled sagebrush submerged underneath. That would be tough dragging. "Well, Jon, here goes." We rode straight toward the bison, our horses' necks arched, their eyes wide. The bison looked at us, then parted cooperatively and let us pass. Indelibly etched on my brain are the bison, the horses, the winter meat we dragged, and directly ahead of us at the edge of the clearing, high in a pine, a bald eagle perched where he could watch the scene.

It is strange what stress can do to you. Primed with stories of

15. Author dragging out a cow elk with Rockytop.

extremely tough, even unfair, law enforcement during these special Gardiner hunts, we had jumped to the worst possible scenario. We had forgotten a simple fact, and it did not hit me until we had dragged my elk right to the rear of the horse trailer and tied up our horses. It still did not hit me as I walked with a convict's dragging feet toward a game warden's pickup, looked him in the eye, and told him we had two elk down and a tag lost in the snow. "Oh, yeah, well you'll have to run down to the check station and buy another tag." I must have looked at him strangely. "Yeah, another tag. You can buy a replacement for five dollars when you lose one. Then go up and tag your elk."

Only this and nothing more? All our worries worth just five bucks? What about admonitions that elk be tagged immediately, stories of wardens locking people up for shooting a minute before legal light, interrogating hunters for hours on the merest suspicion of some impropriety. And only then, walking back toward Jon with the first grin of the day, did it occur to me that the warden could be so casual because of the check-in procedure at the beginning of the hunt. Jon had shown a warden his valid tag and his permit for this weekend's hunt. Both had been logged in. There was no suspicion that he had shot an elk earlier in the season and was now trying to take another illegally.

So we did what the warden asked and then returned to the parking lot. We had one last moment of anxiety when another warden hailed us. "Your elk," he said, "has been drug out. It's over there." He pointed toward a pullout at the side of the road a couple hundred yards above the parking lot. A warden patrolling on a snowmobile had found the elk, read our note, hooked onto the elk and brought it in.

On the drive home we stopped to show the elk to our friend Hopkins by his cabin south of Livingston. We stood briefly in

16. Hopkins at Gardiner with another questionable dragging stick.

a wind typical of that area, reliving the hunt as we leaned on the pickup tailgate, and then, fighting drowsiness as afternoon came on and the pickup heater took over, we headed home.

There had been other Gardiner hunts, and there would be more to come. On one, the three of us, sons Steve, Jon, and myself, fought bitter cold and were totally skunked. On another, much earlier, Hopkins had handed me a "better dragging stick," a larger one than the green willow I was using, and I leaned downhill, pulling a cow elk by a rope attached to the middle of the stick, both hands behind me and my head pointed downgrade, and catapulted into the snow as the stick snapped in the middle. The dive was not as spectacular as Jon's, but was memorable nonetheless. Hopkins has been frequently reminded.

17. Son Steve with his second elk, taken with the .35 Whelen.

There was the hunt on which Steve used my .35 Whelen for the first time, making a good shot on a cow while we salivated over several huge bulls, off limits to us.

On still another, in late December, we found at the top of the mountain in the middle of elk tracks a tangled string of Christmas lights. A bull elk had wandered through the town of Gardiner, rubbed his antlers on a seasonally decorated juniper bush, and then carried the lights up onto the mountain. We hoped that for a moment, until the extension cord ran out, the lights had stayed illuminated, the bull briefly a true Rudolph.

No, this Friday the Thirteenth hunt was not poetry, was not

the ultimate, was not the sort of hunt for which we strive. It was too much like a footrace, and, with the lost tag, too full of anxiety. It was a meat-gathering expedition that started well, turned sour, then came out just fine. And we'll remember it just as long as we remember any of our hunts: quality time, if stressed, between a son and me; a picture of a boy gutty enough to get up from a long toss into a deep snow bank, yet clean off his rifle and down an elk; and creatures, shaggy ones and human, whose horns proved ultimately friendly.

9

Moose

Major's shod hooves, slipping on the wet rocks, make metallic scraping sounds. To my left, down twenty yards from the ledge trail, the river froths and rumbles and tumbles its way down the mountain, its roar deafening. The rope to the lead pack horse turns just once over the horn of my saddle, then snakes under my knee where I can release it instantly by a lift of my leg. The pack horses, Sugar in front, the tall black named Marauder, then the young black mare called Rodeo, are connected to each other by breakaway loops of twine. The thought of one animal going over the edge and pulling the rest with it is frightening beyond belief, so any possibility must be prevented.

Although they are nervous, all four horses are handling this better than I am. The sound of the river along this steep, narrow trail is like a heavy curtain that shuts out all else for them, so they methodically step exactly where Major steps, quietly following. They do not have my worries, one of which is meeting another pack string on this treacherous stretch. Finally, we advance to that single pine tree at the right of the trail, that crazy solitary pine that somehow grows out of a crevice no larger than a dinner plate in the granite cliff, that pine I have kept fixed in my sight for the last two hundred yards and which marks the place where the trail breaks out of this corridor into which it is squeezed with the river. Then we are free. The river widens to a pastoral trout stream, the trail now soft soil and pine needles under the horses' hooves, the woods to my right dark and quiet.

18. A yearling bull moose.

I have won the lottery and am just now beginning to revel in it. No, I did not win the Montana Power Ball nor, for that matter, the Publisher's Clearing House contest. But after many years of applying, many summers of hoping, my number has been drawn for a moose permit in the Stillwater drainage of south-central Montana. Each year just five such permits are granted, the biologists having determined that the moose population of the drainage can best be kept healthy with that number culled each year. Apparently they are right. This is a drainage heavily used by backpackers and fishermen in the summer, its first lake accessible enough that the physically limited can easily reach it on Sunday afternoon day hikes, and almost everyone enjoys seeing moose. That does not mean converting one to winter meat is automatic, however. I have heard too many frustrating tales of someone drawing a permit, seeing moose everywhere during the summer, then having them strangely disappear when hunting season came.

The only down side of my good fortune has been a dearth of companions to come with me. My sons are grown or in school. My friends are all tied down by work, those who are teaching not anxious to blow their precious few days of personal leave so early in the year. I am fortunate enough to have three days available, enough to give me from Wednesday, the season opener, through the weekend. Emily has no such privileges. But she has been involved, nonetheless, for she helped me over the weekend pack in the heavy items of my camp to a special, pre-chosen place in a meadow near the river eight miles up the drainage. We set up the wall tent, left the woodstove and two plywood boxes of heavier supplies, but no food, lest it draw bears. Then we fixed a good meal and spent the night. It was a nice interlude in the best of all seasons when the aspens are golden and the woodstove cuts the chill in the tent. The ground was white with frost the next morning. We rode rapidly out, our packhorses unladen.

So today I arrived at the trailhead in an early morning rain with four horses in the trailer but with no human company. There was a flutter in my stomach. Undertaking a solo pack trip and hunt is no small thing. True, I have confidence in skills learned during years of packing our family into the wilderness on many recreational trips, but much can go wrong with a group of young horses and no helping hand. Soon I had the packs on and adjusted. Major looked upwind into the canyon, the wind ruffling his foretops. His demeanor was that of a confident war horse, and by the time I tied my saddlebags on behind the cantle, I too was ready.

For a Westerner there is little left in life that can match the feeling of sliding a good rifle into a saddle scabbard, swinging aboard a first-rate saddle horse, and grasping the rope of the lead horse in a packstring that contains everything needed to go anywhere in the backcountry. In an instant you are one with the Plains Indians who ascended these canyons to cut lodgepole pine and pick berries in the fall, with Lewis and Clark, with the beaver-trapping mountain men. You are using the same skills, the same transportation. Things look and smell and taste the same. You are able to temporarily forget that so little of our country is still like this, that so much is now paved and lined with endless shopping malls and fast-food restaurants and streets with stoplights choked with traffic.

Very soon the wilderness absorbs me. I relinquish all else, just as I have in the past when I've nudged my canoe into the swift current of the Yellowstone River. Now, in fall, the Nike tracks on the trail have disappeared, recreational hiking having gone with the fair weather. This time of year the use of this trail drops to a trickle: a few die-hard fishermen, lucky people like me with special hunting permits, and packers taking the long way into Slough Creek for the early elk bugling season.

On the entire trip to my camp I see humans only twice. First I overtake a tall, dark woman carrying a pack over which is slung a hunting rifle. In spite of the season she is wearing shorts; in every other way she looks well prepared. Nearly simultaneously I see her husband up the trail twenty paces. I stop briefly to visit while they rest and drink from their water bottles. I learn they are from Kentucky, that they have bighorn sheep permits and will soon turn out of the main valley up the steep feeder creek into a rocky drainage they scouted last summer. They seem as knowledgeable and capable as they are physically fit. I wish them luck and leave them, a happy Orion and his pretty Artemis.

Although the season is now officially open, I do not look seriously for moose on the way in. It would be anticlimactic to find one so quickly. Also, some of my equipment for the rather challenging task of processing a moose into meat is still in the storage boxes at camp. I do eyeball the clearings in each place where the Stillwater widens and slows, the swamp grass openings where moose often stand in the water and search with their long noses for just the right tidbits. Each time I check a clearing without seeing a moose, I am relieved.

The horses have settled into an easy, flat-footed walk, the pull of the grade having its effect. The three packhorses are lightly loaded, beneficiaries of our earlier trip to set up camp. The ride in is relaxing, for the trail is good and I know it well. I backpacked up this trail with David just before he turned six years old, a strong little guy who carried a ten-pound pack, the packing task helped by a dog named Friendly who carried his own food and another ten pounds of our stuff in his packs. This has been the trail for many other family trips and a couple other solo ones. It is not, however, devoid of change. The terrible fires of 1988 licked their way down this valley, so I pass through bands of forest that were burned. The regeneration is remarkable. The places that suffered the hottest fire have the thickest regrowth of baby pine. But it is still sad to see huge spruce trees now turned into bare, black shadows of themselves.

I am seven miles up the valley and nearing camp when I meet the only other people I see on the way in, a string of dudes followed by a pack outfit. The lead rider is a middle-aged woman who smiles and says "hello." She is followed by a half dozen more women, then a male wrangler who looks familiar but whose name I don't know. Bringing up the rear after the packhorses is Wanda, the guide and outfitter for the trip. She recognizes me and stops to talk, her face a small, animated disk under the felt brim of her big hat. "Dan, I think your tent blew down. The wind ripped through here last night, and it looked at least part way down when we went by."

"I'm not surprised. I don't really trust that pole set. Quite a crew you have here."

"Bunch of women from back East, wanted a fling in the mountains without their men. Snowed on 'em the first night, but they've had a ball."

"Seen any moose?"

"A couple up by the Wounded Man trail when we first came in. No big bull."

"Take care, Wanda."

"Have a good one, Dan."

The news about the tent worries me, so I press Major into a running walk and we cruise quickly to the campsite. One of the tent's internal poles has slipped, but I can see at a glance it's quickly repairable. The sun is now shining, the valley, with the dudes gone, mine.

There is much work to do, but I relish it. First, I will unsaddle the horses. The saddles will go onto a tarp, each upside down (easier on the saddle trees) and piled with my riding saddle on top, then covered with another tarp. Two horses will be hobbled and turned loose to graze, the other two picketed to a highline, which I will quickly construct between trees with a sling rope off a packsaddle and a cinch around the tree on each end to protect the bark. Then will come organizing my gear and cutting firewood, some in short lengths for the folding steel stove in the tent. For an outside fire there is a shallow pit to dig, the sod laid carefully aside to be pressed back in place when I leave the site.

It all goes quickly, the physical exertion feeling good after confinement in the saddle. I have brought a pretty sumptuous camp. Since much horsepower will be required if I succeed and must pack out a moose, it has only seemed logical to use that same packing capacity to have a fine camp. So instead of my backpacking tent, a cocoon into which I could crawl wet and tired at the end of a hard day, Emily and I have set up the big wall tent. Inside are a woodstove and a table made of the inverted plywood pack boxes. I have a folding campstool. Soon there is a strategically located stack of stove wood near the head of my bed so that I can reach out during the night, open the stove door, and pitch in a stick to rejuvenate the fire. I have everything I could need and am glad of it, for there have already been early wet snows up here. My camp must be both a support system and a haven after a hard day's work.

I take a short rest on top of my sleeping bag, doze, my dream a hazy replay of the trail up the valley as it looked between Major's ears. Then I awake with a start, shocked that I have wasted precious daylight during moose season when I have a permit in my pocket and a camp in paradise. I retrieve my folding saw from the woodpile, return it to its case, and strap it around my waist. Before I leave camp I switch the horses, hobbling the two that were on the highline and tying the other two in their place. I take time to carry the grain sack around, giving each a couple mouthfuls, which they munch. Then I sling my rifle over my shoulder and head up the trail.

I look less for moose than for sign of them. Moose are not above using the convenience of forest service trails when they want to move quickly up and down the drainage, but in a two-hour circle around camp I see none of their cow-sized tracks. Their absence is certainly not because of hunting pressure. Only five permits are given for a huge area that contains this primary drainage and many smaller ones along the moun-tain front. The one other moose hunter in this valley seems to have been the woman at the trailhead parking lot whose guide and outfitter were packing up to leave as I saddled my horses. I talked to them briefly. The guide said they would camp just a couple miles up. They left right behind me but never caught my fast-walking horses.

We stereotype moose as critters that spend all their time in the marshy clearings, but the truth is that they spend a lot of it running the high ridges in dense timber. That, apparently, is where they are now. I return to camp just before dark, light a lantern, fire up the woodstove in the tent, fill a small pot with chili from a can, and set it on the stove, then, beside it, my coffee pot. Later, after the food, coffee in hand, I find even the large tent confining and go outside to build a small fire. The big white tent, filled with the light of the gas lantern, illu-minates the entire clearing, so to better see the stars I duck into the tent and kill the lantern. The Milky Way is a stunning highway of stars. The argument of Huckleberry Finn and Jim comes to mind, how so many stars could be made, and Jim's contention that perhaps the moon laid them, for he had seen a frog lay "most as many."

The clearing is large enough to give me a panorama above,

the air so clear each star looks close enough to reach out and touch. To the north, straight down the valley, I find the Big Dipper, its lip pointing faithfully toward the North Star. Once I was camped in a similar clearing high in the Sierra Nevada Mountains of California, a Marine officer charged with teaching two companies of men the skills of mountain warfare and survival. The men were from New York and New Jersey, mostly black and Puerto Rican, good Marines but initially as intimidated by this high, open, wilderness environment as I probably would have been by theirs. The howl of a coyote the first night in camp terrified some of these muscular Marines, who would have defended without question our camp against humans with guns.

My classroom was an aspen grove. The elevation was very high, 9,300 feet if I recall correctly, for the timberline is higher farther south. Occasionally a band of sheep would visit, milling through the men, followed by sheep dogs and the Basque herder, his coyote rifle slung muzzle-down over his shoulder. Once I described the simple matter of finding the North Star via the Big Dipper. I drew blank stares from the troops. I asked whether they were not told about this in boot camp, and they said they probably were, but that they did not recall for sure. "Okay," I said, "anyone who wants to see the Big Dipper and North Star come over to my tent at twenty-two hundred tonight and I'll show you."

I really did not expect any of the Marines to take me up on this, since I left it voluntary, knowing the tenets of Marine leadership—you do not mess with people's chow, pay, or liberty (time off). The evening was their own time during this part of the training, their time to sit in small knots in front of their tents and exchange stories. So, I was surprised that night when approximately fifty men strolled over into "officer country," the little knoll on which our tents were located. I showed them the Big Dipper, showed how approximately four lengths out from the two stars that formed the side of its cup opposite the handle, in the direction the two stars pointed off the lip of the cup, you could find without fail the North Star, the star that never lets you down. They were positively tickled. They watched the stars for two hours, an explosive cheer accompanying the fall of each of the many meteors they witnessed. One said to me, "Captain, Sir, you got to understand most of us ain't never seen stars like this." Since that night I have never taken for granted the privilege of seeing the stars in the Western sky.

It is strange to sit alone by a campfire in a clearing in a mountain valley, telling stories to myself. There have been many campfires. I remember tiny ones, kindled with the "heat tabs," the little cubes of solid alcohol fuel with which we warmed C-rations in the military. In the hilly backcountry around Quantico, Virginia, in the cold and humid February wind off Chesapeake Bay, we would get into sheltered places and kindle a few sticks over heat tabs to make mini-fires that warmed the hands and helped the stories flow, making the noon break a good time.

There have been many campfires with Emily and the boys on pack trips, one in a camp very close to where I am now. There were discussions about whether life existed somewhere out in those stars at which we stared. We were here in this clearing just before the Fourth of July in 1988 and watched one of the fires that combined later with others into an inferno that tinder-dry summer, watched it grow from a lightning strike in a patch of pine across the valley, never large enough during the time we were there to be a threat.

And there has grown in our lives another tradition involving campfires and friends, a "spring bear hunt," the quotation marks being necessary because we have never gotten a

19. Emily in her "bear hunting hat."

bear and are not trying very hard. In a group that goes on this spring ritual there are one or two who actually hunt, one or two more (myself included) who go as far as buying a bear tag but spend their time enjoying camp instead, and a couple more who come to fish and b.s. The tradition started with one friend and myself, grew and continued after the friend moved to Alaska, a fluctuating group that has not always been stag, for Emily and another hunter's wife have come, too.

Around the campfire on these outings, lubricated by a particular drink, the stories flow. (The drink is this: take a Sierra cup and pack it with snow, always available in spring in the mountains, at least in the timber on shady north slopes. Mix into the snow equal parts of Yukon Jack and unsweetened grapefruit juice. Serve.) Now, alone on the Stillwater, I remember one of the stories and laugh out loud.

Roger told it. I guess I can, too, for the statute of limitations has certainly run out by now. When Roger was a boy back in the 1950s, he and his dad took a Model A pickup out looking for deer. Roger has never been a very enthusiastic hunter, but went as a matter of course. His Norwegian father, like many of his countrymen, really preferred mutton to venison, had worked with sheep before becoming a town dweller. But times were a little tough for the family, and a mule deer would keep the larder stocked.

They asked permission to hunt on a ranch owned by folks they knew, then spent a fruitless day searching the coulees and finding absolutely nothing. As the afternoon waned they had to face the fact that they had been skunked. Roger's dad steered the old pickup back on the two-track dirt road over the rolling hills toward the ranch house. Suddenly, at a low place in the road, they drove up on a single sheep, a ewe. Roger's dad stopped the pickup and stared at her for an instant. Then he said, "There's some mutton. Yust get out and knock her in the head."

Roger thought he was kidding. Any such illusion ceased when his father grabbed the 30-30 carbine, stepped out of the vehicle, and neatly shot the ewe behind the ear. "I was horrified," Roger told us. "I suspected my old man had gotten close to the edge of the law a couple times, but I couldn't believe he'd shoot a man's sheep, especially the sheep of a man who had been nice to us and whose house was only a half mile away."

But there it was, the sheep dead as a doornail and his father beckoning to him. "Well, don't yust sit there, Boy, help me pitch her into the back." They dropped the tailgate of the pickup and swung the ewe into the bed. Then Roger's father covered it with a tarp.

"I was beside myself," Roger said. "It was bad enough we'd done this, but the old man wouldn't even hurry. He just got back into the pickup and casually drove back toward the ranch house. My greatest fear was that as we passed the ranch house, the only way we could get back onto the county road, someone would hail us and walk over to see if we had any luck hunting. Well, I started thinking we just about had it made because we were right abreast of the house and no one was out in the yard. Then, you wouldn't believe what the old man did. He turned into their driveway! I asked him what the hell he was doing. He turned and looked at me as if amazed I would ask such a stupid question. 'Well, we have to stop for coffee.'"

Roger had been raised with the Norwegian necessity of stopping for coffee, but this blew his mind. With a dead, poached sheep in the back of the pickup covered only by a thin tarp the old man was going to park next to this house and go in for coffee! "Yah," elaborated his father, "They'll think it's funny if we don't stop for coffee. We'll yust stay a little while. I haven't had a cup since breakfast."

The ranch wife welcomed them and did the customary thing, busily assembling not just coffee but oatmeal cookies and lefse spread with butter and sugar. "It was my favorite stuff, but I could hardly force it down, managing just enough to keep from hurting her feelings. We sat there with the whole family, the old man joking and telling stories, the kids, who I knew from school, enjoying it all, me so sick to my stomach with fear that I thought I was going to throw up. I thought someone would at least ask if we got any deer, then, if we said we got one, ask to go see it. But I guess deer were no big deal to them, because no one ever did. Maybe they figured if we got a bragging buck we'd have said so."

So they visited in the ranch house for nearly an hour, everyone having fun but Roger. After his dad drained the third refill of coffee he announced his regrets at having to leave so soon. Finally, the ewe still undiscovered, they motored slowly away from the ranch. By the campfire on the bear hunt Roger told us, "I never did go hunting with the old man again."

It has turned cold now on the Stillwater. I have pulled my coat over my down vest and find myself reaching toward the depleted pile of firewood I have gathered for outside purposes, odd small pieces I had not wished to saw to stove length. "Better save it," I tell myself. "Tomorrow might be a hard day." It is not so bad to be alone by a campfire, I decide, with good stories to recall. I go into the tent, stuff the little stove full of wood, shut down its vent, and turn in.

Two days of hard hunting follow. Each day the tiny travel alarm rings long before daybreak. Each day I rise and cook a big breakfast over the woodstove in lantern light, make my noon sandwich, and set out, either on foot or horseback. I see no moose and no moose tracks. I could hike the timber, but am not attracted to that because there is so much of the timber and so little chance of stumbling onto a moose. Far better, it seems, to look for tracks on the logical trails and crossings where I have seen them the many times when I had no moose permit and was not looking for them.

On the second day, riding Marauder to spare Major, I spot in the timber to my right above the trail a shiny black form and think for a moment it might be the back of a moose. But that illusion disappears when the animal throws up its head and identifies itself as a black bear. I have dismounted. Marauder grazes quietly, never seeing the animal, and it never sees us either. A little rain has fallen during the night, just enough to green up whatever the bear intently eats, for he grazes voraciously. He feels winter coming and needs to add the fat that will see him through a long sleep. I lean over Marauder's back and watch the bear with binoculars, an unexpected bonus.

Throughout the time I watch him I feel a slight chill, a tickling of the hairs on the back of my neck. We are here together, the bear and me, the horse, fine as he is, a flight animal that would clear out in the face of confrontation. And although black bears are rarely aggressive, I feel his power, watch the rippling of muscle under sleek hide as he grubs around the rotten tree stumps. So I reach to the end of the saddle scabbard and touch, just touch, the butt of my rifle.

It is a very reassuring rifle. Purchased in 1967, the Savage 110 started life as a .270. But those who fancy hunting rifles can never leave well enough alone, and when I tired of the rifle and caliber and contemplated larger creatures such as moose and elk (although the .270 had done perfectly well on the latter) I bucked the high-velocity, mega-magnum trend. I sent the rifle to ER Shaw for rebarreling to .35 Whelen Improved.

So I watch the bear this morning, the nearby rifle a stalwart friend of many years, the large hole in its muzzle and the 225-grain bullets with which it is loaded tilting the potential balance between the bear and me, as to which is predator and which prey, decisively in my direction. Then, grateful there is no quarrel between us, I leave the bear.

It is that night when I begin to think the two trackless days will extend into a third, my last full day to hunt, that I may never see a moose on this long-anticipated trip. True, the season extends for some time, so weekend forays up the canyons will still be a possibility, but there will be no time, no leave available from school, for another fully equipped expedition. So when chores are done by lantern light, the horses grained and secured for the night, I cheer myself by cooking a first-rate meal on the woodstove in the tent. I split and fry Polish sausages made of elk and pork but so lean they scarcely make the necessary juice for frying the thinly sliced potatoes I throw in with them. I cook a can of corn and slice a big piece of Emily's homemade brown bread. I pop open a can of beer to wash it down. No meal in a French restaurant, no wine in their cellar, could combine just the way all this combines and be so fine. Afterward, after cleaning things up, I pour a nip of brandy from an unbreakable backpacking flask I have brought and crawl into my sleeping bag thinking that even if I never see a moose, me, myself, and I will have had a good time.

But my serenity lasts only a little while into the night because past midnight sometime all hell breaks loose. A sudden blast of wind and snow rips down the valley, and one side of the tent caves in. I hastily pull on my boots, then, clad only in underwear, wage a running battle with the wind and the tent. I have too few hands to both hold up the pole and tie off the guy ropes that secure the side of the wall tent. It is touch and go for half an hour. I get one thing secured only to have another come loose, the wind roaring the whole time. I am like a single sailor on deck in a storm, trying to secure the sheets. Finally I get it done. The rest of the night I sleep fitfully, awakening at every gust.

But when the alarm jingles all else is quiet except for the gentle water music of the Stillwater River. Outside there are two new inches of snow. This could be the break I need. I hastily eat and, feeling lucky, saddle Major and put a pack saddle on Emily's Sugar so that if I am successful I can bring part of the meat back to camp. I wait a nervous twenty minutes until light just cracks over the mountain wall on the east side of the valley across the river. Then I quickly walk out to the main trail, indecisive, trying to decide what course to take. That issue is readily decided since there are fresh moose tracks in the new snow on the main trail, up the valley a hundred yards from camp.

So I ride rapidly south following what turns out to be two sets of tracks, a small one and large one, a cow and calf; not legal for me but exciting anyway, for moose are no longer phantoms. I catch them at Roosevelt Lake, a lake in name only, really just a sunken marsh surrounded by timber deadfall. I dismount and watch the two of them. They seem to see me, but apparently mother moose has read the fish and game regulations and knows she is safe. At one hundred yards away she looks absolutely immense. It is sobering to think of what a task I will have on my hands, working alone, if I am successful.

In another half mile I see more tracks. The snow has been the signal to the ridge-running moose that their lark up high has ended, that it is time to get serious about the business of feeding in the marshes and staying fat before winter. I tie Sugar and Major at a trail junction and ease left into the timber toward the river. I hunted this two days ago, marveling at the beauty of the trout pools in this stretch where the river is separated from the trail by a thickly timbered tract. I have marked it mentally for future fishing. I circle quietly, find nothing, then shortcut back toward the trail through the timber.

When it happens it is so fast that only a blurred second goes by. There is in the dark timber an antlered moose, not a trophy but the legal game I want, and then it is down and I do not remember dropping to one knee or the report of the powerful rifle or the recoil on my shoulder. I walk cautiously up to it and feel that tinge of remorse felt by all good hunters and also the humility and thanks. It is not only Native American hunters who respect and thank the animals they eat, who revere them, who wish to take them with as little suffering as possible. John James Audubon knew this, as did Aldo Leopold as did Teddy Roosevelt, hunters all, hunters and lovers of the things they hunted.

20. The woods were dark and very quiet after the bull moose died.

So I sit twenty paces from where the moose lies and lean back on a tree and try to quiet my thumping heart. I have drawn, I realize, a dividend on my investment, a premium from this big and beautiful but not always friendly environment in which I live. This is an entry on the other side of the balance sheet, opposite eighteen years of working two jobs for modest pay, for ranching in the dark all winter around the edges of my other job. To have come to this valley with my horses, to camp by a clear river and hunt moose is a great privilege. Close to home and performed with equipment I already own, the hunt has cost me peanuts, not the thousands of dollars a nonresident guided hunter would expect to pay. Sitting leaning back against the tree, I know I am a very lucky man.

But I can't stay sitting long. There is a staggering amount of work to do if all this wonderful meat is to land safely unspoiled in the freezer at home. (It would be both illegal and immoral to waste any of it.) I find a route out of the woods to the trail, a route I'm certain the horses can negotiate. How lucky this is, to be able to take the horses right to the moose. (I shudder at the thought of shooting a moose in a marsh.) Then I trot down the trail a quarter mile to the horses, untie them quickly, and return with them to the moose. I tie Major and Sugar to trees nearby, the two of them eyeballing the downed animal cautiously. Then, before it begins, I gulp down my noon sandwich.

I start at exactly noon. At exactly four p.m. I am ready to head back for camp, and I feel as tired as if I had run a marathon. In that four hours I have field dressed the moose; cut it into two parts; skinned each half as it lay in place; split the quarters apart by sawing down the spine; wrapped both hindquarters in cheesecloth and suspended them as high as I can on two spindly trees (we are in a burn, and the thin remaining trees are fire-damaged and weak); and loaded the two front quarters into Sugar's panniers. Montana moose (Shiras moose, to be specific) are not nearly so large as their Canadian or Alaskan cousins, and this was a young bull, perhaps three or four years old. But coping with his mass alone, on the ground, with no one to hold anything while I sawed, has been exhausting. It has been a lesson in the true meaning of the term "dead weight." I estimate the hindquarters to weigh well over a hundred pounds each, the front quarters nearly that much, and the rule of thumb is that skinned, dressed quarters weigh about half the live weight of the animal, which would have put the moose at around eight hundred pounds.

Because of the spindly trees, the block and tackle I brought has been useless. I have horsed each quarter up as high as I can get it, then tied it off. I can only hope coyotes or a bear will not find them, for skinned as cleanly as I have been able to do working on a tarp laid on the forest floor, the quarters are beautiful meat. The other concern is that they cool quickly, but I am quite convinced they will; they are hanging so air can circulate around them, and that air will drop to well below freezing in a couple hours.

While I'm hefting the hindquarters I remember the story about my friends Roger and Marcus, back when we were all foolish enough to let a six-pack accompany some tasks that really required a more sober concentration. Marcus had butchered, skinned, and split down the backbone the carcass of a huge crossbred steer and now had to quarter it. "Wrap your arms around that front quarter, Roger," he said, "and I'll just cut her loose." Roger was a coach, always in good shape, at the time making frequent use of the weight setup in his basement. He did a bear hug on the front quarter and said he was ready, probably not stopping to think that the quarter weighed considerably more than he did. The instant Marcus sawed the quarter loose, it was as if a hammer pounded Roger to the ground, where he lay helpless and kicking, pinned by the front quarter of beef:

"Well," Marcus said, "it's obvious those weights haven't done a damn thing for you." After letting Roger suffer a moment longer he helped lift the quarter off his friend and into the back of the pickup truck. "Since you aren't up to the job, I'll hold, you cut this one loose." So Marcus did his bear hug on the other front quarter, anxious to show up Roger, who took the saw and cut it loose. Marcus also slammed to the ground, pinned by the quarter, cussing, and it was now Roger's turn to laugh, telling Marcus while he squirmed that the scene reminded him of a cartoon where some critter got hit by a safe pitched out of a third-story window. This was a another campfire story told many times, one that tended to get just a bit better each time.

My plan is to pack the front quarters of the moose back to

camp on Sugar and hang them there to cool. By then it will be nearly dark. Early in the morning I will secure and clean up my camp, saddle all the horses, then pack the empty plywood boxes onto Marauder's Decker saddle. I will lead him back up the trail, the four miles to the moose, and manty the hind-quarters into the plywood boxes. They will protrude from the boxes' open tops, true, but the boxes will still give the manties (canvas-covered bundles that sling to the pack saddle) form and make them easier to sling. Then I will return to camp with Marauder, load the front quarters back on Sugar, load the valuable things that must come out from camp on the young mare, and head home. Later Emily and I will return on a day ride, feasible, though a long sixteen-mile round trip, and retrieve the camp.

It all goes exactly that way. When I ride up from camp the next morning the moose quarters are undisturbed. The man-ties I make around them are very heavy. The big black gelding will handle them with ease, but slinging them to him by myself is a challenge. Once done, the rest is easy. The horses are flaw-less, impeccable, and I am proud of them and of my packing job, for I scarcely adjust a knot on the entire trip home. The sun shines, the fledgling snow now gone. Red buck brush and golden aspens garnish the green of the pines as I lead the horses at a brisk walk down the trail.

I enter the tunnel near the trailhead where the trail is squeezed between a granite wall and the frothing river, and this time I do meet a pack string. It is Wanda again, riding her pinto horse, heading upriver with a hunter. She sees me well in advance and gathers her horses in the one place on this stretch wide enough to pass with confidence, notices the weight of the packs and the moose horns riding between Marauder's man-ties, and as I pass, because the roar of the river makes words useless, smiles and throws me a thumbs up.

21. The young bull resulted in the best wild meat our family had ever known.

We whip into the trailhead at a running walk. I *am* Chaucer's monk, returning after a hunt with my hounds and my "dainty horses." I have gone to the wilderness and no, not conquered it, but melted into it as no one can who merely looks at it through plate glass. We will eat its bounty through the winter, every bite containing the tang of the wilderness, and that bounty will be tonic against the long, dark days.

In twenty minutes I am in the pickup headed home. I top a ridge and reach for the new cell phone (a recent concession to safety on my long commute). It just might work here, so high. I dial home and get a crackly voice of my son Steve. All is okay, I tell him, and I will soon be home. Through static I hear a garbled sentence and make out its last word, ". . . moose?" And I return, hoping he will hear it, "Yes, moose."

10

The Women

"Danny, did you catch a deer?" I could count on that question. After long days in the mountains, sometimes alone, I would steer the hoodless old Ford to a squeaky stop by the burn barrel in the vacant lot, grab my rifle and head into the house. She had usually heard me, and her face showed relief that I was home. Clad in a "house dress" (common then even for day-to-day chores), she looked up from the mountains of clothes she was washing to keep up with her brood and asked the question, a smile on her face.

"Nope," was the most common answer. And then I would try to correct her. "Mom, you don't catch deer. You shoot them. You catch fish." She acted faintly interested in the distinction, but I knew she would ask me the same question in the same words again. I could never tell whether she was disappointed for me or happy for the deer that escaped "catching." A little of both, I suppose.

Her upbringing had been an interesting medley, but it did not include hunting. Born in Madagascar to a missionary father in an area so remote that his 1920s vintage Harley Davidson motorcycle was the only vehicle in the province, Mom's early years had been close to the land in this exotic, poverty-stricken part of the world. There were adventures. She had been lost once as a little girl and was rescued by a Malagasy family who fed her well from their evening meal, a meal, she was told later, that consisted of locusts. There were monkeys, she said. One morning the brown arm of a mystery visitor slid in through the kitchen window during breakfast, wrapped its hand around the colorful curtains, and snatched them. (The prowler left tracks of a club foot in the earth below the widow.) Mom's brother captured, tamed, and raised from a puppy what was described to me as a wild dog.

But then, at age seven, there was a year in Paris followed by upbringing in Minneapolis. Her primarily urban orientation never completely wore off, even after years of helping my minister father through his stints in the Dakotas and Montana. I don't think she ever completely approved of hunting, particularly on Sundays, but she, like my father, appreciated the meat. And, as a mother of eight (while I was still home and of ten ultimately), she had learned to roll with the punches. She survived by keeping the lid on, not by attempting to maintain order in all things. Our home was chaotic, but we all survived. Some would say we prospered.

But I suppose it went the other way, too. Living close to the land as a child, in what we'd call today a third world nation, left on her the imprint of nature. Although pretty much tied to our house during the time I most remember, and tied also to church duties—organist, unofficial secretary, organizer of my father's stuff—her stories showed a love for things outdoors. She talked of younger days with Dad, early parishes in the Dakotas, when the two of them picked out a different butte to climb each Sunday after church. She cooked cheerfully for all of us on picnic tables in Yellowstone Park during our annual camping vacations. She did not understand hunting, but she did not protest. In this and in many other ways she was "the wind beneath our wings."

That supporting role, as it pertains to hunting and to much else, is no longer enough for many modern women, and that's all to the good as far as I'm concerned. I am told that women constitute the fastest-growing segment of hunters. Fewer are the fathers who take their sons but not their daughters hunting. Mary Zeiss Stange, a professor of women's studies at Skidmore College, spends part of her year teaching in an atmosphere charged with political correctness and the rest of it in Montana, hunting whenever she can. She sees hunting as equally natural for women and men, debunking the notion that because men were the primary hunters for eons, the hunting drive runs more strongly in their genes. Roles assigned for each sex by social structure have had more to do with it, she says.

Whether I buy Professor Stange's arguments on this point must wait for a fair reading of her work. (It's hard for me to believe that those eons during which tribal men were the primary hunters failed to imprint something on our makeup.) But I don't really care. I'm just glad Stange and others like her are hunting and writing about it. Magazines about hunting used to be primarily male domain, but we now have good female writers, and their copy seems to be relished by readers as much as that of their male counterparts.

If hunting in my immediate family has been primarily male activity, it's only because of luck of the draw. I had three sons, but no daughters. I'm a little envious of fathers who can experience all the nuances of hunting with daughters as well as sons.

The woman who has been my friend for fifty-three years and my wife for more than forty has never been enthusiastic about hunting. Actually, that's not correct. She's never enthusiastic about shooting anything. She has, however, taken a little game, and she has frequently accompanied me while I've been hunting and has always enjoyed it.

Emily does like to shoot, however, particularly if the target is a tin can. I do remember one critter she did in with her dad's old pump action Winchester .22. I was trying to teach her to shoot it, and I pointed at a small flock of magpies perched nearby in a chokecherry bush. (At the time magpies were unprotected, considered to be undesirable destroyers of the eggs of songbirds.) "There, line up your sights with the front blade in the groove of the rear sight and squeeze the trigger." She did so. At the crack of the .22 a magpie tumbled out of the tree. "Good shot!" I said, astounded.

She didn't seem happy, and I thought it was remorse at killing the bird. "It's just a magpie, and we've got plenty of those."

"No," she said. "It's not that. It's just that the bird that dropped wasn't the one I was aiming at."

But it is target practice with handguns that Emily really enjoys. During Marine training at Quantico, Virginia, I bought our first two revolvers, a Smith and Wesson Model 28 in .357 magnum for myself and a little Ruger Bearcat .22 for her. During a portion of our lives dampened by anxiety, separation, and knowledge of the war, we enjoyed outdoor time on the big Quantico reservation and nearby state forests by driving to remote places, setting up a cardboard box for a target, and practicing with our revolvers.

Recently I pulled out the little Ruger, not having fired it for years. Feather light, with a long, hard, creepy trigger pull, the little gun is challenging to shoot, not a good beginner's handgun I realize now, decades later. No wonder, then, that Emily did so well with Steve Hopkins's Smith and Wesson Model 29 .44 magnum when we introduced it to her (with some trepidation).

It was back in the 1970s during the Jordan years. The *Dirty Harry* movies had become popular, and Model 29s were extremely hard to find. Indeed, they sold for considerably more than the suggested retail price, Clint Eastwood wannabees snatching them off the shelves as quickly as Smith and

Wesson could make them. Hopkins, however, had managed to acquire one. He had loaded up some hard-cast 240-grain bullets with a load a little below maximum but still well into the magnum range in velocity and recoil. Emily admired the handsome revolver and expressed a desire to shoot it.

Yes, we gave her all the warnings about recoil, but she was adamant. She liked the revolver's two-handed heft, and the trigger pull, tested by dry firing, was a dream compared with that of her little Bearcat. Jordan had an old-fashioned town dump, a big pit full of trash ringed with more trash ready to be dozed under. Hopkins waded out through the stuff and assembled six bottles of various sizes in a line at about twenty-five yards. (A landfill, of course, is the *only* place where it's responsible to shoot at bottles.)

Emily donned ear protectors, held the big handgun with two hands out at arms length and took aim. The revolver waved this way and that, then settled, then rocked her back in recoil. The first bottle disintegrated. I made eye contact with Hopkins. Fluke? Before we could congratulate Emily the big revolver bellowed again, and another bottle vaporized. This was getting interesting. Then it happened four more times in fairly quick succession. Six shots, six bottles, and Emily, grinning, saying, "It doesn't kick very much."

We shouldn't have been so surprised. Women are often good shots. There seems to be less ego involved, less tendency to think of the firearm as an extension of power. They simply listen to their teachers, line up the sights, and squeeze. Besides, good shooting, like horsemanship and proficiency with a musical instrument, is a matter of finesse, of fingertips, not of muscle.

I spent many years teaching at a school sixty miles from the ranch. During the shortening days of November I began my long commute in darkness and came home in a race with the sun. I usually lost. I watched the brown hill grass grow golden as the daylight faded, while the snow on the Beartooth Mountains turned briefly pink before the sun ducked behind them. Then the ranch came into view as the last of the light slipped out of grasp. By then, with a sigh of resignation, I had turned on my headlights. The legal time for shooting was gone, so my own hunting would have to wait until the weekend.

My sons were luckier. When their practice schedules for sports and band allowed they could slip home at 3:30, don orange vests, grab their rifles, and head for the river bottom in search of big bucks. I had accompanied each of the three, of course, for their first deer, and they'd been with me before they were old enough to hunt but happy to ride to the hills in the old GMC pickup and take walks with me to check the coulees. Each of the three in turn grew to the stage at which we could trust him to hunt alone.

Emily jokes that the real badge of a Montana mom is not whether she has helped her children get to soccer practice, but whether she's helped her sons drag deer out of the woods. "The family that drags together, stays together," she says. Maybe there's something to that. She recalls with fondness a couple of such incidents with each son.

Jonathan, now a Boeing engineer, remembers jumping his first four-point whitetail and attempting a shot on the run. "He flipped at the shot," Jon says, but then got up again. "I'd led him too much and had shot off one of his horns." Hitting a buck on the horn often has that effect. The shock is transmitted to the skull like a fighter's punch on the jaw, the animal goes down, the hunter begins congratulating himself, and then the buck gets up and runs off.

Two quick following shots with his 7mm-08 put the buck down for good, however. Jon doesn't remember for sure whether Emily had driven them over in the first place, or whether he hiked back to the house for help. He does remember his mother's help dragging the buck back to the pretty little depression on the ranch we call "the basin," where the two could reach it with an old Land Cruiser wagon we owned at the time.

David, today a professor of economics, got help from his mother dragging a mule deer down from the juniper-covered hills east of the ranch buildings. He also recalls relying on her for some mechanical help when his plan to neatly sandwich a whitetail hunt between school and basketball practice met with a snag. He writes:

I'm not so sure this story is as much about Mom as my misfortune. It was the first day of basketball practice, which was to start sometime around 7 p.m. I remember sitting in class planning the rest of my afternoon. I would jump in my Mighty Mike [his little pickup] and drive home for a quick hunt in the woods for the "Ayatollah" [1980s talk for the giant of all whitetail bucks]. I would walk the woods from the road entrance all the way to the end of the basin, turn around at the end of shooting light and walk back with plenty of time to spare to run home, catch a quick bite and head off to practice. I even left enough time in my plan, should I have shot something, to dress him out, run back to the pickup, drive to the kill, load him up, head back to the house and off to practice.

Everything started out great. I parked and entered the woods. I had a nice hunt but didn't have any opportunities to shoot anything. Until I hit the basin. Then I sneaked up on a modest whitetail buck, dropped to my knee and shot him. Nice clean kill, as I remember. I gutted him out (glancing every minute or so at my watch to make sure my plan was on schedule), quickly wiped my hands in the dry grass, picked everything up and headed back at a jog for the pickup. I glanced again at my watch; everything was still on schedule, but just barely. Once at the pickup, I got in, took another quick glance at my watch and took a deep breath. Still on schedule. I turned the key. Nothing. Damn, I had left the lights on and the battery was dead. My plan was shot. I ran over to a neighbor's house and made a call to Mom. She came and helped me jump-start the pickup and get it running again. We then drove to the buck, loaded him up, and headed home. Al, our rather strict coach, was probably just taking roll. Of course with my last name, I would be called first with no response. I could just imagine Al saying some smart ass remark about "Aads needing to get his ducks in a row."

Mom took care of the rest of the deer, maybe hanging it up herself or waiting for Dad to get home. I ran into the house, quickly changed my clothes, grabbed my b-ball shoes and headed into town. I laced up my shoes in the Mighty Mike and ran into the gym. The guys were already scrimmaging. I had missed a few drills (which wasn't such a bad thing). Al looked disappointed, gave me a short lecture and told me to get in the game. I quickly got into the flow of the game, which seemed a bit surreal after all I had gone through the past hour. After playing for a few minutes, I remember looking down at my hands and smiling. I had forgotten to wash my bloody hands.

Steve, our youngest, is a Master of Music, an operatic tenor, who remembers best a team effort with his mom in a race against my return home from school. They wanted to prove what they could do on their own:

22. David with one of the many deer his mother helped drag.

My anticipation grew as the Nissan pickup went down the road toward the clearing. I was frustrated with being too young to drive, yet I was glad I had a mom who was willing to take me hunting. We planned to scan a short group of fields next to the woods, just below the road. The fields were quick to check. They covered a fairly small area, but were plentiful with deer. Either the buck would be there or he wouldn't.

Simultaneously, Mom and I discovered that the buck was definitely there. He was a nice 3-point whitetail, nothing huge, but nice. He was grazing about 150 yards away and standing just a few feet outside of the brush. Mom turned the pickup off the road and stopped just short of the gate into our field. I quickly hopped the fence onto our property, sat down, and shot. Nothing happened. By the time I had another round loaded the buck was gone.

I ran straight for the woods, staring at the precise spot where I last saw the buck. I couldn't see any blood from where he stood. Since I was somewhat confident in a hit, I decided to go after him. Both the buck and I knew that crossing the river in the center of the woods was the ultimate escape route. I sprinted straight for the river and began scanning its bank for blood. After several minutes I finally found a few blood drops on a leaf at my feet! I looked across the river, saw nothing, and guessed that he had crossed. I ran through the river and climbed onto the other bank as fast as I could. I thoroughly searched for more blood, finding nothing.

Feeling rather guilty and disappointed in losing the animal, I crossed to the original side of the river and started back to the pickup. I wandered around the drops of blood one last time. Then I saw the buck. He had doubled back from the river and had not crossed at all! He was already dead, and had picked an extremely hidden, low area to lie down in the trees.

Mom and I tagged him and immediately began dressing him out. Dressing an animal is certainly my worst skill as a hunter. [Emily remembers this assurance from Steve: "I can do this, I can dress him out. I've watched Dad a hundred times."] By that time we were racing against fading daylight. I remember asking her for constant reassurance as I clumsily progressed. However, we were determined. She and I set a goal to complete our retrieval and hang up the deer before my dad got home.

We finished dressing the deer, and with Mom's help, we lifted him into the back of the Nissan. We went home and quickly hung the deer while we watched for Dad, an easy task compared to before. Our mission a success, Mom and I went back to the house. When Dad got home he congratulated me on getting my first whitetail buck. Mom and I could tell he was impressed.

I'm sure there are mothers who would consider all this indelicate, even improper. But our boys grew up on a ranch where there are few illusions about nature, about cycles of life and death, about the conversion of things living into Swiss steak simmering in the pan. Emily's memories of helping her sons with their hunting exploits, of being a mentor during hunting as elsewhere, are among her most poignant.

11

Hopkins's Goat

We were descending a timbered mountainside on a smooth but steep forest service trail that switchbacked every hundred yards or so, heading in the general direction of two white spots, mountain goats, that we'd seen through binoculars on a far-off mountain. My gelding Little Mack was cruising in his ground-eating flat walk about as fast as it was safe to go. Behind me was the voice of Steve Hopkins saying, "Easy-easy-easy-easy-easy . . ." In one respect he was doing the right thing, since I'd told him emphatically not to use "whoa" unless he wanted to stop dead still. Use "easy," I had told him, if you want the horse to merely slow down.

But after a long cadence of "easy" offered to Major, an old mountain veteran who would keep his nose near the tail of my horse no matter what Steve did, I finally reined to a stop. "Steve," I said, "he doesn't give a damn what you tell him. He's going to stay up with me either way. Besides, we've got to get to your goats sometime before dark." I slackened Little Mack's reins, and he was off again. Then came a touch of regret. Here was a friend of thirty years, now in portly middle age, his hair whiter than mine, riding a horse for the third or fourth time in his whole life and terrified by it. "Dan," I told myself, "you're being a Marine again. He's doing his best."

But the remorse didn't last long. I was talking to Hopkins, after all. Hopkins is not the pouting kind, and he'd get his own back—I was bound to hear later how I'd been a hard-ass outfitter who barked orders, that I made him saw all the firewood, sleep on rocks, and carry all the water, all this while denying him booze and other sustenance. Good friends are those among whom you need not feel as though in all your words and deeds you're walking on eggs.

It had started as many fine hunts start, with a permit in the mail. Steve Hopkins, Jim Benvenga, and I had a pact. If any one of the three of us drew a goat permit, we would all go, two of us in support of the lucky one. As the only horseman in the group, I'd offered to furnish horses and camp, the two of them contributing to the expense. Then there was a wait, and then an excited phone call. Yes, Hopkins had drawn. We would go for the season opener on September 15. True, the white coat of Rocky Mountain goats grows more beautiful as the weather chills, but it's a trade-off. Wait until mid- to late October, and snow at those high elevations just may prevent you from hunting at all.

And so to my repertoire of hunting experiences I would add this one: as an unpaid outfitter I would take on a wilderness pack-in high altitude hunt "clients" who were experienced hunters but very inexperienced in the ways of equines. I would try to remember everything, to pack well, to keep things safe, and to do it without turning into Captain Bligh. Jim, an athletic school administrator and coach, had been on a horseback hunt, where he had been given a horse supposedly night-blind (but, by the description, probably merely loco) that with no warning whatsoever would turn off the trail and head down the mountain through the timber. I'm proud of my mountain horses, and they impressed Jim greatly, but he would have been impressed by horses of far poorer quality, indeed, by anything that didn't seem to him downright suicidal.

Hopkins had sat on a horse only once or twice in his life, at our ranch, back when he was much younger and much thinner. I would turn him over to Major. Major would handle not only his weight but his inexperience, for Major has been there, done that, and gone back again. Big, strong, and smooth-gaited, Major carried me over two mountain passes when he was only three and later yanked home a cow elk on the end of my lariat rope through two feet of snow as easily as if he were dragging a child on a sled. As long as we could get Hopkins onto his back and keep him there, Major would do the rest.

But old Marines believe in training, and I'd insisted that a condition of my furnishing the horses was an orientation ride on the ranch in advance of the trip. I went through currying, saddling, bridling, and above all, techniques for staying safe. I didn't expect my two friends to remember everything, because humans aren't made that way. Horsemanship is a lifetime quest, a medley of skills learned so thoroughly by endless repetition that you do the right thing without thinking. However, within these limitations, Steve and Jim did well on a short practice ride on the ranch, Steve game enough, though apprehensive when the pace picked up to a brisk walk. Riding in the mountains would, of course, be an entirely different thing from a slow saunter across a hayfield.

Hopkins is not a timid person. He really had every right to be frightened of something so relatively unknown to him and so potentially dangerous as horses. Horses are big, strong creatures. They can and will hurt or kill you, though rarely deliberately. Skill and knowledge will usually prevent disasters, and Steve had neither. Further, middle age tends to fatten the torso while weakening the legs. This is not good. The heavier torso makes you top heavy while the weaker legs make for a poorer support system, since downward pressure on the stirrups is needed for stability.

I knew all this. I'm a worrier anyway, genetically 100 percent Norwegian, directly descended from those Norseman who lay awake during long northern winters to listen for things that went bump in the night, who were sure they would soon face Ragnorak, the day of doom. Well, maybe I'm not that bad, but when I'm the responsible one, details and worst-case scenarios rebound in my brain like cheap refrains from television commercials.

All this said, the horses were the ingredient that would make this trip possible, and we agreed later we could not have accomplished it without them. Hopkins and I were not in shape for a full-fledged wilderness hunt via backpack. Besides, even had we been in that sort of condition, age tends to change ones' attitude toward sleeping uncomfortably, toward eating second-rate food, toward doing without the little luxuries a horse camp can provide. To give Hopkins a fighting chance, we needed a base camp at eight thousand feet elevation within striking distance of two goat-rich mountains.

Since Jim could free himself from work one day earlier than Hopkins could, he and I would pack in the camp and get set up. I would pony Major down to the trailhead the next day to pick up Steve, and goat season would begin the subsequent day.

The trip in with Jim and the packhorses was a little too eventful. I've often been able to brag about taking a pack string from trailhead to campsite without having to adjust a single sling rope or cinch, but this was not to be one of those times. Major, carrying a Decker pack saddle with two heavy manties, had problems almost immediately—all of them my fault. I'd mantied two wooden boxes heavy with food and had not been careful to distribute their cargo with a low center of gravity. Then, I had basket hitched both manties a little too high.

I had instructed Jim, who would be following the pack horses, to watch the D-rings on top of the Decker saddles, to holler at me if they moved off the center of any horse's back. On a ledge trail through timber, at a particularly bad place, he hollered. Major's pack saddle had completed a 90 degree turn. One manty straddled his back, while another hung under his belly. A lesser horse would have blown his cork, scattered packs, people, and other horses up and down the trail, and perhaps killed some of us by knocking us off the edge.

Instead, Major just froze. If I could have read human thoughts into his big eyes I would have seen something like, "Goddam, Dan, did ya forget how to tie a basket hitch? How the hell is a horse supposed to carry a load up the mountain with a deal like this? Get back here and fix it."

That, unfortunately, was problematic. The trail was extremely narrow, a cliff up on one side and a near-cliff down on the other, no place to walk *except* the trail, and no room on the trail because of the horses. I wrapped Little Mack's reins around a tree root projecting from the earth on the high side of the trail, hoping he wouldn't take off at the worst possible time. Then, hanging onto him, I edged my way back toward Major, my heels at the drop-off. I remembered rappelling out of a helicopter during my Marine days, standing on the rear ramp of the chopper, my heels right at the edge until the jumpmaster signaled to go. At least then I was hooked to something.

With some sweating and cussing I got the packs back in place, then walked the tightrope back to Little Mack. Tired of waiting, he headed upgrade at a nice flat walk. The breeze cooled the sweat on my face, the packs rode well, and all now seemed right with the world. That is, all seemed well until we attempted to find the pretty campsite Jim had located earlier, a spot near the base of a slide on which Jim had seen many goats in the past.

Unfortunately, Jim, like many experienced hikers, had little concept of the capabilities of horses or the needs of a horse-oriented camp. Getting to his chosen site involved crossing a creek that fingered into many tiny branches, mossy, soaked tundra between them. A hiker could skip across from rock to rock, but horses don't skip well. The third time Little Mack sunk to his knees, I turned the outfit around and managed to get us all out of there before we hopelessly bogged down a horse. "We'll have to camp somewhere else, Jim."

So we continued upgrade, finally coming to a thin spot in the timber that let sunlight and blue sky show through. A quick reconnaissance on foot revealed a spot we'd noticed on the map, a tiny lake made smaller by years of drought and surrounded now by a ring of inviting grass. This was the place: water and grass for the horses, a reasonably level spot for the camp, and goat mountains on each side of us. The elevation was eight thousand feet. There was firewood aplenty, and Jim went right to work on it. We made a fine camp: spike tent set up, my "kitchen" on an inverted pack box to which I attached legs, a fly overhead. We built a highline and kept three horses tied to it, alternately hobbling the remaining two to graze.

The next morning, ponying Major, I rode down the trail to meet Hopkins. He was there and beaming, toting a package of first-rate frozen steaks that I stuffed into my saddlebags. I swapped Major's now-surplus pack saddle for a riding saddle I'd locked in the horse trailer, and I retrieved my spare saddle scabbard and mounted it for him. Then he placed into the scabbard his diminutive .260 Remington. "Steve," I said, "What's happening to you? You shot a goat during high school with a .338. What's this pea shooter? It's not much bigger than a .243." He took all this with a smile.

Goats are supposed to be tough to kill. I thought about going further, about suggesting that Hopkins's recent affection for light calibers might be tied to some inevitable drop in testosterone caused by the aging process, but I figured I'd better not go there: he's five years younger than I am. His reply was an academic one. "Hey, it's loaded with 120-grain Barnes X bullets backed by 45 grains of 760 Winchester Ball powder. It will do the job."

Hopkins is a very fine shot, and in truth, I had no doubt that should he get the chance he'd place that indestructible Barnes bullet exactly where necessary for a humane kill. But it wouldn't have been any fun to tell him that. With the help of the running board on the horse trailer, we got him success-fully mounted on too-tall Major, and we headed for camp. Steve and I talk a code most accurately called Holbrook/ Twain, that is, dialogue from Mark Twain as interpreted by Hal Holbrook. So I wasn't surprised to hear him say, "*I'd prefer an excessively gentle horse; a lame one if you have such.*"

And my reply, looking at Major's patient face as Hopkins settled into the saddle: "*Yes, it appears that he's planning some outrage. But maybe he's only asleep.*"

We headed up the trail, Little Mack pushing the envelope, his somewhat pacey running walk made more square and smooth by the uphill grade. It was a fine day, too warm for hunting, really, but beautiful for everything else. I learned later that the pace up a trail, past several intimidating drop-offs, kept Hopkins in a steady state of terror, but I was enjoy-ing myself too much to be aware of that. He claims I leaned over the edge to point out a beautiful waterfall, but that he wasn't about to look.

The first night in camp was a festive one: steaks, beer, and fried potatoes followed by brandy—too much brandy—by the campfire. I slept well. In the morning "our powers were under a cloud," as Twain would say, particularly those of Hopkins, who had imbibed somewhat more generously than Jim or I.

But I soon learned first-hand of the joys connected with being the nonhunting wrangler/cook. After fixing breakfast

I watched Chingachgook and Natty Bummppo head up the mountain to look for a goat. I sat down on a stool and opened a book of short stories. It seemed a fair exchange. They would check in periodically by walkie-talkie. I had merely to tidy the camp, alternate the horses so that all could graze, and take our drinking water containers down to a clear spring a mile below us. Jim's muscular manipulation of my water filter had broken the handle, and the little lake was rather too lively with critters to seem attractive for drinking. Indeed, water taken from the lake the night before and mixed with cognac and brandy has since been tabbed by Hopkins as the cause of his malady that morning. If he wasn't already sick, scooping up a sample and noticing its heavy load of biological samples was probably enough to kick it off.

I accomplished the water run aboard Little Mack, stuffing my saddlebags with whatever containers would fit and riding down to the clear spring and the little stream that bubbled away from it. It was a fine thing to do on a mountain morning. High altitude air seems to intensify the smell of wet earth and pine needles and horses and saddle leather. But on the ride back I did have a sobering moment, a split-second of equilibrium between the Jekyll and Hyde of the mountains, the pastoral side and the side that can reach out and bite you hard when you least expect it, particularly if you are alone.

There was a boggy place on the trail, unavoidable, the steep slopes on both upward and downward sides of the trail prohibiting a detour. Worse, the boggy spot terminated with a large square rock, a step up on the trail of a foot and a half or so. The horses had all negotiated it well enough on the way into camp. I had been careful to give the packhorses plenty of time to handle this obstacle, and each had accomplished it with a little jump out of the boggy place and up the natural step in the trail.

This time, however, just as we came to the rock and Mack lifted his front feet into the air to deftly clear the hurdle, I felt his hind legs sink into the bog. There was a split second with the horse balanced on his hind legs, with me leaning forward as best I could, terrifying images flooding my mind of the animal coming backwards onto me, slamming me into the unyielding trail, and probably killing me in the process. There is nothing more dangerous in the entire equestrian world than a horse coming over backwards onto you. I reached out to a wrist-sized aspen sapling growing in front of me at the side of the trail and pulled hard. Mack's balance swung forward, he gave a little leap, and all was well again.

And so, we were headed toward the next drainage, because Steve and Jim had indeed seen goats, two white dots they picked up by binoculars against the slate cliffs of a mountain several miles away. Their morning hunt had been exhilarating and challenging (Jim), or exhausting and terrifying, where the slightest misstep meant sudden death down a cliff where even recovery of your body would be questionable (Steve). I split the difference as best I could but was game for their one agreed-upon deduction: yes, there were at least a couple of goats in the next drainage, and perhaps we could get to them before dark.

Cruising down the mountain trail as fast as possible without losing Hopkins off Major seemed the appropriate course. The trail wound down the mountainside and bottomed out in a pretty little valley, then started to gain elevation again. Navigation from here was dead reckoning. Our first impulse was to tie the horses and head east on foot through the timber toward the base of the cliff we had seen from afar. It quickly appeared, though, that the stand of timber was thin, penetrated by an old trail, and that we could ride farther. After advancing off trail for a quarter of a mile or so, we emerged into a giant clearing and tied the horses in one of the most spectacular settings I've ever enjoyed. We faced a cliff perhaps five hundred feet high but unique in its length because it stretched right to left in front of us for a couple of miles, wrapping slightly around us, putting us in a sort of amphitheater. From our position we could not see all of the cliff, because small foothills ran up to it, rippled by coulees.

We scrutinized the cliff but saw no goats. A plan emerged. My responsibility lay with the three horses, so I would stay with them, enjoying the view and the late-afternoon sun, while the hunter and his assistant would climb the hill to our right to gain a better view of the south end of the cliff. The ground around us was encouraging: the strange, nearly square tracks of goats were everywhere, on every trail.

Jim and Steve had not been gone long when a white spot appeared on the very top of the cliff, a mile from me. I was sure it had not been there earlier. The binoculars revealed it well, a billy goat, even from such a distance looking confident and powerful as he walked briskly on skyline. He would have been well out of Hopkins's reach—getting to him would have required advance mountaineering skills—so there was no need to attempt to catch and alert the hunters. Instead I could enjoy this quick flash of mountain goat, this revelation of the animal to me, before he walked off skyline and was gone.

Time passed, and the western sun, broken by tall shadows of the trees, began to light less brightly the face of the cliff. We were edging toward the point when shooting a goat could well mean a trip back to camp in the dark, something I didn't relish with two inexperienced riders. And then it came, staccato shots, each echoing off the cliff just as the next one came, three or four of them in quick succession. Something had happened over the hill.

I double-checked the tie-up knots on the three horses and started climbing in the general direction Steve and Jim had advanced, sure that when I topped out I'd be able to see them. The climb was relatively steep, and the route through scattered timber longer than I expected, given the proximity of the shots. But before long, things opened up. I could see at the base of the cliff two orange dots on each side of a white one. Hopkins had his goat.

From here, stories differ. I'm quite sure that the truth was something like this: Hopkins nailed the goat right in the boiler room with the very first shot, but as goats will do, the critter, not knowing it was dead, kept running. Hopkins wisely kept shooting. Eventually the goat went down. Simple enough.

I remember arriving at the scene out of breath from the long climb, examining the goat, a very fine specimen with horns that later measured 9⅝ and 9¾ inches respectively, and congratulating Hopkins on the good shooting. Oddly, he remembers something completely different. He says I labored up the hill, took a quick look at the white goat's perforated hide, and said, "Looks like it was shot with an Uzi." Since I was quite impressed by his ability to hit a goat at long range with a rifle of such modest caliber, then connect on follow-up shots while the goat was running, it seems doubtful I'd have invoked the image of mowing something down with a submachine gun, but that's what Hopkins claims. Jim's testimony is noncommittal.

We skinned the goat in place, boned it out, and left it all spread out on the rocks to cool, hoping a coyote or bear would not visit before morning. The late afternoon sun was now touching the cliff with a pink glow. It was time to get back to the horses. At one point on the walk back down, when Hopkins had taken a slightly different route and was thus out of earshot, I said to Jim, completely without malice, "You and I will ride back in the morning with Redstar as packhorse to get the meat and hide. No sense in bringing Hopkins. He won't be much help, and he might be a hindrance."

I meant no harm or insult by it. But I'd seen the steepness of the terrain I'd just walked, and I thought we could ride horses right to the goat, then lead them back down over the worst of it. Given Steve's reaction to far less dangerous endeavors on horseback and his difficulty getting on and off big Major, I thought the recovery would be more efficient if Jim and I rode rapidly and got the job done. I was several years retired from teaching, from teacher's lounge banter, and it never occurred to me that my remark might be made known.

It is in situations like this one, with darkness coming soon, that we gaited horse aficionados revel in the animals' ability to get you back to camp rapidly and smoothly. We hit the trail in a flat walk that on the smoother sections of trail, with release of an ounce of pressure on Little Mack's reins, became a silky running walk. The lodgepole pines flew by like slats in a picket fence. Behind me there were murmurs of unease, even from Jim. For a while I ignored them, but eventually said, "Guys, just trust the horses. Just hang on and enjoy."

We switchbacked up the mountain, frequently ducking branches on this little-used trail. I reined Little Mack to an abrupt stop when I heard behind me a sharp, "Damn!" from Hopkins, and then, "My hat." A branch had reached out and grabbed his hat, which now lay on the ground behind Major. Knowing Steve's difficulties getting off and on Major, Jim cheerfully hollered, "I'll get it." He vaulted off, grabbed the hat, handed it to Steve, and mounted up. I released Little Mack, and we cruised up the trail again.

We'd gone not two hundred yards when I heard again, "Damn! It's my hat again." Jim, his voice slightly less patient, said, "Oh, I'll get it. No problem." He retrieved the hat for Hopkins, threw in a harassing word or two, and again we were off. The sun was now long gone. In the dusk a great horned owl lifted from his perch just over our heads and silently threaded his way through the timber. We would make it to camp at just about dark. I would light the lantern and begin cooking a celebratory dinner.

But it did not take long for it to happen again. "Damn," he said, but this time he added, "Oh, hell with it, just leave it." I was beginning to release Mack to tool up the trail again, when there came, now more quietly, in tone a touch plaintive, "Even if it is my lucky hat."

I can't remember what Jim said, but that's probably all right, since little of it would be printable. But he got off and picked up that hat. (Later, Hopkins would claim that little magnanimity on Jim's part was involved, that he, too, was attached to the hat, because it bears a New York Fire Department logo and was sent out by his brother as a gift for Steve after 9-11. I'd rather think Hopkins's plaintive, slightly whiney tone had more to do with it.)

No matter. The camp was festive that night: the food, the sundowners, the campfire, the sense of mission accomplished, friendly barbs between us adding spice. Retrieval of the goat in the morning went like clockwork. Since the goat was already boned, I knew a single packhorse could easily handle it, and for this purpose the sawbuck saddle with two nylon panniers seemed the easiest approach. We did ride up a grade steep enough to have us leaning over the horses' ears, but beyond that there was nothing particularly hazardous about getting the horses within a hundred yards of the goat, just to the edge of a granite slide, where we could tie them to scrub timber. All was well with the goat, no predator having found it, the meat well chilled by the mountain night.

23. Hopkins, the "Uzi," the hat, and the goat.

The boned meat, in a plastic bag, went into one pannier, the hide and head in another, while Redstar stood blissfully unconcerned. We were back to camp by late morning. Hopkins had put in some quality time with my Oregon pruning saw, and the result was plenty of firewood for one more celebratory night before pack-up in the morning. I decided he looked good in the hat, that much as we teased him, it would have been a shame to leave it on the trail. I could not have foreseen that two years hence he would kill a six-point bull elk while wearing the lucky emblem of the NYFD.

Fast forward. Just over a year has passed since collecting Hopkins's goat. I am covered with sweat, hot and cold at the same time, because I'm dragging a hindquarter of a big cow elk I've shot in the vicinity of a cabin shared by Jim, Steve, and another friend. The cow was bedded in deep timber, strategically locating herself under a big tree where she could watch for any approach from below through a coulee that runs down to private land. I'd been able to get above her. The powerful Ruger #1 single-shot did the rest—with a single shot.

Through the miracle of the cell phone (which I curse in airports but revere for backcountry situations such as this one) I've been able to contact Jim, as he's asked me to do should I down an elk and need help. I've dressed the elk and quartered it, hide still on to keep it clean, then have begun laboring through deep snow and buck brush dragging one quarter at a time to an open area. I'm working on my second quarter, laboring hard, breathing like a steam locomotive, when my cell phone feebly rings.

I pull off my glove and punch one of the phone's tiny buttons. Through a crackle I hear the voice of Steve Hopkins. "Hey, good going. Jim says you got a cow. Need any help?"

"Thanks, Steve, but I think we've got it covered. Jim should be here shortly, and he said his friend might bring a snowmobile. He could drive it to the edge of the brush, so I'm working on getting the quarters down to the fence line."

"Well, if you're sure." I can tell he's genuinely willing to help, but also that he's tired from work, comfortable at home, and not terribly anxious to come unless he's truly needed.

He asks me for details of the hunt, and I tell him as much as I dare, given the fading of the phone's battery. The conversation closes this way: "I'd be glad to come out and help you guys if you need me."

"No problem, Steve. I'm sure we've got it covered."

"Well, I probably wouldn't be that much help." Then this, after a pause, with a twinkle in his voice, "And I might be a hindrance." I'm startled. And then we both laugh.

12

Whitetails

There are two species in the deer family that consistently leave me speechless with admiration, struck dumb by their ability to leave me holding an empty bag. It's not that the tactics of whitetails and elk are particularly similar. It's just that both are so very good at what they do. With whitetails my chagrin has come in many ways. The biggest bucks appear in September before hunting season, sometimes in large gangs with smaller bucks, their magnificent velvet racks displayed carelessly as they browse the last of the green in our open fields. Then, as rifle season nears, the biggest and next biggest in these gangs simply disappear. The smaller bucks remain, those we call "three-points" in old-style Western count (three points plus a brow tine on each side, eight-pointers by Eastern count), and it's usually these that fill the freezer. The consolation is that such whitetail bucks, two or three years old, sport a solid inch of fat on top of their hind quarters. There is no better meat in the world.

Where do the big ones go? We're told that whitetails aren't migratory as mule deer and elk can be, though I think our western whitetails cover more ground than their woods-bound eastern brothers. But there's every reason to believe that the biggest bucks in our little valley stay put. They simply have the patience to hole up somewhere and stay there, even if you walk by within feet of them, and to come out only during darkest night (if at all). Some will eventually make a mistake in late November during the height of the rut, unable to turn their backs on that hot destination that frequently causes tactical blunders among males of many species. The very largest bucks, perhaps, learn to resist even *that*.

While I was teaching high school English, my hunting students and I created a fantasy to explain this disappearing act of the largest bucks, a fantasy that grew in detail throughout the season, creative contributions coming sometimes even from boys who normally spent their English classes with eyes glazed and heads nodding toward their desktops. It was like this: The biggest bucks retired during hunting season to vast underground excavations, huge caves, normally located right underneath areas with the highest density of hunters. Presiding over this underground assembly was the Grand Dragon, King, and Emperor of all whitetail bucks. Beside his magnificent rack all Boone and Crocket record holders (and according to one student, all the racks on the walls of Cabela's in Mitchell, South Dakota) would look spindly in comparison.

For the five weeks of the Montana rifle season the bucks loiter in luxury in their underground haven. Moreover, through advanced technology they're able to keep track of the foibles of human hunters seeking them. On one wall is an illuminated topo map of the hunting ground above, with each active hunter highlighted as a moving LED light. Apprentice bucks, those with smaller three-point and four-point racks (eight- or ten-point Eastern) are not allowed below, but the big bucks in the cavern watch as even these younger ones successfully outwit the hunters. Guffaws of buck laughter break out when such an apprentice waits until a hunter nearly steps on him before exploding across the clearing and into the thick stuff. The hunter never gets off a shot, stands open-mouthed, wondering whether he just saw an apparition or a real deer. (Large-screen television has come recently to the underground hideout, so such fiascos can sometimes be observed live in living color.)

Above the map behind the desk of the Grand Buck is a head and shoulders mount of a hunter, a pudgy white male in his sixties. He cradles a Model 70 Winchester on his arm. The look on his face left by the taxidermist is one of sad confusion.

"Wait a minute, Doctor A. What kind of scope is on the rifle?" The question comes from a student named Jimmy, one I'd lost during the on-task part of the English class. He has gradually come to, first paging through his literature book to find the story he thinks we're discussing. Now he has caught on. "Seems to me it would be a Leupold. Everyone knows they're good scopes, and these bucks would have a good hunter mounted on the wall, not a slob. Otherwise he wouldn't be much of a trophy."

"Well, if he's such a good hunter, why did he die?" shoots out one of the girls, rolling her eyes.

"He was a good hunter, but an old one," Jimmy retorts. "In his younger days the Grand Old Buck jumped out from behind a bush and surprised the hunter so bad that he dropped dead of a heart attack. But this hunter had done such a good job of looking for the Grand Old Buck for several years that the buck admired him and had him mounted." This explanation settles the dispute. Kendra goes back to her reading assignment for the next day, the task that's actually been assigned.

But we can't resist, so we continue. Occasionally, during the hottest time of the late-November rut, a shapely doe walks by the above-ground camera, the wide screen television below revealing momentarily a flash of her tail. When this happens some of the younger of these underground bucks let out soft moans, then look accusingly at each other in denial while the oldest among them stare sternly. (I get uncomfortable at this point—you can only legally get so graphic in high school

English classes. The boys are sitting up a little too straight and enjoying this a little too much.) But another boy points out what the old bucks would say. (I paraphrase because this student wasn't particularly poetic.) "Forget about that. Forget about it if you want to live. Think instead about the first flush of green alfalfa peeking out of the ground at you in early spring when your big antlers are gone and the hunters are gone and you can taste the succulent stuff at your leisure."

At this point, somewhat to my relief, the bell rings and the students pack up for history class. If their minds are like mine, the fantasy lives on. It will be renewed after our literature lesson the next day.

There is a local myth that whitetails are not native to our area, that they began filtering into south-central Montana around World War II. This is incorrect. Our ranch's old outbuildings contain door handles and coat hangers made of whitetail horns that date from early in the twentieth century. Skip back a century earlier and you'll read in the Lewis and Clark Journals references to "common deer" and "jumping deer" or "blacktail deer" sighted across Montana. The common deer were whitetails—the deer with which the Corps of Discovery were familiar. The others, obviously, were mule deer.

But something must have happened to whitetails to make them disappear during the Great Depression. People were hungry; that explained much of it. But whitetails are vulnerable to a disease called Blue Tongue, and I suspect those that escaped the frying pans of hungry Montanans succumbed to such an illness.

That the species has come storming back here and elsewhere is an understatement. I wouldn't argue with anyone who claims there are more whitetails in Montana than ever before, and I'd agree that they've come to occupy country we used to think of as mule deer Mecca. The wide open spaces of eastern Montana hold whitetails in scant patches of buck brush in shallow coulees where an eastern member of the species would shake with agoraphobia. In such country whitetails have altered their habits. Flushed out of hiding, they evacuate the area just like mule deer or elk, running for miles to more friendly terrain.

No larger mammal, save perhaps the coyote, has the survival skills of whitetail deer. Only in regard to speeding automobiles do the beasts appear completely stupid. Everywhere else they invoke the admiration of any hunter who really studies them. When stressed there's little indecision about them. They commit to a particular plan of action. Flush a whitetail buck and he goes full bore, no hesitation, no looking back. He runs in bob and weave style, two lopes, a jump, a dodge to the side. Swift as they are, pronghorns are much easier than whitetails to hit on the run. The pronghorn runs level like a gaited horse in a running walk, and if you can figure out how much to lead them you can connect.

The iron nerve of a big whitetail buck when discovery must seem imminent is of caliber to be coveted by any undercover CIA agent. Horseback with Elmer forty years ago, when whitetails were just beginning their frontal assault on our ranch, I spotted the antlers, then the head and shoulders of a big buck in thick chokecherry brush at the bottom of a coulee next to the trail. He was no more than fifteen yards from us. We both stared. I could detect no movement whatsoever, and I finally asked Elmer, "You suppose he's dead?"

"No," Elmer said knowingly. "Just wait." We did so, resting our horses, chatting about other things, eyeing the buck, looking for some movement in his visible eye. It never came. Convinced we did not see him, or perhaps that any movement would be fatal, the buck let us ride through the coulee on the trail that passed within ten feet or so of him. An hour later, after working our cattle, we returned along the same route. The buck was gone.

Some of the whitetail's survival acumen might be explained by his age as a species. According to Ron Spomer (*Sports Afield,* January 2006) whitetail fossils four million years old have been found, fossils that perfectly match modern whitetail bones. This means the species has survived relatively unchanged far longer than humans have and means, too, according to Spomer, that whitetails "once roamed this land with mastodons, giant bison, cave bears, and saber-toothed cats." In other words, this critter has been in the survival business a long, long time.

During my boyhood the ratio of mule deer to whitetails favored the mulies, and most of us cut our eyeteeth on smallish mule deer bucks. These were the most accessible deer. Yes, I know that the true monarchs among mule deer, the huge bucks of the breaks and sandstone buttes, of the deep mountain canyons, are smart and wary, surviving to grow those magnificent antlers by spending their lives where they can watch from afar the approach of anything dangerous. But talk about the rank and file of deer, compare the talent of average individuals, and I firmly believe whitetails are in a superior class.

I was nearly thirty before I shot a decent whitetail buck. Before that I'd been outwitted by a couple of big ones, and I'd had one heartbreaking loss. This occurred on the ranch during my years in eastern Montana, when the teacher's association was still foolish enough to schedule their conventions on the first Thursday and Friday of the rifle season, thereby virtually assuring a mostly female audience at the various workshops teachers were supposed to attend. This particular year the convention was in Billings, near the ranch, so we stayed in our country cottage and I split my time (not very evenly) between convention sessions and the woods.

We'd experienced early snow and cold, true winter, not just wet fall snow. I fished out my irrigating boots and planned an early departure across the river in hopes of ambushing a buck in the little basin due west of the house. I had hunted a little that afternoon under wet trees that dropped snow in big clumps on me and on my rifle as well, something I didn't consider as I followed my usual custom of hanging the rifle out in the woodshed to prevent it from condensing moisture inside the cottage by the oil stove.

For late October it was bitterly cold the next morning. The ground, though, was not yet frozen under the snow, so there was no crust, and I proceeded through darkness into the west breeze nearly silently across the river and through the cotton-woods on a path I knew well.

It was almost perfect. The deer feeding through the snow on the buckbrush in the basin never knew I was there. I'd approached in the direction from which they'd come, the woods and river to which they'd normally retreat, and from my position behind a cottonwood trunk just into the woods I could see among them a big buck. My heart started thumping. He was a couple of hundred yards away, not a bad range for the .270. I worked the bolt as silently as I could, leaned against the tree, and squeezed. Then I squeezed harder. Then I pushed against the tang safety and squeezed still again. Then I pulled, hard. Nothing. The rifle wouldn't fire. The buck, restive, eyeballed the edge of the woods. Finally, another try, a death grip on the stock, and the rifle recoiled, but at an instant when the crosshairs did not look quite right.

I recovered from the recoil. He was running straight away, west, up the hill, and I could see that he favored one front leg. I turned instantly sick, cursing the rifle and cursing myself.

One of two things had happened, and I'll never know which. Savage 110 bolt actions have a three-position safety, a nice feature. Pulled to the rear the safety locks both trigger and bolt. Pushed all the way forward to the fire position both bolt and trigger are free. Half way in between is a position in which the bolt can be cycled but the rifle will not fire. Perhaps in my excitement I pushed the safety only part way forward and actually had it in the middle position. More likely, the rifle's wetting the night before, followed by the cold night in the woodshed, had resulted in ice frozen around the trigger and sear mechanism. None of it mattered now. The buck was out of range, clearing the top of the valley wall. I had hurt him and would likely lose him.

It was at this point that he commenced to educate me, and that my background as a hunter of mule deer did me wrong. I followed him straightaway. I knew intellectually that these woods were a security magnet to him, that he'd probably circle and try to return to them, but he had left with such commitment, had run such a straight course, that I was convinced he'd head across the flat above, then up the next ridge and over into the neighboring valley.

Yes, there were occasional sprinkles of blood along his tracks, nothing bright that suggested lung or messy that would indicate guts. I was sure that in yanking the recalcitrant trigger I had pulled the rifle left toward his front, that I'd hit him too far forward rather than too far back. I labored up the hill through the snow, longing for sight of him. When I cleared the crest onto the flat, expecting to see him working his way up the next ridge to the west, I realized I'd been played for a fool. (It would not be the last time.) Through the binoculars I could trace his tracks in the new snow where they made a long arc to the north, then turned abruptly east, where the buck, with equal decisiveness, had sprinted back to the security of the woods. While I was climbing he was running, masked from my view by a small intervening grove of trees that ran down toward the cottonwood bottom.

There is, in the place where the buck had entered the woods, a patch of thick brush no larger than one hundred yards square. My brother calls it the deer motel. Nowhere in it can you walk upright. The brush is honeycombed by tunnels just the height of a deer. The buck's tracks, still showing occasional sprinkles of blood, entered this brush patch. I knew what would happen if I followed. When I was tied up, unable to see or to move quickly, the buck would exit the opposite side, cross the river, and be gone into thick woods on a neighboring ranch where I could not go.

I did the right thing. I circled the brush patch to the side by the river, never striking fresh tracks. He was in there. He was in that patch, perhaps within yards of me. Maybe he could hear my breathing. I listened for his, but heard only the gurgling of water under new ice behind me.

I longed for a partner, for someone who could enter the brush patch on the buck's tracks while I watched the river side, someone to smoke him out for me. But I was alone. Emily was at the house with the babies. Even if I could break her loose, leaving my position for even a minute would give the buck the escape route he needed. By the time I returned with Emily he'd be long gone.

A better hunter than me, a man with more patience than I have, might have prevailed. He might have brushed off a log, sat down and said, "Okay, Buddy, I've got all day." But even in that there would have been danger. There was nothing to keep the buck, if lightly wounded (which I'd come to believe) from exiting the side he'd entered and then running south along a line of chokecherry bushes and, with a sprint across a small open meadow, into the woods.

I suppose I threw in the towel. I suppose the buck proved to have a superior resolve. I'm a terrible "stand" hunter, and in those days, young, in good shape, only a few years out of the

Marine Corps, it was even harder for me to stay inactive physically. So after a half hour I made my move. If I started a very slow circle back to the west around the north perimeter of the brush patch, not going all the way, just easing that way far enough to pressure the buck, perhaps he'd make his move. He'd run, I was sure, straight to the river and across. He'd go balls to the wall, never looking back, and I, hopefully, would still be close enough to the openness along the stream bed to sprint fifty yards and catch him while he crossed.

So I started to ease around. I took two steps and listened. Another two steps and listened, my nose thrust toward the brush to catch a whiff of him, mouth open to hear more distinctly. Nothing. I reached the limit. That is, I'd gone as far as I thought I could go and still be close enough to the river for my necessary sprint. Silence. And then I did it, two things he was waiting for. I took two steps, listened, two steps more (one over a fallen log), heard nothing, and sighed. That's all, but it was enough.

There was a tawny flash through the chokecherry brush and a mighty crackle of branches. I sprinted, jumped the log, and ran toward the river like a man possessed. He'd done better than a straight sprint toward the river. He'd angled slightly south, keeping the largest mass of brush between him and me, and when I reached the river bank it was over and he was gone. He had broken the new ice and dragged water up onto the snow on the other side of the stream. He was gone.

I sat down on the snow at the edge of the cut bank of the river and watched the water bubble in and out of the holes the buck had made in the ice. I don't believe I cried, but I felt like it. Any consolation came from my conclusion that the buck was not badly hurt. He had limped on the leg, but he had not carried it. The blood was dark, muscle stuff, coming, I guessed, from the front of a shoulder. He would probably recover. Maybe we would meet again. But I doubted it. I stayed on the riverbank until the cold and wet seeped through and numbed the skin on my rear, and then I walked home.

It was the next year, I believe, that I shot my first really good whitetail buck. I found him very close to the brush patch used so skillfully by the one that had eluded me. There was less drama involved this time, though for five minutes or so this one, too, had my heart pounding.

I'm convinced that the reflection of light off the required blaze orange (if not the color itself) is like a flashing warning light to deer. However, I've noticed that when the daylight fades to a certain point the warning light switches off. In Montana legal shooting light ends one half hour after sunset. Late in our long season the light and the colors change, and not too subtly, each minute of that final half hour. At the tail end of that legal window there are five or ten minutes when something happens to the way a whitetail sees. Blaze orange no longer fixes his vision.

I had hunted our favorite edge, a bank above the cottonwood bottom that runs a half mile south toward the little basin, intending to arrive there just at the end of shooting light. It was one those blustery days when it seems futile to dope the wind. I've always thought those days weren't all bad. I suspect strong shifting winds disperse scent or at least impair a deer's ability to tell your location from it.

I arrived at the basin a little early, found nothing, and began my trek back during those last minutes of daylight. I walked rather carelessly, though by habit I continually scanned the terrain a quarter mile ahead of me. I suspect the buck had lain in the brush and watched me pass on my way to the basin. Now he'd slipped into a little hollow strategically located below the bank, an acre or so of lush browse where he could snatch forbidden mouthfuls yet remain hidden from most angles of approach. At first I couldn't believe he was there against the patch of buckbrush four hundred yards in front of me. I dropped to one knee and glassed carefully. He was no apparition, but the light was fading fast enough that he was hard to make out without the binoculars.

I dropped below the bank, out of his vision, and sprinted the first hundred yards, then slowed. My race was with the clock as well as with the buck. I walked as quickly as I could and yet maintain some semblance of tactical quiet, thankful now for the wind that watered my eyes. Finally, I crawled up a little bank that would put me a mere hundred yards from the buck. I could not believe he would still be there.

But he was. Broadside but slightly quartering away from me, angled uphill, the buck was still feeding. He fell to an easy shot from the .270. He had a good, mature typical rack, four points on each side plus brow tines, and his body was fat and huge. After dressing him out I could, but just barely, drag him twenty yards up the bank to a flat place I could reach with the pickup. As they say in the South, he'd eat really well. There must have been two inches of standing fat on top of his hind quarters. My hands were sticky with his fat-laden blood.

I remember a quiet contentment, sympathetic but thankful, full of admiration for this beautiful animal. I had waited for him a long time.

Over the years I have shot some decent bucks. Nothing I've ever killed would make Cabela's wall, and that's perfectly okay with me. Smart whitetail bucks have enriched my life, and their flesh has enriched our table. (For some reason, whitetails are the one species of the deer family whose flesh does not deteriorate during the rut.) No, they're not super beings. They do make mistakes, big fatal ones, particularly when the females command all their attention.

I do have in my office a nice European mount of a buck with eleven total points, nice long brow tines, and a satisfying symmetry. The antlers are not large or heavy enough to be trophy class, but their presence in my office pleases me and recalls the long, precise shot I made on him.

Sons Jonathan and Steve have killed better ones, and Jon's was taken in the same area as my first one. He writes:

As best I can recall I wasn't walking the edge as usual, but I was about 30 yards into the brush. I don't remember a whole lot of action until I got to just below the haystack where there's that thick brush before the clearing to the south.

I saw a pile of deer that had "made" me and were getting out of there as quickly as possible. In that pile I saw this guy's rack. For the first time in a long time, my first reaction was not to put the glass on it, count the points, agonize over whether or not it was big enough to be worthy of my tag. My only reaction was, "Get him! Get him now!"

They were out of sight in a fraction of a second. I pulled my rather unorthodox (but proven successful) whitetail hunting technique of lowering my head and charging at full speed. I knew they were dumping into the clearing ahead and from there they would turn left, jump back into the brush, cross the river and be gone. I had to get there before they could do that.

As I went through the small dip before the clearing my eyes were to the left, hoping they'd still be in sight. They weren't. I figured I'd been too slow. Wait a minute, no I wasn't, the does foolishly went to the right—into the nice open hillside instead! Amazingly enough, the buck had followed them. Thank goodness it was the middle of the

24. Jonathan with one of the best whitetail bucks taken on our ranch.

rut—he never would have made such a mistake two weeks prior.

But he did, so I still had a chance. The second I emerged into the clearing, they all realized their mistake and began streaking south along the hillside so they could reach the bottom of the basin and then go to the brush.

I know I fired three times. I can't remember if I hit him two or all three times. I can honestly say that was the last time I've ever had to pull the trigger more than once to fill a tag. Anyway, he finally went down at the south end of the clearing right at the bottom of the basin.

He had almost made it to the trees. Almost.

Steve also killed a fine one by waiting until the last few minutes of daylight in the entire five-week Montana season. This buck, crazy with the rut, had been making flash appearances in the clearing across the highway from our house. He would come flying out of the woods, sniffing like a hound dog along a doe's trail, oblivious to everything else. But he wouldn't stay long. I'd seen him a couple of times when I walked out to our mailbox, had made brief eye contact with him, laughed at his preoccupation but also at myself: he was making his appearances when I was ill-prepared to do anything about it.

Steve counted on the buck appearing one more time. He hid himself in the remnants of an old sheep shed, where just two partial walls remained amongst a jumble of roofing tin and rubble lumber waiting to be burned. Shooting light was slipping away, and so was Steve's season. He began to berate himself for putting his hunting that season at such low priority, for waiting so long to get serious about it.

But the buck did appear, nose to the ground in his hound dog imitation, sniffing the trail of a hot doe, thoughts everywhere but where they needed to be. He fell to Steve's .270. Like Jon's buck this one was a fine typical specimen.

There have been so many others. I shot a couple from my brother's tree stand, but I will not do so again unless it's with my longbow. In each case I squeezed the trigger with reluctance, with regret, motivated only by the opportunity to collect fine meat with surgical precision. I felt flat afterwards.

There was the buck Steve Hopkins and I nearly lost, even though we both knew he'd nailed it perfectly at long range with a .300 Winchester. It had stood near the river bank and had disappeared at the shot. Although the range was around three hundred yards, I knew better than to think that Hopkins, from a steady sitting position, would miss a standing whitetail, and the caliber was certainly more than adequate. But we searched and searched to no avail.

This was a head-scratcher. The river's surface was about ten feet below the bank. Had the buck been able to cross, he'd have left a tell-tale trail of wet tracks on the exposed cobblestones of the other side, and no such trail existed. Finally, when we'd exhausted all possibilities, Steve noticed a stick bobbing in the good fishing hole below us, a small forked stick that seemed stuck in the deep water. Gestalt!

The buck, hit hard, had made one giant leap into the river and died, sinking into the deep hole until just two points of his rack on one side protruded. Hopkins claims he is the only one who got wet during retrieval of this buck. I can't confirm that, and it doesn't seem likely.

But in addition to a nice set of symmetrical antlers with three points plus a brow tine on each side, the buck sported another decoration, an earring consisting of a red plastic ear tag identical to those with which I mark my calves when they're born in the spring. It bore the number forty-four. I told Hopkins that the ear tag made it one of my herd, that we should look for a brand as well.

But there was something even more remarkable. A week earlier my brother Steve—I know it's confusing; we have so many Steves we practically have to spray for them—had shot an identical buck, also with a red tag, this one numbered forty-five. We sent the tags to Montana Fish Wildlife and Parks with a brief account. We got back an interesting, detailed letter. The bucks were twin fawns tagged two and a half years earlier near a town ten miles up the valley.

My friend Bernard was a hunter and probably a poacher. He lived just far enough back from the highway, across the river and through the cottonwoods, to get away with it. I suspect he and his family lived on whitetail bucks, preferring them even to the beef he raised on a small scale. His ranching operation was much too small to fully support a family, so he supplemented their situation not only with ample venison but with work at a local mine.

My father-in-law, Elmer, did not hunt, but Bernard, knowing his taste for venison, took care of him. Early in the morning, long before daylight, Elmer would awaken to the sound of Bernard's Jeep slowing by the mail box. There would be a rattle of the tools Bernard hauled in back of the Jeep, a grunt or two, footsteps, and then the heavy thud of a body dropped on the front porch. When Elmer heard that he knew he had his deer, dropped by Bernard on his way to work at the mine, but he knew, too, that he'd better get up and do his butchering before daylight. These delivered deer rarely bore legal tags.

"You can't sneak up on them, Dan," Bernard told me once. "You've got to jump 'em. You've got to know where they are and just jump them and shoot one during the confusion." Festooned as Bernard's sheds were with impressive whitetail antlers, I couldn't question his effectiveness, though his methodology was worse than marginal. Bernard used his Jeep. Painted a flamboyant red and yellow, mufflerless, the vehicle was about as clandestine as a marching band. No matter. Bernard knew the little clearings where the bucks hung out and knew how to weave his Jeep at kamikaze speed among the cottonwood trunks right into their living rooms. He had a .270 mounted with a puny three-quarters inch tube scope that looked as if it belonged on a .22. But he was fast with it, and by the time the deer figured out they'd been invaded, a buck was usually down.

I mention Bernard because I must confess that not all my whitetail hunts have been classic, sporting affairs. There was, for instance, the "penis buck," referred to with that ignoble handle by all our family and close friends. Just the other day I went to the stack of antlers under a lean-to against a boxcar we use as a granary here on the ranch and plucked his antlers from among the pile. Heavy, crudely formed, nontypical antlers, they sport one brow tine that forks twice, the other brow tine absent but replaced by several unorthodox points on its lower reaches. The rack is narrow but heavy, gnarled, with one side somewhat palmated. Had I not let slip one tiny bit of information, everyone close to me would to this day admire my bagging a buck with such impressive if somewhat malformed antlers. His body, too, was huge, and his loins superb on the table. Also, the shot that took him was perfectly placed.

But, as is characteristic of me, I let slip a little too much information. First of all, I didn't find him after a long and arduous stalk. Truth is, I was fixing fence when it happened. The Montana hunting season is long, and for rancher/hunters the work goes on. With a valid deer tag in your pocket, you go nowhere unprepared. The rifle rides in its pickup rack, and your hunting knife stays handy.

I was driving the old GMC pickup along the river looking for a the spot in a fence where a couple of cows had escaped, cruising along a little too fast for the terrain, the fencing tools rattling in the bed, not at all intending to "pull a Bernard." But my eyes caught white tails waving, and among them, a bigger-than-usual body with big, light-colored antlers that caught the morning sun. I slammed on the brakes, grabbed the rifle, and rolled out of the door into a kneeling position, working the bolt as I moved. The shot seemed wrong, coinciding as it did with the buck's great leap over a log. I sprinted toward the river, certain he'd cross.

Probably no more than ten seconds had passed before I reached the edge of the water just as he did, fifty yards downstream from me. This time the shot was perfect, right behind the shoulder. His momentum carried him into swift, but shallow water. I was too happy to be overly concerned with the icy water that invaded my boots and soaked my jeans as I plunged into the river, grabbed a horn, and snaked him back to land.

I feared I may have hit the buck badly on the first shot, perhaps in the guts, or worse, through his two prime hindquarters. But a close examination showed no such thing. Except for the one perfect shot just behind the shoulders I could see nothing—at first. Then I noticed, as I dressed him out, a notch out of the bottom side of his penis. There was no blood, just a burned-looking, cauterized groove where the bullet had stung past under him at three thousand feet per second.

I let this fact slip, and thus doomed myself forever to reminders of a bad shot I made. Never mind my impeccable immediate reaction drill, my perfect sprint to the river, the shot on the run that killed him instantly, his savory chops, or his interesting, nontypical rack. When the buck is discussed or his horns examined by family or close friends, when the beer is cold and the summer sun sinks and the barbecue releases the aroma of steaks sizzling with Emily's marinade, I can expect to hear it. "Oh, yeah," someone will say. "The penis buck. Thank God you got him right afterwards. He wouldn't have wanted to live." Oh well. Live by the rib, die by the rib.

As a rancher I pride myself in raising good alfalfa. I love cutting the stuff with the swather when it's thick and dark and so very green, and its aroma fills the air. It cuts cleanly in front of the sickle bar. It reminds you of luscious cake being sliced.

Alfalfa is prized because of its protein. Deer are protein-seeking machines. Thus deer, particularly whitetails, eat much of the expensive protein I raise. Stand a stack of first-cutting alfalfa hay next to a stack of grass hay, and the whitetails will not even touch the grass. They'll eat only the alfalfa. In turn, stand a second-cutting stack next to that first-cutting stack, and the later alfalfa, being higher in protein, will get all the attention. The deer will turn up their noses at the first-cutting stuff.

Long before the alfalfa is baled the deer take their toll. They graze on the plant as it first pokes out of the ground in the spring, then really nail it late in the summer when I'm irrigating my brains out trying to get the second-cutting to grow tall enough to justify cutting it. Sometimes it actually recedes, and that is no mystery. Drive out into the fields during the night, and it's not uncommon to see a hundred whitetails on a forty-acre alfalfa field.

During winter the deer surround our house and eat from the bales stashed for the corralled horses. Occasionally they study us through the glass door. Sometimes they bed right against the house. The cost in lost feed, expensively raised with sweat and diesel fuel, would be staggering were you able to calculate it. So, since ranching tends to be an economically impossible occupation anyway, I should hate the deer. But, of course, I don't. I may curse occasionally. I surround my haystacks with tall wire mesh to cut down on the damage. But on February mornings when it's twenty below I find myself thinking, "They've got to eat, too. We've all got to eat." The whitetails eat me, and I eat them. It works out.

When I close my eyes and think about hunting whitetails I see a kaleidoscope of tails flashing through the brush, of antlers carried out of range, of near encounters and of occasional success. But it isn't only the big ones that stand out.

When Emily and I first tackled ranching, when I commuted

sixty miles each way to a teaching job while she milked cows and tended to little boys, when we both ganged up on ranch work on the weekends, daylight being denied me much of the week, venison was a staple. Money was very short. True, by world standards we were far above poverty level, but this didn't mollify Emily when she searched through dresser drawers to find small change for the boys' school lunches. In those days I may have coveted antlers, but I hunted for meat.

One year I had let my second (antlerless) tag go unfilled nearly to the end of the season not because of neglect but because of work. I simply hadn't the time to go looking for a doe or time to do the butchering after I'd found one. (We never took our deer to a processor, and still don't when we can avoid it. In those days the cost would have been prohibitive to us.) Besides, there were plenty of deer, weren't there?

But even the most plentiful game has a way of being absent when you really need it. So here I was, on the last weekend of the hunting season, needing meat, and the deer had grown suddenly scarce. Worse, I was sick with flu. I could walk but ten steps through the snow before breaking into a profuse sweat, my breath coming in heaves and growls. So I walked very slowly down through the cottonwoods along the same route I'd taken when the buck in the basin got away from me.

The river in our woods breaks into two branches. Both, this year, were shallow enough to cross in my irrigating boots, thin ice clinging to each bank but still easy to break with my walking stick to make a path. I crossed the first branch very carefully, my rifle slung on my right shoulder, my left hand feeling with its stick for easier footing on the cobblestone bottom. Between the rivers I found a fallen log, scraped off the snow, and sat down to rest. It began to snow heavily. These were the woods of Robert Frost, filling up with snow, and I understood what he meant, why they lured, why he was tempted to stay there. But I, too, had promises to keep.

So I stirred, knowing I could do this, knowing I could find a doe and bring her back if I just took my time and paced myself and did not draw too deeply the cold, wet air into lungs that reacted with violent coughing whenever I did so. There were few tracks in the new snow. Something, I was sure, would be in the basin.

I could not have hunted long, and it did not take long. I eased into the breeze, my condition forcing upon me good habits of "still hunting," a term that confuses many because "still" refers to the game, not the hunter. (You assume the game is stationary and approach slowly, unlike in "stand" hunting, where you take a position and hope that game moves past you.) I had no choice but to move slowly. True, I was not in a survival situation, but I couldn't help but recall Boone's quest for the "white buffler"—mountain goats—in *The Big Sky*, when the men are starving in the snow of a mountain pass. We weren't starving, but we needed the meat enough that I was doing this when I should have been in the house by the woodstove.

I found her as I eased toward the second branch of the river. She saw me and stood there on the other side of the stream, an alfalfa-fattened lone doe, either dry (lacking a fawn) all year, or deprived of it by a hunter or an automobile on the highway. She was a full-sized, savvy doe that should have known better than to stand and stare at the orange vest of a hunter emerging from the woods and leaning now against a tree to steady the shakes of fever. She never had a chance to question her judgment.

When the doe went down I sat down again, this time on the river bank. Only a shallow riffle separated us, and I'd soon feel rested enough to cross and dress her out. I felt the familiar sense of thanks. I would not claim she had rationally offered herself to my family and me, but it amounted to the same thing.

25. A good, fat, whitetail buck, fine meat of the sort that has been a staple for the author's family.

It would be a long morning. I would cross the stream and dress her out and slowly drag her home on the snow. Each branch of the river would constitute a problem. I'd have to leave my rifle on the river bank so that I could drag with both hands, the water swift and deep enough to swing the doe's carcass downstream where it might tug hard, trying to free itself from my grasp. Then I'd cross again to retrieve my rifle.

On the east side of the east branch there is a place to which I could drive the pickup. Once I got her there, I'd be okay. Emily could leave the babies and come with me, helping to load the doe into the pickup, then to hang her from a single-tree in the wooden shed. For supper we would feast on her loins.

13

Wapiti

I was out of breath from climbing the mountain through deep snow. Hopkins progressed up the same slope, but across a big coulee from me, his orange vest occasionally peeking from a frosty aspen grove as he climbed a course parallel to mine. It was very cold. I breathed through my nose and through clenched teeth to avoid as much as possible the dump of icy air deep into my lungs, overworked from the climb. There had been no easy elk today, no elk hanging lower, so we would climb to them, hoping that by splitting up we would improve our chances of bumping into something.

I entered a spruce grove on a trail that elk had broken through deep snow and ducked a few low branches framing a portal into a clearing not much bigger than my living room. It all came at once. There was the heavy, musty, beautiful aroma of elk, and simultaneously he was there, the big one, not twenty yards from me, rising from his bed with an air of surprised arrogance. He stared at me for an instant, nose outthrust, black horns back, eyes bright. I had not been given permission to enter his chambers.

I glanced to my left through a window in the trees, hoping Hopkins, too, could see this tremendous creature, and when I looked forward again the bull was gone. I hadn't heard him leave. He just melted away.

In my wallet was an elk tag good only for an antlerless animal, but I've sometimes wondered whether the outcome would have been the same even if I'd had a bull tag. So overwhelmingly powerful was this creature twenty paces away, so unexpected

26. A big old bull near Gardiner, Montana. (Typically, the author had only a cow tag but has few regrets about leaving this monarch on the mountain.)

was his presence, that I wonder whether I'd have reacted quickly enough. Would the rifle have come up automatically as my thumb nudged the safety forward? Would I have been able to see more than a patch of hair through the scope?

Elk have my number. I have yet to take a decent bull, and while I've shot many lesser specimens of this big American deer, and have enjoyed the superb eating that results, I've concluded that somewhere the elk gods have conferred and concluded that Dan Aadland will be denied. He will see many big bulls when he has only a cow tag in his possession, the gods have declared. And he will even more frequently see only cows when bulls are the legal game. He will ride for miles seeing no elk at all, only to see a herd eighty animals strong standing safely on the wrong side of a fence that marks private land. He will often be at the wrong place at the right time, or at the right place at the wrong time, but rarely in the right place at the right time.

It's not as if I want that much. I don't care about a Boone and Crockett bull expensively mounted for my living room wall. All I want to accomplish antler-wise is to make up a certain deficiency on the front of the bunkhouse.

This requires some explanation. The bunkhouse is a log cabin behind our ranch house that dates back to the 1930s. Built of massive cottonwood logs, the cabin is of that design that projects the front logs out over a small porch. On the end of three of these logs, the two outside ones and the middle one, is bolted a respectable set of elk antlers. Or, I should say, used to be. Some years ago one of these elk racks fell down to the ground, my favorite one it happens, the one with a bullet hole neatly punched through a somewhat flat place on one of the beams. I was laggard about remounting the antlers on the log, instead merely setting them on the porch and adding the task to my endless list of jobs to do "when I got time." But

I never got a chance, because someone pulled into our place while we were gone and stole this loose set of antlers. And the bunkhouse has seemed lopsided to me ever since.

There was a historical attachment to them, too. From what my father-in-law said, the elk were shot by an old trapper named Benny Jones who lived in this bunkhouse for many years and worked for Emily's uncle. Elmer told me the man was high on his Savage 99 .250-3000, claiming it punched a neat small hole through the elk without wrecking much meat. Today we'd consider the caliber inadequate for elk, but no one had told that to Benny, and the evidence he left was pretty convincing. I suspect fine stalking, close shots, and perfect bullet placement had something to do with his confidence in the caliber.

So my mission in seeking a nice six- or seven-point bull is not to shatter world records but to simply restore symmetry to the bunkhouse. Benny and Elmer, if they could know, would be pleased by that. And thus far I've been denied.

Elk may not be as good as whitetail deer at using scant cover or at surviving right in the shadow of civilization's accoutrements. But they're big, strong, and incredibly tough, and no creature is better at sensing pressure and fading away from it. Their physical attributes are legend.

We have near us a mountain named Old Baldy, a nearly bare dome sprinkled with boulders and a little scrub timber. The mountain is not ringed by cliffs, but its sides are extremely steep. Old Baldy rises a couple thousand feet from canyons on each side, one of which holds several ranch houses. The canyon to the west has no structures, but a well-used forest service trail passes there in deep timber at the foot of the mountain. A couple of miles south of this mountain lies a trailhead that is extremely popular with hunters, particularly on the first morning of Montana's rifle season.

An elderly friend of mine was at that trailhead one opening morning, a cow tag in his pocket, a faint hope that the teaming crowd of hunters emerging before daylight from campers and pickups, piling onto four-wheelers to check the forest service roads, and dispersing on foot in every direction, would run elk to him. It almost happened. A big herd he estimated at two hundred head was flushed out of the timber. Several bulls were taken, but the majority of the herd escaped to the north toward Old Baldy. What amazed my friend (who was able to watch the entire drama through his binoculars) was that a cow, crippled on one front leg either by gunshot or by some earlier, natural circumstance, led the entire group right over the top of the mountain.

This handicapped cow could have chosen an easy course in either of the valleys flanking the mountain to the east and west, but she aimed the group right at the summit of this mountain, up its nearly vertical sides, and over the top. Her determination to do so shows two things about elk. First, physically they're nearly bionic. The mountain was no major obstacle to them. Second, the cow was escaping in a way typical for elk. She was taking the route where there was the smallest chance of pressure from humans. The valley to the east contained the ranch houses, livestock, and fences, though its terrain was still relatively remote. The western valley was heavily timbered, great elk cover, but it also contained that forest service trail. Perhaps hunters and horses were traveling it, and maybe a hunting camp or two was set up in that area. The lead cow was taking no chances. Her escape route made an assault on the herd from any direction extremely unlikely.

It is these two attributes, ability to sense pressure and astounding physical strength that make elk the elite species of North American deer. Like whitetails, they make mistakes. They're a bit more herd-bound than other deer species, and occasionally their herd leader is not as skilled as that lame cow that headed over the mountain. An entire herd can thus run into trouble, especially if caught out in the open. They don't have the steely nerve of a big whitetail buck at hanging tight in cover when you pass them merely steps away. They're somewhat easier to directly track through the timber than whitetails are. Find a fresh track in snow, and if you're very quiet and have the wind in your favor, you can often get into them. (It's best if your buddy follows the track, and you, the one who won the coin toss, parallel its course a hundred yards to the flank.)

I did not begin hunting elk in earnest until midlife, a fact that may seem unusual for a Montana native. But in south-central Montana during the 1950s the elk density was not high. When old man Kelseth came down from the mountains with a cow elk draped over the hood of his tiny Jeep we gawked and talked about it for a week. Yes, the hardcore hunters who set up mountain camps, who packed in with horses, or who lived and ranched at the foot of the mountains, did get elk. But all that was out of reach of a preacher's kid in town.

Then there were the years away from Montana, years in college and the Marine Corps and graduate school, followed by more years in eastern Montana where the antelope and deer were fine, but where there were no elk. (That has changed.) Later yet, I simultaneously ranched full time and taught full time for eighteen years at locations sixty miles apart. Major hunting expeditions were not in the cards. The good news is that during those decades the elk population grew. More restrictive regulations have replaced the over-the-counter either-sex tags we used to buy, tags good anywhere in the state that there were elk.

As a boy, however, I did get close to this animal that I came to regard nearly as a ghost. The small bunches of elk that existed on the face of our mountains did leave occasional sign. I never got one, but I got close enough to smell them and to hear them, and that in itself was an incomparable thrill.

The big mountain basin where Robert shot the whitetail buck (not to be confused with the quarter-mile-long depression on the ranch that has come to be called "the basin") did hold elk, and occasionally we would see fresh sign. Several times I climbed straight up the mountain face, following tracks through lodgepole pine so thick I'd have to turn sideways in places to squeeze through, amazed that such big animals could go so easily where I struggled so hard. I did get close enough to hear elk crash through the timber ahead of me.

Another time one of the Amos boys and I tracked a lone elk, probably a bull, into a beautiful little depression perhaps two hundred yards across with a thick patch of aspen and buck brush in the bottom. The tracks clearly went into that brush patch, and they did not emerge. Quite proud of ourselves we sat down in the snow on the hillside to wait in steady shooting positions for what we were positive was about to happen, the bull losing his nerve and busting out of the brush and into the clear.

He did so, but we could not capitalize. Within minutes of our plopping down in the snow a mountain fog rolled in. The bright sunny day turned to darkest gloom with this fog so thick that we couldn't see a hundred yards. Almost as quickly the fog went away. And so had the bull. When the sunshine returned we looked in dismay at a new set of tracks emerging from the brush, crossing the clearing in which we'd hoped to catch him, then disappearing into the lodgepole thicket above. Two boys floundering in thigh-deep snow were not going to catch up with a spooked bull elk in the timber. We knew that, so we turned home dejected.

In retrospect, the bull may have been watching us the whole

time, or he may truly have been taking a midday snooze. But elk are light sleepers. I have no recollection of the wind, and that's probably what did us in. He probably scented us and then took advantage of the fog.

I'm convinced that the most successful elk hunters (if we're measuring success by bringing home the bacon) have two things going for them. First, they tend to hunt the same areas year after year. It takes much time to really learn an area, to know the patterns of elk behavior in a particular region. True, an elk, unlike the typical whitetail deer, will pack up and leave an area completely if too pressured, taking up residence in the next county (or even farther away). But elk are elk. Residence in an area means certain patterns of feeding, of escape, of bedding. The best elk hunters learn these things, learn where elk are likely to be and where they're likely to go if spooked.

Besides these skill-related attributes (and sometimes in place of them), those who take big bulls often have the luck of the Irish. Two men I knew took their wives on an elk hunting trip near the borders of Yellowstone Park. One of the men was an experienced hunter, while the other man and the two women were quite new to the game. They parked their pickup on a logging road and got out to eat their lunches using the vehicle's tailgate as their table. The tyro male felt the urgings of nature, grabbed the shovel, and headed up into the timber. In fairness to him, he did one thing that even experienced hunters sometimes fail at: he took his rifle along, even though the contemplated jaunt was a short one.

In the deep timber a hundred yards above the pickup truck, the hunter blundered into four bull elk. He shot one. The other three ran in exactly the wrong direction for escape, down through the small clearing where the truck was parked. The second man and the two women had grabbed their rifles when they heard the shot, and they managed to put down the three remaining bulls. The score: two 6x7 bulls and two 7x7 bulls shot by hunters who applied very little skill, who shed not a drop of sweat. Such things do happen—but never to me.

More typical of my hunts (which are always successful—just not always meat-yielding) was one with my friend Billy, a young MD, when we packed into a pretty little triangle of ground where two creeks joined, and set up camp among the aspens. We were in one of those fringe areas that elk use, sometimes, an area in which there are probably always a few resident elk in the timber and occasionally herds in greater number.

It was a good camp. There was plenty of firewood to keep things crackling, beer and a bit of whiskey to wash down the peanuts whose shells kept replenishing the fire as we sat on stools under the stars. We wondered at them, at their brilliance against the black sky, and we wondered too how anyone could look up at them without thoughts of a Being greater than we.

During the night came clouds, and with the clouds six inches of wet snow that sagged the fly over our cooking area and motivated us to get saddled and head up the trail. This was the break we had needed. The weather had been too nice, the terrain too bare. Snow is so key for elk hunting, at least for the way we carry it out in these mountains. Snow tells you if elk are using the area, where they're headed, and where they bed. The very best trackers can learn these things without snow, perhaps, but snow on the ground multiplies your chances many times.

So we rode with eyes glued to the trail for new sign. Branches laden with snow hung too low for my tall horse, so I continually lifted them over us, often catching their wet load squarely on the back of the neck as I did so. I was soon thoroughly soaked, but I didn't care. Somewhere along this trail or within the clearings we crossed we'd find elk tracks, I was sure, and the tracks had to be fresh.

But it didn't happen. We rode until the trail began to peter out in scrub timber. There were new deer tracks, many of them, but the big, rounded tracks we so coveted had not appeared even though we'd now sampled a couple thousand lineal feet of elevation. Maybe the storm just had the elk lounging in their beds this morning, we thought. That can happen. Or maybe they just weren't here at all.

Eventually we stopped, the high altitude having made for far deeper snow. The horses were breathing hard, their hides soaked and sending up great clouds of steam. We rested them, snapping photos of this deep white wonderland. But the only life was an occasional raven that squawked past us. We turned back toward camp, the horses celebrating that decision with shakes of the bit that said, "C'mon, give me some rein, let's get the hell out of here."

A mile out from camp we saw, superimposed on the tracks our horses had left on the trip up, the single track of an elk, a big elk, probably a big bull. He had used the trail during the time we'd been ascending the mountain above him, not bothered by the new horse tracks or the scent we must have left. We tracked him a half mile down the forest service trail before his prints turned off the trail into some thick scrubby timber. From what we could tell he had never hurried. He had sauntered. "So there it is, Billy. We got up early and did the right thing. But if we'd slept in, cooked up a big breakfast, and waited for the sun to shine we'd probably have met this guy half way up the trail!"

Billy laughed and nodded. In retrospect we probably should have tied up and followed the track into the timber, but we were wet and cold and needed the camp to regroup. And that's elk hunting: being in the right place at the right time.

For the most part, though, elk hunting on public land in the West as we know it means getting out of camp during darkness, riding to where you think elk will be and attempting to catch them before they hole up for the day. I am told that elk are heat machines, that in weather that makes us reach for a down vest, elk are actually hot. They seek deep timber on north slopes for two reasons, for security, yes, but also in order to stay cool.

We were in the northern Bighorn Mountains of Wyoming, Teddy Roosevelt country, in a true safari camp. There were four of us, my sons David (an economics professor) and Jonathan (an aeronautical engineer) and David's friend Justin, his buddy for many backpacking and hunting trips. I was cook and wrangler by design, but by sheer chance, I was also the only bull hunter in the party. I'd applied on a whim, the odds being low. I was ready to enjoy furnishing and tending the horses, cooking, packing out any elk we were lucky enough to get, and perhaps even doing a little reading while the young guys beat the brush. But the Wyoming Fish and Game computer deemed otherwise: I got the either-sex tag. The boys would be hunting cows.

Hunting as a nonresident is nearly new to me, though there were two hunts years ago, the first in Colorado with my brothers Steve and Luther, the second with Luther and me alone in unfamiliar territory (a mistake I'll not repeat). We tried hard, frustrated by tales of big herds below us on forbidden private land. But this situation was very different. David and Justin knew this area thoroughly, and I had been able to scout it with David a year earlier. I had met him there with a light camp and two horses. We heard elk bugle in the middle of the night and were adopted by a lonely bowhunter who shared beer and peanuts at our campfire, telling us everything we could want to know about hunting elk and NASCAR, two things he found curiously allied.

On this trip to the Bighorns a year later, with David, Justin, and Jon, we were camped by our vehicles, not a storybook situation, but a convenient one when much gear is involved. At 8,800 feet the main concern was a snowstorm that would make exiting the area impossible. Conversely, weather as nice as we were experiencing has its own problems. It wasn't that the elk were too high; they really couldn't go much higher than we were camped. The problem is that elk activity slows down when the weather is warm, and most of the ground was bare, making tracking difficult.

Riding out from camp in the dark assumes knowledge of the land and trails and confidence in good, competent horses. We had the competent horses, all right, and three of us had been down this trail before. But our late arrival the afternoon before the season's opening day and the time consumed in setting up a sumptuous camp (two tents, a cooking canopy, and a portable corral for the horses) wiped out every bit of daylight. Justin needed to be checked out on an unfamiliar horse, saddle scabbards had to be mounted properly, everything assembled to minimize chances for a wreck on the trail. So I vetoed leaving early. We'd have our breakfast in the dark, but we'd leave as light hit the mountaintops.

And less than an hour out from camp it happened for the second time in my life: we rode smack into a herd of elk right on a forest service trail and still came up empty. Justin warned me. "We're almost to that first clearing," he said. He didn't suggest getting off and walking into it, rifles in hand, but I should not have needed such a suggestion. Instead I stayed aboard, slowing my pace, and within seconds faced a bull elk at less than a hundred yards, the sun just catching his dark face and black horns.

Where horses are concerned, no one has ever accused me of being slow. My life is in constant interaction with the critters, and I don't believe more than a few seconds were occupied by piling off, yanking the Ruger #1 from the saddle scabbard, darting forward ten steps over a small rise in the trail, and jacking a cartridge into the rifle's chamber. Somewhere along the way I barked to Justin to hang onto my horse.

But it wasn't enough. By the time the crosshairs settled on the bull's tawny body he had made it to cover, all but his rear third hidden behind a pine. A cow, still in the open, offered a brief target, but with a highly coveted either-sex tag in my pocket I couldn't pull the trigger on a cow on opening morning. Hopefully there would be opportunities later in the hunt if I didn't get a second chance at a bull. And there was little sense in following these elk farther than the quarter mile or so we tracked them. They had dived off an extremely steep slope into elk jungle, and we were convinced that better opportunities might lie ahead.

The near miss opening morning was in no way a downer for us, even though we rode a long distance to a fabled park and back to camp without seeing any fresh elk sign except where the bull and his group had startled us earlier. But we were elated. We had "gotten into elk" right away, and that had to be a good omen. So camp that night was fine, even if the wind blew so hard that we added additional guylines to both tents. We didn't even consider a fire. No matter. We sat in the wind as long as we could and then took our stools into the wall tent to semicircle around the sheepherder's stove and make plans for the next day.

We agreed that we would make a wider footprint hunting in pairs, cover more ground and discover more sign, and that the big park we'd checked out, full of knee-high timothy but devoid of elk sign, was too low for the elk in such warm weather. I listened to the three young men plot strategy, enjoyed their enthusiasm, and wondered how long I would

27. Skywalker, Jonathan, and Redstar high in Wyoming's Bighorn Mountains.

28. Skywalker and the author, glassing for elk.

be able to do this. But I did not dwell on that. I have become a little more able to live for the day.

And these days in camp, a whole week of them, were fine. Jonathan and I rode up the north valley wall and saw two big moose in a huge burn grazing within a hundred yards of (of all things) a hunter in a tree stand. In the center of this huge clearing, his orange vest looking like the bulls-eye in a target, a hunter we later met spent a week in a tree stand within sight of the county road. From Wisconsin, this hunter knew but one way to approach things, and he assumed they'd work as well in Montana as they had in Wisconsin. We gave him an A for determination, but an F for common sense.

One day Justin and I tackled the new Dutch oven and glowed over the results. Into it went two whole chickens, some chicken broth, chicken soup, potatoes, and carrots. We all hunted hard until after dark and were greeted at camp by the aroma of one of the best meals we'd had. We repeated this culinary tour-de-force with beef the next day and were equally pleased. We flunked only on Emily's beer bread, which she'd premixed for us. We added the can of beer, put the pan in the Dutch oven when we left, but returned to find a doughy brick instead of bread. We'd left too soon, before the coals really got going, and our fire had blown out.

On the hunting front there were encouraging signs. David and Jon got into elk on foot to the west, where timber was broken up by several nice parks. Once when alone David could have shot a bull in one of those parks, but he lacked the correct tag. Justin and I rode up that trail we'd used the first morning, watched a park until dark, then rode out through the timber and into the open where a magnificent moon lit up the landscape like a headlight. The moonlight was so bright that we cast long shadows that looked like those of quixotic knights on our horses that champed at their bits, cruising in running walks toward camp and their evening's ration of hay. And the next day the two of us walked the parks and spotted a cow and a calf crossing a tiny clearing well out of range.

We were pleased to have so much action when the weather was so warm. Our camp, located by the public road, was far from remote, and we had many visitors. Nearly all complained that they had seen nothing at all. But then, nearly all appeared to be driving these high-altitude forest service roads and getting out of their vehicles rarely if at all. And then there were the four-wheeler jockeys, hoards of them. From what we could tell they pretty much respected the motorized vehicle bans on many of the roads and trails. But it also appeared that many of them drove their ATV's a lot and walked very little, their butts epoxied to the seats of their camouflaged machines.

It was the brothers who finally came back to camp with hands bloody and voices jubilant. In very tight timber where either might have gotten a shot, David had a brief window through which he sent a .35 Whelen bullet toward a cow. She went down hard, and that was that. It had been a team effort, and as their dad I was glad to see the great pleasure Jon took in his older brother's elk. Jon, the middle son, had some good elk hunting opportunities with me during high school and shot several, but David, more heavily involved in sports, was too busy meeting the demands of his coaches, so he got fewer chances. This young cow was his first elk.

It was a merry camp we had that night. Some things haven't changed in eons. Young men kill game, come triumphant back to camp, and the rest of the evening consists of drinks around the fire and telling, then retelling, and then telling again. And we plan.

Early the next morning Jon and Justin will hunt their way to where David's cow lies field dressed in the little clearing at the end of the finger of timber that hid the two hunters

29. David, Jon, and the author with prime elk quarters packed out on
    the horses.

when they took her. They will begin quartering the cow. David
and I will hook up the trailer and haul the horses to the far-
thest point up the logging road where a turn-around of the
big gooseneck is possible, and then we'll ride two horses and
pony the other two with Decker pack saddles ready to receive
elk quarters secured with basket hitches. And sliced elk tenderloin, carefully cut free by Justin, will simmer that evening
in the pan.

It is the last hour of shooting light on our last day in the
Bighorns. I have long since decided (again) that a cow elk
will do just fine. Besides, I am very lucky. Our Montana elk
season, usually a notch later than Wyoming's, still lies ahead.
Another chance for a bull may come then, and if not, I've

been as lucky with Montana's lottery as I was with Wyoming's and have drawn a cow tag for an area near home.

I have elected tonight to hunt alone. Justin, pressed by his business back home, has had to leave the camp. David and Jon will make a long circle north into territory they haven't yet explored, hoping to find an elk for Jon.

I have meandered my way up and over the ridge I've hiked twice already, once with Justin and once with my sons. I'm betting my last chips on the long clearing in which David saw the bull and from which Justin and I watched the cow and calf. It is a beautiful place, a fine place to watch the daylight ebb whether an elk appears or not. But it is not an easy park to watch. Averaging a couple of hundred yards in width, it is perhaps eight hundred yards in length, and it slopes down relatively steeply from west to east. Since the wind blows along its length, one direction or the other depending upon the time of day, conventional wisdom would be to watch the park from the downwind end. But that would cut off your view of much of it, and the far half would be out of range even if you could see it.

I elect to hide on the north edge about two-thirds of the way up on a rock ledge where I can sit quite well camouflaged by bunches of buckbrush. I wait and I wait. The magic time, the last fifteen minutes of legal shooting light, approaches. Nothing. The only sound is the gusty wind that worries me, that seems to have shifted so that it blows from the northwest, from behind me.

I'm haunted by the fact that from the position I've chosen I cannot see the bottom third of the park. Finally it gets to me. I rise but stay bent at the waist and ease down the rock ledge, playing hide and seek with an invisible opponent, gaining fifty yards before dropping to one knee behind a bush and staring at the far fringe of the park below me. They are there. A yellow mass seeping out of the timber and into the open, the tightly grouped herd might be an apparition, so I blink and look again, then steal a very quick peek through the binoculars before darting across the ten feet of open that put me into heavy timber. There, in heavy cover, I pant for a moment.

The elk are out of range, particularly in this cruel wind, even for the .338 Ultramag. If I can gain just a hundred yards through the timber and emerge on a little high point I know from the previous hikes, if they'll only stay where they are, the shot might be doable. I sprint through the timber and gain fifty, can't stand it, and peek again. They're still there, but with restive body language discernable even without binoculars.

Back in the timber, I gain the last fifty yards as quietly and swiftly as I can. Rifle in front of me, I penetrate the last little stand of cover, ready to plop into sitting position. But they are gone.

As the daylight gives way to the moon I sit on the lower end of the shale shelf and watch the place where they were. My binoculars tell me that they were never in the open for very long, that they merely kissed the tail end of the park, crossed its bottom end, reentered the timber, and headed up the next ridge. I may have screwed it up, and I may have done everything right, and I'll never know. Had I sat tight they might have drifted into the park, working their way up as they fed, and given me a shot. But the wind, which probably betrayed me in spite of my best efforts, votes otherwise.

Adios, Auf Wiedersehen, Arrivederci, Goodbye. You were most worthy. You leant to me the sight of your big yellow bodies against the black trees, you gave me a chance, and that was enough.

Postscript to 2005: The Montana elk season has come but not quite gone. I have hunted hard in brief stretches, but life and work go on as well. The ranch has its demands, as do several magazine editors with rather inflexible deadlines. I have the brass to complain that I have too little time to go hunting because I must put in so many hours writing about hunting, a paradox met with not one whit of sympathy from Emily, Billy, or Travis, my horse trainer and ranch hand.

Brother Steve and I have had a brief pack-in up a creek that used to be a well-kept secret, but which today is too well hunted. All hunting camps had deserted the drainage, a welcome sign in some ways, but an ominous one in others. We rode up nearly as far as it's possible to go horseback along the creek in the shaded, timbered bottom where just enough snow remained to let us easily spot sign of any elk crossing the valley. We saw wolf tracks and deer tracks, but no fresh sign of elk. Local belief is that a small, new pack of wolves has kept the elk in and out of this area. They spook down to the private land downstream, and then, when human pressure becomes too great, filter back into this drainage. The pack contains only three or four wolves, but they've kept elk restive over an area the size of some counties.

The second night we enjoyed antelope steaks under a starlit sky, turned in, and heard rain, hard rain for several hours. When the sound of rain stopped I heard instead the soft hiss of wet snowflakes sliding down the tent fabric, and I feared we might be in for it: wet snow on top of mud, the county road from the trailhead likely to be iffy.

So morning's breakfast was cut short, and we hurriedly broke camp and packed up. It was not the best packing job I've ever done. On the way out we had to twice make adjustments, which angered me. And there was the usual irony I've come to expect while elk hunting, because after fruitless searching and this morning's rotten weather, the clouds now cracked, the sun came out, and there were several sets of fresh elk tracks in new snow that crossed the forest service trail and beckoned to me. Should we have followed them? Probably. But Steve is not a rider, and long hours in the saddle the previous two days had done unpleasant things to his body. I was not particularly chipper myself, and anticipation of the muddy drive out pulling a big gooseneck horse trailer kept haunting me. Again we said it: Another time, Elk.

So this is it. The regular season has closed, and my either-sex tag has become a cow tag, good for two more weeks. Travis has secured permission to hunt a huge, fabled ranch, a ranch where sparing permission is occasionally granted after the regular season to those who hold cow tags. The ranch spans the land between two mountain drainages and butts on the south against national forest.

For several days we have chickened out. One morning the thermometer outside our dining room window read -22. The weatherman continued to forecast a warm-up, but always delayed it. I'm not afraid of cold weather, but extreme cold makes not only for unpleasantness but for genuine danger. If your horse slips and falls on you and breaks your leg at twenty above zero, that's one thing. At twenty below, staying alive until help comes can be problematic.

But finally the cold has broken, though not completely—the morning has started out crisp enough. We have unloaded Skywalker and Redstar on the county road on the western side of the ranch and will ride a big circle looking for a herd we've been told numbers more than a hundred head. This morning the geldings, having suffered the equine version of cabin fever, are ready to go. An ounce of slack in the reins puts them in a running walk, and we fly up the valley wall and across the sage flat into the ranch.

Travis knows the country and has eagle eyes, a happy combination. Soon those eyes are wide with enthusiasm. He spots three bull elk on a hilltop bedded down a mile away. I have trouble finding them, but eventually can discern their ample antlers sticking above the buckbrush in which they're bedded. They are watching us, but don't seem particularly concerned.

But that's not all. From a hilltop we spot a fourth bull elk to the south, little bigger than a dot appearing to head toward the national forest. Then, below him, a half mile from us, two dots move rapidly across the snowy landscape. "Those have to be wolves," Travis says, and sure enough, the binoculars reveal them as such, one nearly black, the other lighter, loping gracefully but purposefully south. A quarter mile beyond them, from a quaker grove, still another dot darts out, and this one, the binoculars tell us, is a cow moose, no doubt staying clear of the wolves.

We're having a fine time. A half hour on horseback and we've seen four bull elk, a cow moose, and two wolves. The wolves, we've heard, have soiled their nest by refusing to limit their diet to the hoards of mule deer we see later in the timber or to an occasional elk. They've become beef eaters, and the U.S. Fish and Wildlife Service (which put their parents in Yellowstone Park, over the mountain, in the first place) has authorized removing them. If our encounter is any indication of their awareness I have to conclude that getting a rifle shot at one is going to take some doing.

Since none of this menagerie represents legal game to us, we begin our long clockwise circle toward the south. Along the way two of the hilltop bulls decide to change territory, and our presence is not much of a deterrent. They pass within two hundred yards of us, stopping a couple of times to eyeball two men on horses. This ranch has not been hunted for bulls at all this season, and these two show it by their near indifference toward us. I long for the ten-power optical zoom of my sophisticated digital camera which, unfortunately, resides safely at home. I reach for my pocket camera, then nix that—through its lens the bulls would be mere spots in the snow. I'll carry their picture in my mind instead—two handsome, healthy bull elk, dark against an expanse of snow, steam rising from their nostrils.

There is, underneath the pleasure of riding through game-rich mountain terrain under a bright sun, some sobering news that nags us. The ownership of this ranch is split into many entities. They've been offered, we're told, forty-one million dollars for the place. This may well be my first and last experience on these spectacular acres.

The man offering to buy has a seemingly bottomless well of ambition and money. He already owns a giant swath of land facing these mountains, a swath containing hundreds of thousands of acres. His ranch originates down in Wyoming and proceeds north, then bends west into the headwaters of our valley. He does not subdivide, and that part is good. But he does the reverse, which is equally unsettling. He buys all ranches in his path and bulldozes their sometimes historic buildings, destroys every shred of evidence that a ranch ever existed there, and sometimes extracts from the rancher an agreement that he'll never again live within a certain distance of the borders of this ever-expanding empire. No one knows his motives. But we do know that upon the land he buys, none of us are likely to ever tread in the future.

We ride south, then begin to bend west on the next leg of our circle. We know elk hunting too well, know that just as it's possible to search through cows all day and never find a bull, the opposite can happen as well. Our method is simple: ride until we find fresh tracks, and then pursue them, either on foot or horseback as the terrain dictates. But there is a dearth of fresh elk tracks in the fresh snow, and we begin to wonder if the ultimate irony may happen. Perhaps on a day when we could have shot any of three respectable bulls, and viewed another from a distance, we just might get skunked.

Mule deer are everywhere. There are so many that timber hunting is difficult, because we constantly see motion in front of us. We spot mazes of tracks in the snow from afar, ride to them, and find that deer alone have pockmarked the hillside, with not an elk track to be seen.

At the point that we begin to veer north again, on the last leg of our circle, a bald eagle, two crows, and a flock of magpies rise suddenly from the base of a big pine below us. The object of their dining turns out to be a nice cow elk, dead perhaps for a couple of days, a bullet hole, now enlarged by the birds, neatly punched behind shoulder. Somebody's shot was picture perfect.

A long range shot, perhaps, from a hunter who thought he had not connected? Deliberate vandalism is unlikely, because this place is very remote and difficult to enter without permission that includes being given combinations to locked gates. At the very least, the cow's death suggests that someone failed to follow up a shot. Elk are tough animals. One should never assume he missed without a thorough investigation. We regret the waste, but are sure that the eagle, the crows, and the magpies see it differently.

We stop by a gate through a fence in the timber to eat our lunches and confer. The weatherman's promised warmth has finally come, and we find ourselves unzipping our coats. I tell Travis that if we see no elk between here and the truck I will still mark this day as one of the finest I've spent in the saddle. And I mean it.

But on the way back things suddenly happen. We've ridden through a shallow, semi-open coulee, idly staring at the ground for tracks, just as we have for many miles, when Travis suddenly stops and leans far off Redstar's side. He moves the horse this way and that, peering more closely, and I see them too, elk tracks, fresh ones in the snow. We follow them for a couple hundred yards on horseback, whispering, then pile off and tie up our horses. We know we are close. We can feel it.

We walk less than a hundred yards before we see the tail-ender, a cow (we think) in the shadows of the timber that would offer a shot if only I could see her more closely. There can be no mistake. My tag is good only for a cow, and I can't see her head clearly enough to be sure. Then she is gone.

"Do we take the horses or follow on foot?" Travis asks.

I make the call. "On foot." Travis takes off on the trail and I do my best to follow. Travis is twenty-three years old and clean living. I am sixty-one, and . . . well, never mind. We ascend the ridge through the timber, top out, and see them. They're standing looking at us, and Travis says he's certain they're all cows. The range is no more than two hundred yards, maybe less, but on this sage flat I can't sit down and still see them, and an offhand shot is out of the question. I'm breathing like a windbroke horse. Kneeling, I can see the top thirds of their bodies, no more, and I pick one cow that is facing me and squeeze off, wracked by pessimism.

For many years I had a string going. I tended to make bad shots when there were no witnesses. In front of others, I hadn't missed for a long time. (This is a happy scenario, because early in my life it was the opposite—I missed in front of others and shot well when there was no one to see and report.) The last cow elk I shot at before this one was picture perfect. I waited, deferring, while the rancher's friend, who had only a bull tag, blazed away at three hundred yards at the one bull in a bunch of elk until the bull ran over the ridge, leaving several cows. Then I touched the trigger and my selected cow rolled down the hill. I acted casual while the two men stared. I very nearly blew smoke away from the muzzle of my rifle, but couldn't quite bring myself to such an excess.

Today, though, with Travis, I just flat miss a shot that I fear I won't get again. Another, now at much longer range as the elk moved out, has a similar lack of effect. I'm heartsick. A long hard season, one chance, and I've blown it. We confer quickly. Travis will go back for the horses, and I'll follow the tracks on foot. He's hopeful I'll get another shot before he joins me. "They really aren't all that spooked," he says, and he's right.

In the fifteen minutes or so it takes Travis to return with the horses I proceed slowly on the tracks of the elk, which has turned out to be a group of eight or ten young cows. We've noticed no calves among them. There is no blood with the tracks. And then Travis arrives riding Redstar and ponying Skywalker. I climb on and we take off through timber sparse enough to allow the chase to resume totally on horseback.

And a chase it's become. It's hard to explain to riders of arena horses just how a seasoned Tennessee Walking Horse can cruise through the timber when you really allow it to. I'm convinced we were gaining on the elk, even if they were trotting or loping, as we duck low branches and dodge dead-fall. The instant we break out of the timber, Travis whispers, "There they are."

The range is now longer, considerably longer, but circumstances are better. I'm not winded, and there is an armchair-sized boulder over which I lie, a veritable bench rest. At the shot Travis says, "She's down. I heard it hit." Then, "She just has to be down." It turns out the cow is down, then isn't down, in several alternating episodes. She is hurt badly enough to stay behind while the group drifts away. I feel for her. Several times she lies down, and we tell each other, okay, let's move up, only to see her rise again before, with a finisher shot, she stays down for good.

It is not the picture-perfect kill I always seek, and I wonder why. I've definitely hit her far enough forward, and the new gun is an impressive one, a .325 WSM propelling 200-grain Nosler partition bullets. The explanation comes when we examine the bullet's path. The cow had quartered away more steeply than she appeared to have. The bullet entered behind the shoulder, but emerged between the shoulder and the neck, thus missing the vitals. I regret any suffering and am thankful it was brief.

We have crossed a drift fence, and there's no gate for the horses, so the first part of our drag will rely on human power, not equine. I tell Travis the story about Hopkins's dragging stick, the larger dead one he insisted I should use instead of the green one I'd chosen, how he carried the rifles while I dragged the cow down a steep snow-covered slope, how I slingshotted down the slope into the snowbank at the snap of the stick. "We won't pull a Hopkins," I say, picking out a burley stick. We drag to the fence, each with one arm on the end of the stick, alternating sides periodically to rest the arm that aches. We marvel at the dead weight of this cow, even though she's probably only three-quarters grown.

We rest by the fence. Travis puts his rangefinder to work. We determine that my rest rock was between 325 and 350 yards from the elk when I fired, and we'd both estimated closer range, perhaps 275. The discrepancy explains why my second shot merely nicked the cow's underside. (It's wonderful to have such alibis.)

The rest is easier, at least on us. Had we killed this cow more miles away from the truck, or on ground bereft of snow, we would return to my ranch for a couple of pack horses. But the snow and the relatively short distance to the county road, perhaps a couple of miles, mean we can drag the elk without damage to the meat. Neither horse has dragged an elk, but Redstar, the elder, and Travis take the first and toughest heat at it, through a couple of coulees and up a couple of steep slopes. Redstar handles it well, but not without considerable sweat.

On top of the sage flat I relieve Travis and Redstar for a while, anxious to see that Skywalker learns to drag as well, and I'm quite gratified. He objects not in the slightest. We ride briefly through a neighboring ranch, a ranch that has also sold to the same man now offering millions for the big spread on which we've been hunting. And then, very quickly, we drop down into the valley where the horses stop by my pickup and horse trailer and let out sighs.

So, the 2005 elk season ends this way for me, gratified in a good hunt with a fine companion (or three of them if you count Redstar and Skywalker). There will be tenderloin again and much more from this prime young cow along with summer sausage from my smokehouse when I get time to make it. There will be memories of brilliant sunshine on snow, of bulls off limits, of two foxy wolves, and, perhaps, of a hunting ground that may soon disappear.

The big bull will have to wait. The bunkhouse will stay asymmetrical for one more year, the log on its south side still bereft of ornamentation, a sort of quiet challenge to me from a hunter of the past whose heritage I share. He's probably grinning and saying, "Don't worry, Dan. You'll get him next year." And he, like me, knows that even if I don't, it's okay. There's so very much more to it than that.

14

A Beautiful Bow

He walks through the timber and up toward my perch on the ridge, grey hair showing underneath his cap, this brother who was present when I shot my first deer nearly fifty years ago. Festooned in camouflage he leans against a scrub pine, catching his breath. I tell him, "Your bull call has no testosterone whatsoever."

He opens his mouth, either to breathe or to reply, but with my big brother mean streak still intact, I steal his words. "I know, and my cow call has absolutely no estrogen."

He's ready now to talk. "I didn't want my bull to sound too macho. I wanted bigger bulls to think they could beat him up."

"You sure as hell succeeded." But the truth is it wouldn't matter anyhow. The elk herd that resides here much of winter and on through calving season, stealing sustenance from the hayfields below, is nowhere in the area. We've seen nothing, heard nothing, and found not a single fresh dropping. But it's been a beautiful walk up a hill, through a clearing, and then to the top of this mini-ridge where elk have been taken in the past. So it really doesn't matter. It's been a fine morning, and we feel no failure in deciding the elk are simply not there, that it's best to amble our way back toward the vehicle.

I, too, am dressed in camouflage. I have never worn the stuff before, except for my later years in the Marine Corps Reserve. Even during Viet Nam in 1968 we wore plain USMC Green utilities, camouflage not coming to the Corps until later in the war, and I've never worn it rifle hunting because

30. The author's longbow by Chaparral Archery.

doing so seems pointless when law requires you to wear a blaze orange vest. On top of this ridge today I feel just a little clownish, not comfortable in garments that seem more appropriate for the Cabelas catalog than an old Montana hunter.

But then, at least since high school, I've never been a bowhunter. I grew up with bows, crude ones we fashioned from green willows and slightly better ones bought at stores, entry-level solid fiberglass, always right handed, with arrow rests on their left sides. Forced by circumstances I learned to shoot reasonably well, left-handed but with the arrow on the wrong side of the bow, twisting my right arm clockwise to hold the arrow on the rest. That early bad training is something I've known I would have to overcome if I ever took up the bow again.

But in spite of my boyhood fascination with the lore of archery, through much of the rest of my life I've had little motivation to take it up again. I was not quite sure why. I've thought of myself as a rifleman, and I've taken pride in my skills and my attention to the accuracy of my rifles and their handloaded ammunition. But there was more to it than that. My cursory attention to archery hunting via a few friends and through articles in hunting magazines showed that bows and bowhunting had become something strange to me. The photos in the magazines were no longer of boyhood heroes like Fred Bear. Instead they showed people bedecked in elaborate camouflage, faces painted black and covered with see-through nets, carrying contraptions of wheels, pulleys, and extra strings that were apparently bows, though scarcely recognizable to me as such.

But one day some years ago I was horseback with several friends pushing our cows up the highway toward our home corrals. Our ranch, unfortunately, straddles a major highway, and we occasionally must move cattle on the pavement, waving our hats at hurried drivers who resist slowing down until the last possible minute. Where it's feasible we try to move the cows to one side as a courtesy to let passing motorists through the herd. At a wide spot in the right-of-way I had been able to make a gap through the cows for a vehicle patiently idling behind me, and I motioned the driver through. As he passed I noticed the license plate. It said "LONGBOW."

The pickup's windows were down, so I kicked Little Mack forward into a running walk, caught up with the vehicle as its driver carefully threaded his way through the cows, and told him, "Stop by and show me one of those longbows sometime!"

He grinned and said, "I'll do that." I didn't take him very seriously. But a few weeks later the same vehicle showed up at the ranch. The man had taken time to stop and show me a bow as requested. He did not sell longbows, it turned out, but merely built a few for himself and for friends. He had stopped strictly to share a passion with a stranger who had expressed interest, and I found that remarkable.

Had my heart been set on taking up his passion, I'd have been crestfallen the instant I pulled back the bow he handed me, one with a modest weight of pull, fifty pounds or so. Before the bowstring touched my cheek I felt in the top of my shoulder a sharp pain, not a pain of new injury but a pain the said, "Remember, and don't push it."

We were horseback, Jonathan and I, on a March day when the wind bent the trees in sporadic gusts that made you grab your hat and duck the blowing dust. There was no snow on the ground, but there was still frost that made riding tricky. In cowboy language it was a good day to get bucked off, the kind of day that makes even gentle horses wild and that makes green horses downright dangerous.

I was riding a green horse. A black roan with a blaze and socks, Ace was smooth as glass, spirited, and a bit quirky to train. But he had gained my trust on an elk hunt through deep snow, when I also gained admiration for his grit. Jonathan and I rode out from the corrals toward a field of calving cows where we would separate off a half dozen pairs, cows with small calves born the previous week and now ready to be moved into an adjacent pasture.

There was a growing tension in the colt that I could feel. I should have been warned. In horses, as in people, stress can grow, can expand like yeast until there's no containing it. Eventually something blows.

The day itself, the wind, the noise, and the unfamiliar job the colt was asked to do were the primary causes of the incident, but I had made the situation worse. An orange electric fence tape lay on the ground. It was not charged, I knew, and even had it been it would have been grounded out and incapable of shocking a human or an animal. But the colt knew what it was—he'd been shocked by electric fences made of such stuff before—and he balked. I was in a hurry to get the job done, so rather than hop off and move the tape out of the way, I forced him to step over, his body further tensing as he did so.

We began cutting out the pairs, I moving each cow with her calf over toward the exit gate, Jon holding them there with his horse. All went well for several pairs, but the colt was dancing, his eyes wide, his body electric with tension underneath me each time we left Jon and the security of the older horse to repeat the job. I was approaching the neighbor's fence to pick up another pair penned between it and an irrigation ditch when a mighty blast of wind practically stopped us in place. But worse than the wind itself was what it did to a big plastic irrigation tarp I had carelessly left lying in the ditch. The tarp rose just under our noses, an orange apparition that hovered for an instant ten feet off the ground. The colt lost it.

He swapped ends and took off in a running buck toward Jon and the other horse, his explosion so sudden he yanked a yard of rein away from me, so that the for the first few jumps the "one-rein stop" was no option at all. And that's about as long as I rode him. I hammered into the ground front first, my shoulder taking most of the blow, my hard Norwegian head the rest of it. I remember pain and confusion, Jon asking if I was okay, and I claiming to be fine while I got slowly to my feet and caught Ace by the reins. Foolishly, I did the cowboy thing and got back on. Ace seemed repentant and somewhat calmed. We eased the separated pairs toward the gate and out where they belonged.

"Well, let's get the rest of them," I told Jon.

"I don't think we better, Dad." He told me later my face was white and my eyes were still dazed. The pain was coming on more strongly now, and I had trouble getting off my horse. Jon sent me to the house, where with great difficulty, Emily helped me remove my shirt. What I saw in the mirror was not pretty. Above my left shoulder was a big, unsightly bulge. I looked like the Hunchback of Notre Dame.

Later, our family doctor just shook his head. He sees me only when I get hurt, chides me about the lack of care I take of myself, then has a way of becoming absent for long periods of time because of his own miscues. A dedicated rock climber, he once fell off a mountain. Another time he smashed into a tree while snowboarding. But he thinks I live a hard, physical life. "It's a classic shoulder separation," he told me.

"Well, what can you do about it?"

"Nothing. Oh, I could wire it together for you, but down the road I'd probably have to do it again. That type of procedure doesn't last too well. If we leave it you'll heal up and it will eventually quit bothering you. It shouldn't hurt your range of motion."

"Sure is ugly," I said, standing to eye his mirror, wincing in pain at every motion. "But then, I'd about given up on winning the Mr. Universe Pageant." Doc just grinned, handed me a fistful of pain pills, and sent me home.

All this happened one year before the man stopped and showed me the longbow. And that is why I could not pull it back without pain.

As years passed I became aware of a movement that eschewed the mechanical advances of the compound bow and favored returning to basics, to the extremely effective bows and arrows that for thousands of years were used by humans to defend themselves and to acquire their food. I began noticing on the larger newsstands a national magazine devoted to this point of view, and then a second title. I would occasionally pick up a copy of one of these, enjoy reading it, but put it aside, remembering my shoulder.

I learned that the non-compound people were classified into two areas of interest. *Primitive* bowhunters do their best to duplicate exactly the bows and arrows of the past. They use the same materials, the same arrowheads, the same glues as their forbears. Since the study of bows of the past involves a staggering body of scholarship, these folks usually specialize, duplicating a particular American Indian, British, Turkish, Korean, or Asian design. I learned, too, that there was nothing very primitive about these weapons. Turkish bows could shoot eight hundred yards, nearly half a mile!

My interests inclined more toward the other group, those called *traditional* bowhunters. For the traditional folks, modern materials, such as laminations of fiberglass and wood veneers glued up with epoxy, are just fine. The idea is to be more practical than purist, but to shoot a bow that has no mechanical multiplication of its draw, that looks like a bow and shoots like a bow. Although such bows vary widely, two types are most popular, the recurve and the longbow, that latter often much improved by two bends that are laminated into their construction. These longbows usually have some *reflex* and *deflex*. Unstrung, they are far from straight, the bow bending back toward the shooter above and below the handle, then reversing direction. Thus these longbows have some of the advantages of recurve bows—great power and reduced hand shock—as they uncoil.

Both primitive and traditional bows are normally shot with a method misnamed "instinctive." No sights or mechanical releases are used. The shooter gradually learns a relationship between his draw and the position in which he or she holds the bow. A certain groove is eventually established through practice (thus the incorrect nature of the term instinctive, which is normally reserved for abilities that require no learning). Be that as it may, instinctive shooters hit their targets exactly the way a basketball player hits a three point shot or a quarterback hits a running receiver. It takes much practice, but the best instinctive shooters are very good indeed.

So what is my problem with the mechanical marvels called compound bows? Actually, I have no problem with them whatsoever. Some of my best friends use them. They simply don't appeal to me. They have many advantages. Through the miracles of compound leverage, produced by pulleys in a pattern only decipherable to a mechanical engineer, these bows not only have tremendous power, but they give the shooter the advantage of lightened weight at full draw. A seventy pound compound bow may have 75 to 80 percent let-off. In other words, you only pull seventy pounds over a small hump, and then the pull eases off, so that when you hold the string back at your cheek you're only holding twenty pounds or less. This makes it practical to hold your arrow at full draw for quite some time while your quarry approaches.

Compound-bow shooters normally use mechanical releases and a series of sight pins. They peer through a small peep sight attached to their string, line it up with the proper sight pin for that range (most use rangefinders to determine distance), and fire away. Gaining minimal competency with these bows requires perhaps one tenth or less the amount of practice needed for shooting instinctively with a traditional bow. Instinctive shooters concede that they'll never compete with the compound bow at stationary targets when the range is known.

But there are advantages in the other direction. Instinctive shooters adjust the shot to the range by muscle memory, and thus don't need sights. They can shoot from many different positions—sitting, kneeling, even prone—because their bows need not be held perfectly vertically, a requirement of the compound if the sights are to work properly. Traditional bows are much lighter to carry, and they're quieter, a feature that sometimes allows you to get off a second shot. They're much faster when it comes to positioning and releasing the arrow.

As to power, there is really not much difference between the two, because they do their work in different, but probably equal, fashion. The compound bow shoots a light arrow at high velocity, an advantage for flatness of trajectory. A long-bow shoots a heavier but slower arrow. Longbow shooters believe these heavy arrows penetrate better than the light ones flung from sophisticated compounds, but the truth, as far as I can see it, is that both types frequently send arrows all the way through the rib cages of elk-sized animals. If the broadhead is sharp, that animal will die very quickly, and it won't make one whit of difference which type of bow sent it on its way.

Still, common sense should have drawn me to the compound bow, particularly with a questionable shoulder and with a schedule that allows little time for practice. I could have become competent far more quickly, and that limb-saving let-off would probably help guard my separated shoulder against renewed pain. But I steadily inched toward traditional bows, and I faced the fact that not much about hunting, about relating to the outdoors, has anything to do with reason. Hunting is supremely sensual and tactile. At no time are your senses more alive, more aware, and I suppose that includes your aesthetic sense along with the others.

So regarding the compound bow and my problems with it I won't claim anything factual or rational. I'll just paraphrase Robert Frost: "Something there is that doesn't love a compound." And why? Because the damn things are ugly. They're not just ugly, they're butt-ugly. Camouflaged contraptions of metal, cable, and pulleys, compound bows have all the aesthetic appeal of jammed freeways on Sunday afternoon.

And why should that make any difference? Well, I would not go fly fishing with a piece of white PVC pipe for a rod, even if such could be made wickedly efficient. My rifles, even those with synthetic stocks, are smooth to the touch, are shaped for the body, are attractive enough that I handle them with a certain tenderness. It seemed to me, too, that if were to go back to hunting with a bow, to put aside for part of our long Montana season the efficiency of high powered rifles with telescopic sights, that I'd just as well go the whole way. For thousands of years Man hunted with a bent piece of wood, cleverly shaped by lessons learned during centuries of human experience into something that could bring down a buffalo. If I were going to hunt with a bow it was that collective experience I wanted to tap.

However, I can't say I'd given this all that much thought. It's just that something had kept me from gravitating toward bowhunting for decades, even long before my shoulder injury, and I suspect the deterrent was bows that had grown to be unrecognizable to me, implements that did not invite my touch. Then one day I saw a small advertisement in *Traditional Bowhunter*. Its black and white photo was modest next to the full page color advertisements of larger companies, but that photo showed a bow that asked to be touched, to be carried, to be drawn. I emailed the company a note that simply said, "Your bow called the Kaibab is the most beautiful bow I've ever seen. I expect I'll buy one someday." The reply, profuse thanks, came quickly from Chaparral Archery.

Shortly afterwards Travis came to work wanting to show me his new compound bow. "What does it take to pull it back?" I asked.

"Seventy pounds," he said, "with 80 percent let-off. Go

ahead and pull it, but don't let it go." (No bow should be "dry fired," pulled back and released without an arrow in place.) I grasped the bow and pulled, my teeth clenched. Surprise! I passed the seventy pound hump without pain, and then held the bow briefly at full draw. Maybe my doctor's promise fifteen years earlier, that eventually the pain would go away, wasn't idle. It had just taken a whole lot longer than I'd expected.

Meanwhile, my friend Billy told me he was selling his compound bow and had ordered a recurve, the second model of bow made, it turned out, by this same small company in New Mexico called Chaparral Archery. Well, that did it. I ordered the bow, a left-handed reflex/deflex longbow, knowing that the thing was pretty enough to justify its existence as a wall ornament even if I never learned to shoot it. I'd measured my draw length right at the common twenty-eight inches. I'd read that archers switching from compounds to traditional bows should drop back 25 percent in draw weight. Pulling back Travis's compound and several others had given me a meager point of reference. I wanted a bow strong enough to cast heavy arrows for elk, yet one my aging body could learn to shoot well. I settled on fifty-seven pounds, the company promising they'd build the bow within two pounds of that, plus or minus. (It turns out they nailed it—fifty-seven pounds at twenty-eight-inch draw.)

I am standing in a shady grove of cottonwoods, watching the timber below me. My neighbor's south fence is forty yards to my left. Behind and above me, through a dense maze of chokecherry bushes, is the highway. The occasional noise of speeding cars does not add to the aesthetics of this hunt, but I tune it out, because I know from experience that I'm camped on a hot crossing. Daily at this time whitetail deer come up from the river bottom, over the highway, and east toward our alfalfa fields. I have extra tags for antlerless whitetails, and I'm determined to fill one with my bow.

I am not a patient man, so I'm surprised that several times this day I've been able to stand behind this big cottonwood tree for a full hour and a half, from the time of late sun until the end of shooting light, scarcely moving. I suppose a tree stand would be better, but this big cottonwood works fine. I've already had several close encounters. The first arrows released at game from my new longbow have been sent on their way from behind this same tree.

There were two arrows, actually, the doe frozen on me, curious but incapable of discerning me. She turned out to be a tad farther than I estimated, perhaps close to thirty yards rather than twenty, but that's no excuse, because my "instinctive" rangefinder compensated for the extra distance. The problem was that I just plain missed. The first shot went just over her back. She rose as if on tiptoes, straining to see me. The second shot went just under her brisket. A little lower on the first shot or a little higher on the second, and I'd have had my first deer with a longbow, because my windage for both shots was right on for the heart/lung area.

So now I wait again behind my cottonwood trunk, because they'll certainly come. Before my eyes the sunshine on the cobblestones of the river turns tan, then golden, while the shadows lengthen. Finally the earth turns one more degree and the sunlight switches off. Within minutes they are here, below me, a bunch of whitetails, parts of their bodies playing peek-a-boo through another hedge of willow and chokecherry. And then the boss jumps into the open.

She's a big, muscular doe, and she knows I am there. She stares right at me where I stand in the shade, not completely assimilating, perhaps, but dead aware anyway, pissed off, snorting, stamping her front foot, telling me she'd chew me up and spit me out if only she knew where to start. Our eyes are locked. There is no way. There is no way I will be able to draw this bow and launch an arrow before she's out of here.

I learn firsthand how hard it is to draw a bow of nearly sixty pounds when you must do so slowly and quietly, using nothing of your body but your two arms. But I get it done. "She will jump the string, she will jump the string," goes a refrain in my mind, and when I release she does just that, swapping ends and sprinting a body length during the nanosecond it takes the arrow to travel from the shelf of the bow to her vicinity.

But she doesn't stop her war with me. She's a Marine of a mother deer. She gets down behind the hedge of brush and herds the other does and their fawns all out of there with stamps and snorts, gets them all on the run down the safe side of the hedge before she, the leader, the last one out of the hot landing zone, consents to leave herself. She gives me one last resounding snort. She has kicked my butt, and I'm grinning all over.

It's an intimate business, I discovered during my fledgling beginnings as a traditional bowhunter. It's getting back to basics in spades. You carry a bow weighing little more than a pound, a bent stick (albeit a sophisticated one), its remarkable energy held temporarily in check by a string. Because you must be extremely close to the animal before you draw, you adjust your aspirations. Now a doe or a very small buck is a trophy. To be that close means other things as well. You see as you rarely see during rifle season, smell your quarry, study subtle differences between individuals. And then you try to reach out and touch it in just the right place and in just the right way so that death comes quickly.

As a student of the longbow as a hunting tool I'm at best an apprentice. Whether I have enough years left to become a master, or even a journeyman, time will tell. My first season was successful, but not in terms of game harvested. Thoreau, though, would have approved. "Simplify, simplify," he said, get to know nature by sucking the marrow out of it, by touching it and by living it. My longbow is one trail in that direction. It will not hang idle as an ornament on the wall.

But I'll give Dr. Billy the last word. Here is his e-mail, shot my direction during the height of the elk bugling season:

Dan:

No, I didn't fill the freezer—but this morning I had an outdoor experience that was absolutely incredible.

Woke up at 0400, drove out to the campground south of town. There is an area above there that has difficult access, therefore good hunting.

Just South of Mercy Creek there is an avalanche chute that I like to hike up to the plateau. In the dark it keeps me oriented and all I have to do is put one foot in front of the other and keep going up, up, up.

Arrive on the plateau just at sunrise, beautiful sight. At that time take off my sweat soaked shirt, put on the camo shirt, mask, gloves. Eat a power bar, have some water and start glassing.

Immediately note some elk to the NW, about ½ mile feeding out in the open, some bedded down. See some horns on a few of them. Figure out a way to skirt the edge of the plateau and end up downwind of them in the only copse of trees on the whole plateau. Amazingly I do this without breaking my neck or spooking the herd. Spot one lone cow during this trip but she behaves and keeps feeding.

I arrive about 200 yards downwind of herd with a copse of stunted pines at my back. I catch my breath and plan to set up in front of the trees to break up my silhouette. The herd is just over a small rise about 50 yards away. I cannot see them.

The bulls are bugling off and on, sound hot. I hit the cow call and get an immediate bugle. Set for a while, more bugles, hit the cow again and bam, another bugle. Hot bull. This goes on for about ½ hour. He sounds pumped now, bugling, "glunking" (real guttural grunts), I can hear him probably 75–100 yards away just over the crest of the hill.

All of a sudden I see two antler tips cresting the hill coming right for me. That got the heart going. Next the rest of the antlers, head, neck, and body. Here he comes—and comes—and comes. Stops about 7 yards away staring at me. Beautiful 5x6, dark horns, ivory tips, he is obviously looking for the "cow" and isn't sure what the hell I am doing there.

He isn't spooked but obviously disconcerted. I avoid making eye contact and now the Mexican standoff. He slowly works to my right, not spooked but not relaxed. NEVER gives me anything besides frontal or quartering towards me view. Then gets a little goosey, lopes about 20 yards farther and stops to look again. Now broadside but out of my range. He slowly walks out of my life forever.

I let him settle and I move about 30 yards to a new setup and he starts getting fired up over the cow call again. YES, I may have another chance. By now it is 0830, wind is getting goofy, next thing I know I hear the herd stampeding away. Must've winded me. I move up and watch them take off with binocs and see the herd bull. Monster. Real typical 6x6 with those 5th/6th points at least 16". They go, and go, and go up into the rocks. I never saw them stop and figured they won today.

Side note, missed a spruce grouse by about ½" with a judo point on the way down. Fun, though.

Great experience this morning. Wow, Eastern guy calls in a bull with skills mostly gleaned from books and magazines. One person I told today said I should have shot "at that range you could hit him front on and kill him." No way. My view is to respect the animal, that is #1. Today was awesome, incredible. If I had made an attempt to shoot, it would have been poor presentation, probably running animal—a kill at best, a wounded magnificent bull at worst—that would have soured me on bowhunting forever.

So I hope you are having great luck on whitetails. This is more proof that we can get close enough for traditional equipment!

Billy

15

Sunset?

I have been cutting aspen logs for firewood. It's a cloudy, windy day, and my main problem is situating myself so that the chips and dust created by the chainsaw don't blow onto my face, into my eyes, and down my shirt. I've been largely unsuccessful at preventing any of these things.

The entire grove of aspens is dead. They do that, I've heard, grow together, leaf out together each spring, turn brilliant yellow together each fall, and then eventually die together. Their roots connect beneath the ground, and in a sense, the whole grove is just one tree. These have been dead several years, but they have stayed standing, and they'll be good firewood. It's not always so. Sometimes aspens begin to rot even before they die, but these have not done so, and their wood is milky white and solid. It will split easily and burn well.

So, doing my best to dope the wind, I've cut notches on the uphill side of three of the trees and have felled them toward the pickup. They've fallen obligingly into one big pile where I can limb them and cut their trunks into twenty-four-inch lengths for our woodstove. The felling job is one I'd normally be proud of, the work of the sort I normally enjoy.

Hunting season this year has come and gone. I find that late in our long Montana season I begin to wish for its end. Bird and bow seasons start in early September, the big game season doesn't end until the Sunday after Thanksgiving, and I've had an additional two weeks, until mid-December, to seek a cow elk and whitetail does. Depending on the species, one can hunt for three months.

31. Turkeys in the author's yard have "King's X."

I've passed on the does, even though, as we're fond of saying, they're so thick we nearly have to spray for them, and I've done so with some regret: I love the extra meat for my sausage concoctions. And I've passed, too, on my wild turkey, leaving the either-sex tag unfilled even while flocks came into the corrals and roosted in the cottonwoods that ring our yard. Turkeys, like the whitetails that savage any alfalfa bale left uncovered, have when they're in the barnyard what we called "King's X" in our childhood games.

The turkeys, a big flock of them, had been hanging in a meadow below the road when they weren't making gutsy forays into our corrals to pick up the oats the colts had left. I was watching for the return of the eagles, and so were they, and I'd been telling Hopkins he'd better come down before the eagles arrived. Our turkeys change lifestyles abruptly when the bald eagles show up to perch in the cottonwood trees and feast on the afterbirth our cows leave when calving. Apparently the placentas are caviar to them. I doubt whether they kill many turkeys (though I've seen a redtail hawk perched proudly on one he'd killed), but the turkeys take no chances. They head for the woods. Eagles, like fighter bombers, need swooping room.

Hopkins finally came down to collect his turkey, but he didn't really try. I urged him. He said he'd make a pass across the river while I did my chores, but he returned too soon to have been serious about it. Finally, over a beer, he admitted, "Well, hunting's over." Never mind that by February we'll both be checking the Fish, Wildlife and Parks website each day for Montana's new regulations. He and Billy and Jim and my brother Steve and Travis and my sons David, Jon, and Steve will be plotting and planning, eager for the next year's adventures.

But on this day, cutting up the fallen aspens, it's over. "For everything there is a season," said one of my favorite poets.

And this is not it. As the pickup bed takes on its load of fire-wood I wonder why the physical labor is not working today, why it's not bringing me out of whatever it is that kept me from smiling at the bunch of Huns that stampeded into the air from the spring as I parked the pickup. A Chinese meta-phor sees men on stilts, stilts that grow taller with accumulated experience as men grow older, until balance becomes impossible. This is a tall stilt day.

I recall the bumper sticker that says growing old is not for sissies, and I tell myself to quit moping. It's all the usual stuff. What the hell did I expect? The one parent left to Emily and me is having difficulties, true, but we're lucky to still have him. The old horseman, the mentor who recently died, is no longer suffering as he was, and that's good. And even Al the body shop man, one of the toughest guys I've ever known, who hunted until the end, couldn't live forever. And how about hunting at large? There are times, I confess, that I fear it will not survive, that I fear it all of a sudden might be overwhelmed and die like this aspen grove has, or like Oliver Wendell Holmes's one-horse shay: "All at once, nothing first, just as bubbles do when they burst."

Hunting's adversaries are many: habitat loss, particularly by subdivision; locking up of land; animal rights groups; slob hunters; ATV's; elite hunters who damn all but their selected methods and ethic; hunting videos featuring loud high-fives at the deaths of beautiful animals; a public increasingly bereft of affinity and awareness of the laws of nature . . . I could go on, but today I have no stomach for it.

Al lost a leg when a sleeping driver crossed the centerline and collided head-on with his motorcycle. He saw it coming and tried to lay the bike down and take the ditch, but there was no way it could be done in time. He very nearly died.

When he recovered, he went hunting. For fifteen years he hunted, sometimes covering more ground with one leg and a crutch (he never found an artificial limb that he liked) than hunters supposedly "whole." I used to joke with him during coffee hour after church about various modifications, holsters and such, for his crutch. He pointed out that it was already adjustable like a military ski pole, for walking sidehills, he said.

Al bowhunted in the Missouri breaks for elk, and he pursued turkeys on our place and elsewhere. For longer distances and more difficult conditions, a Montana law allowing handicapped hunters to use ATV's let him shoot over the handlebars. He took a nice whitetail buck just last year about the time lung cancer kicked in. And even then he did not stop. He ended it all with a buffalo, the meat from which he donated to a big scholarship dinner, where he spent his time sitting at the entrance, greeting the hundreds who showed up. Accounts of the buffalo hunt were narrated at this occasion, but most of the talking was done by the friends who were with him. It was beginning to be difficult for Al to speak. A week or two later he was gone.

Some might see a contradiction between the slipping away of this man's life and the continued drive to take the life of the bison. Al, apparently, did not. The buffalo was a gift to him, and he, in turn, made it a gift to others.

On an early December morning the sun emerges, but it does little to warm us. Travis and I are, quite frankly, freezing our butts off. I've left the diesel pickup idling, and we're each unabashed about taking a quick turn inside by its heater before guilt at the fact that Sarah does not do so drives us back out.

She stands hovered over the skewered mare, the mare that

has died mysteriously. We must do our best to find out why. This is not a horse to which we are attached, and that is good. But we're horsemen, and that is enough. Sarah, the veterinarian, is bundled in coveralls and additional layers, but her hands wear only the obligatory plastic gloves as she meticulously extracts and examines tissue samples that Travis bags and I label.

The mare, supine, is opened from stem to stern. In spite of the cold, Sarah never hurries. Even though the state laboratory will scrutinize each sample under considerably more controlled conditions, she examines it too, looks, smells, and probes in an attempt to find something abnormal enough to have killed the mare.

She removes the broodmare's fetus. It is perfectly formed. She measures it, records the results, and estimates its weight. Then she lays it carefully back inside the body cavity. Never mind that it's not likely to stay there during disposal of the mare. For now, that's the correct place for it.

And once, just once, she steps out of her role as scientist. It's only for a second, and if I were to interview her today, perhaps she would not even remember doing what she did. She has laid the tiny horse back inside the mare, and as she releases it, its neck lolls back limp. She catches this in the corner of her eye, pauses for one beat, then swoops down with both hands and corrects its posture. She leaves the fetus a perfect little horse, neck arched, beautiful—if only for a moment. There *will* be dignity and beauty, even in death.

We pass the remaining time as the three of us best know how, doing our work but talking about hunting. Sarah has killed a young bull elk and an antelope a month earlier. Travis and I have still not gone after my cow elk, and we discuss strategy with her. Then, our icy and unpleasant task completed, we go back to the barn.

In traditional archery there is something called the "archer's paradox." This term refers to the fact that the arrow does not shoot exactly where it's aimed, if "aiming" were to mean sighting down the arrow itself as you might the barrel of a shotgun. The bowstring is centered relative to the bow's limbs, but the arrow rest is not. On primitive bows the arrow rests at the outside of the bow handle, considerably out of line. On more modern recurves and longbows with "center cut" arrow rests, the arrow is in closer alignment, but the center of the arrow still usually rests somewhat outside the plane of the bowstring. Thus the arrow, when released, must actually bend its way around a slight bulge.

So arrows are selected for a certain "spine," a certain stiffness that matches the requirements of the bow. They distort when released, wobble briefly in flight, and then straighten out. The traditional archer does not worry about this. The "why" is not really important. He or she simply learns to look where the bow shoots, to understand its nature, and if the bow is mastered, the reverse happens. The arrow hits where the archer looks.

The essence of hunting lies in something I'd call the "hunter's paradox." The paradox refers to reverence for life even though we're willing to kill. It is found in all but the most boorish of hunters. Its existence explains a woman who strives daily to save the lives of animals, and then shoots one while hunting, and a man clinging to life against all odds, but who still feels like taking the life of a buffalo. The hunter's paradox has been known to all of history's great lovers and preservers of wildlife from Thoreau to Roosevelt to Audubon to Leopold.

Particularly in recent years, reams have been written to dissect the hunter's paradox. Oft quoted in such treatises is the foundation work of the Spanish philosopher José Ortega y

Gasset who penned *Meditations on Hunting* in 1942. Modern anthologies such as *A Hunter's Heart: Honest Essays on Blood Sport* (ed. David Petersen [New York: Henry Holt, 1996]) focus the talents of many fine hunter/writers to prompt any sensitive hunter/reader to look inward, to examine why he or she hunts, what ethics are involved, what is acceptable and what is not in an activity that involves taking the life of an animal.

All of this discussion is pretty much to the good, it seems to me. Respect for the animal taken is not something new, something only recently emphasized by these rather academic writers. Respect, reverence, and thankfulness for the meat provided are essentials if we, as modern hunters, are to rise to the standards of earlier, simpler cultures, too often misnamed "primitive." Such feelings about the animals taken were universal among them.

Can hunter introspection be excessive? I've touched on it only lightly in this book, partly because it's so well handled in so many other places. But I think, too, that taken en masse, serious writing about hunting has become collectively a bit too much of an apology, not to the animals hunted (which is entirely appropriate) but apology for one's existence, one's very nature as a hunter. And for that I will never apologize. I will never apologize for the incisors in my mouth—the tools of a meat eater—or for that powerful drive that has kept me a hunter now for more than half a century.

I respect the tears so many modern hunter/writers report shedding at the death of their quarry, because I have felt that impulse, that remorse. I respect, too, more extreme expressions, that, for instance, of the hunter who reports burying his face in the coat of a freshly killed cow elk to inhale her essence, even though that's an impulse I've *not* felt. But there are times, I confess, when I ask myself, "What would Teddy think?"

Theodore Roosevelt, after all, was the father of us all. Without him it's questionable whether hunting as we know it in the United States today would exist at all. This man, so thoroughly modern in so many ways, did more than accept that the hunting impulse was natural in modern man. He considered it *essential.* In his writings he frequently points to cultures in which hunting had disappeared and always, in his judgment, to their detriment, to a resultant loss of human character.

Roosevelt was not a conservationist who was also a hunter. Roosevelt was a conservationist *because* he was a hunter, and he makes no bones about that. The national park system should exist, he made clear, as a protected breeding ground for game animals, so that there will be an ample supply for hunting. Human character, as he envisions it, *requires* hunting.

I do not think the drive is equally strong in all people. Hunting is not, and should not be, for everyone. And I wonder about some of the more extreme renditions I've read of this thing we call hunter remorse. If killing an animal you've hunted must always include a tortured catharsis, a wrenching self-flagellation, the neutral observer might not be cruel in asking why the one who suffers so much had not instead played golf.

And so my own possibly excessive introspection continues on this particular day accompanied by the cacophony of a chain saw ripping through white aspen that was alive a few years ago when I stalked a whitetail buck in this very grove below the spring. And the Ecclesiastes poet, too, keeps speaking. "A time to be born, a time to die; . . . A time to kill, and a time to heal; . . . A time to keep silence, and a time to speak . . ." And he continues, too, through the less-quoted verse that follows these apparent contradictions: "He hath made every thing beautiful in his time."

No, I don't have problems with the fact that I'm a hunter deep down in the very core of my being. The genius of the poem is that its seeming contradictions are laid out in a way so matter-of-fact. It doesn't explain the paradox; it simply *is*. Trying hard to explain something basic to one's nature can be profitable, but it can also be frustrating and even destructive, like the result of lovers trying to analyze and quantify their love.

And it is love, love for the animals hunted, love for the land, for each tree and coulee; love for the campfires and the companions; love for the horses that carry me there, for the smell of their willing sweat, for the creak of the saddle leather, for the feel of a good rifle in a saddle scabbard under my calf; it is love for these things and more that takes me there each season and makes me, when the season is wrong, long to go back.

It will not stop soon. I will not go gentle into the realm of those who have grown too old to hunt. It's time to drop some weight again, just in case I draw a goat permit. (Keeping up with the likes of Justin, David, Jonathan, Billy, and Travis has been a stark reminder of *that*.) And then there's that nagging problem with my single-shot Ruger #1 that shoots tight groups, only to have the point of impact move mysteriously. I must address that problem before I even consider again unleashing its power toward an elk. There is the colt I am training, a strapping black with a silky running walk and an attitude that looks toward the mountains as if there's nothing there he won't be able to handle. I must get with him, because if Billy and I take that early bugling hunt, or if I'm lucky enough to go after a goat, this colt will be along. (Should a goat permit be drawn Hopkins plans to cook, and walk this time instead of ride.)

The pickup box is now full of wood, and I shut the chainsaw down, this time for good. I remove the earmuffs, worn in attempt to hang onto whatever hearing is left after repeated assaults from gunfire and the engines of farm equipment. There is a beautiful quiet. The wind has subsided somewhat, though the tall wheatgrass left by the cows still flattens to an occasional gust.

I drive the laden pickup past the spring enclosure, a couple of acres we've fenced so that we can regulate its use by livestock, opening it to any one of four different pastures. The Huns have filtered back in. I see their tiny bodies, their heads ducking this way and that as they search for the meal of the day. I ease the pickup a little higher on the sidehill away from the spring, hoping not to flush them. Ben, my Brittany, is living briefly in Billings while a trainer works him. For him, too, there will be a season.

In spite of my best efforts, the pretty birds, pressured by the sound of a diesel, flush from the buckbrush. And this time I smile.